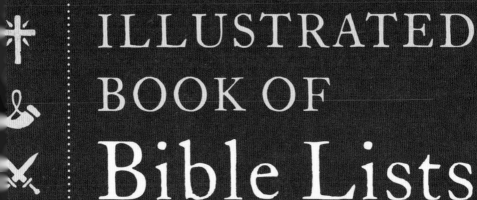

ILLUSTRATED BOOK OF
Bible Lists

ILLUSTRATED BIBLE HANDBOOK SERIES

Christopher D. Hudson

BARBOUR
PUBLISHING

D1599321

Illustrated Book of Bible Lists
© 2013 by Christopher D. Hudson

Print ISBN 978-1-61626-584-7

Cover design: Faceout Studio, www.faceoutstudio.com

Interior design and page layout by Hudson & Associates. Special thanks are given to Jorie Lee.

Published by Barbour Publishing, Inc., P.O. Box 719, Uhrichsville, Ohio 44683, www.barbourbooks.com

Our mission is to publish and distribute inspirational products offering exceptional value and biblical encouragement to the masses.

Member of the
Evangelical Christian
Publishers Association

Printed in China.

Contents

INTRODUCTION

The *Illustrated Book of Bible Lists* offers a fun and informative way for you to better understand God's Word.

You can benefit in multiple ways from this book. With over 200 lists on just about every Bible topic, you'll be able to quickly find answers to intriguing questions such as the following:

- What kinds of clothes did people wear in Bible times? (See page 76.)
- What did Bible characters eat? (See page 77.)
- What did Jesus say the kingdom of God would be like? (See page 157.)
- Where can I find Jesus' parables or stories of His miracles? (See pages 131–133.)

As you browse through these lists, you'll find more than simple facts—you'll discover how understanding recurring biblical themes can enhance your reading of God's Word. For example, you may know that there were twelve tribes of Israel and twelve apostles, but did you realize that other significant Bible details are arranged in groups of twelve? (See page 190.) And while you're probably familiar with the term *Christian*, have you ever stopped to reflect on all the different names God uses to describe His people? (See page 176.) Though the lists in this book aren't always exhaustive, we've tried to include the most significant entries for each subject.

This book will not only add to your knowledge about the Bible but also give you resources to refresh your heart as you find vital verses on subjects like marriage (page 258) and finding strength (page 260). You'll also find a number of Bible reading plans that offer suggestions for reading your Bible devotionally (page 241).

Whether you go through this book page by page or jump around between the subjects that most interest you, we trust you'll find *The Illustrated Book of Bible Lists* enjoyable and enriching as you spend more time in God's Word.

CHAPTER I.

...ation of heaven and eart... ...of the light, 6 of the fir-
...9 of the earth separate... ...the waters, 11 and made
...l, 14 of the sun, moon, a... ...20 of fish and fowl,
...easts and cattle, 26 of ma... ...the image of God. 29
...e appointment of food.

...he beginning God created the hea-
...n and the earth... ...ut form, and
...nd the earth... ...on the face of
...eep. And the Spirit of God moved
...n the face of the waters.
...And God said, Let there be light:
...there was light.
...And God saw the light, that *it was*
...d: and God divided the light from
...darkness.
...And God called the light Day, and
...e darkness he called Night. And the
...ening and the morning were the first
...y.
...¶ And God said, Let there be a fir-
...ament in the midst of the waters, and
...t it divide the waters from the waters.
...7 And God made the firmament, and
...ivided the waters which *were* under the
...irmament from the waters which *were*
...bove the firmament: and it was so.
...8 And God called the firmament Heaven. And the evening and the morning
were the second day.
...9 ¶ And God said, Let the waters under the heaven be gathered together unto
one place, and let the dry *land* appear:
and it was so.
...10 And God called the dry *land* Earth;
and the gathering together of the waters
called he Seas: and God saw that *it was*
good.
...11 And God said, Let the earth bring
forth grass, the herb yielding seed, *and*
the fruit tree yielding fruit after his kind,
whose seed *is* in itself, upon the earth:
and it was so.

12 And the earth brought forth gra...
and herb yielding seed after his kind, a...
the tree yielding fruit, whose seed *wa...*
itself, after his kind: and God saw t...
it was good.
13 And the evening and the morn...
were the third day.
14 ¶ And God said, Let there be li...
in the firmament of the heaven to d...
the day from the night; and let the...
for signs, and for seasons, and for...
and years:
15 And let them be for lights...
firmament of the heaven to give...
upon the earth: and it was so.
16 And God made two great ligh...
greater light to rule the day, a...
lesser light to rule the night: *l...*
the stars also.
17 And God set them in the firma...
the heaven to give light upon the...
18 And to rule over the day a...
the night, and to divide the light...
darkness: and God saw that *it w...*
19 And the evening and the...
were the fourth day.
20 And God said, Let the wat...
forth abundantly the moving...
that hath life, and fowl tha...
above the earth in the open...
of heaven.
21 And God created great...
every living creature that mo...
the waters brought forth...
after their kind, and every...
after his kind: and God sav...
good.
22 And God blessed them...
fruitful, and multiply, and fi...
in the seas, and let fowl mu...
earth.
23 And the evening and...
were the fifth day.

BIBLE LISTS

ANIMALS, PLANTS & OTHER CRITTERS

ANIMALS

Animal	Description	Reference
antelope/gazelle	A clean animal eaten by Solomon's court	*Deut. 14:5; Isa. 51:20*
ape/monkey/baboon	Animals in Solomon's court	*1 Kings 10:22; 2 Chron. 9:21*
badger/hyrax	An unclean animal	*Lev. 11:5*
bat	An unclean animal	*Lev. 11:19*
bear	Attacked the boys who teased Elisha	*2 Kings 2:24; Isa. 11:7; Lam. 3:10*
behemoth	Scholars are uncertain of which specific animal this verse references. Possibilities include hippopotamus (photo above), rhinoceros, elephant, water ox, and dinosaur.	*Job 40:15*
bull/calf/cow	Often used in sacrifice	*Exod. 29:36; Lev. 9:2–3; 22:28*
camel	An unclean animal	*Lev. 11:4; Judg. 7:12*
deer	A clean animal	*Deut. 14:5; 1 Kings 4:23; Ps. 42:1*
dog	Ate garbage and corpses	*Exod. 22:31; Ps. 59:14–15*
donkey/mule	Often a mode of transportation	*Num. 22:21–33; Matt. 21:2–7*
goat	Often used in sacrifice	*Gen. 27:9, 16; Lev. 16:10*
horse	Used as a means of transportation	*Gen. 47:17; Exod. 14:9*
jackal/hyena/fox	Wild dogs and scavengers	*Judg. 15:4; Isa. 34:14*
lamb	Jesus was the ultimate lamb	*Ps. 23:1*
leopard	Frequently mentioned symbolically	*Dan. 7:6; Rev. 13:2*
lion	Frequently mentioned symbolically	*Judg. 14:5–6; Dan. 6*
lizard	An unclean animal	*Lev. 11:30; Prov. 30:28*
mouse/rat	An unclean animal	*Lev. 11:29; 1 Sam. 6:4–5, 11, 18*
ox	A clean animal that worked in the fields	*Deut. 14:4; 25:4; Luke 13:15*
pig	An unclean animal	*Lev. 11:7; Deut. 14:8*
rabbit/hare	An unclean animal	*Lev. 11:6; Deut. 14:7*
sheep/ram	Often used in sacrifice and symbolically	*Gen. 12:16; Lev. 16:3; John 10:3*
snake/serpent	A manifestation of Satan in Genesis	*Gen. 3:1–5; Num. 21:6–9*
weasel	An unclean animal	*Lev. 11:29*
wolf	A wild predator	*Gen. 49:27; Isa. 11:6; John 10:12*

* Translations of animal names are drawn from the New International Version of the Bible

BIRDS

Bird	Description	Reference
crow/raven	It was sent by Noah to check for dry land. Though it was unclean, it was used to feed Elijah.	*Lev. 11:15; Deut. 14:14; 1 Kings 17:4–6; Job 38:41; Ps. 147:9; Luke 12:24*
cuckoo	An unclean bird	*Lev. 11:16; Deut. 14:15*
dove/pigeon	Considered a poor man's sacrifice. (Photo above)	*Lev. 1:14; 12:8; Matt. 3:16; Mark 1:10; Luke 2:21–24; 3:22*
eagle	An unclean bird, often referenced symbolically	*Lev. 11:13; Deut. 32:11–12; Isa. 40:31; Jer. 48:40*
falcon	An unclean bird	*Lev. 11:14; Deut. 14:13*
fowl (rooster, hen, chicken, goose)	Signaled Peter's denial of Jesus	*Matt. 26:34; Mark 14:30; Luke 22:34; John 13:38*
hawk	An unclean bird	*Lev. 11:16; Deut. 14:15*
heron	An unclean bird	*Lev. 11:19; Deut. 14:18*
hoopoe	An unclean bird	*Lev. 11:19; Deut.14:18*
ostrich	An unclean bird	*Lev. 11:6; Deut. 14:15*
owl/nighthawk	An unclean bird	*Lev. 11:16; Deut. 14:15; Jer. 50:39; Mic. 1:8*
partridge		*1 Sam. 26:20; Jer. 17:11*
peacock	Imported from other nations by Solomon	*1 Kings 10:22; 2 Chron. 9:21*
pelican	An unclean bird	*Lev. 11:18; Deut. 14:17*
quail	Provided as food for the Israelites in the wilderness	*Exod. 16:13; Num. 11:31–34; Ps. 105:40*
seagull	An unclean bird	*Lev. 11:16; Deut. 14:15*
sparrow	Considered a poor man's sacrifice	*Lev. 14:1–7; Matt. 10:29; Luke 12:6*
stork	An unclean bird	*Lev. 11:19; Deut. 14:18*
vulture	An unclean bird	*Lev. 11:13; Deut. 14:12–13*

Spotted eagle owl

Turkish stork

Falcon

CLEAN AND UNCLEAN ANIMALS OF LEVITICUS

Animal	Clean or Unclean	Reference
bull/calf/cow	clean	*Lev. 9:2–3; 22:28*
goat	clean	*Lev. 4:23; 16:10*
grasshopper/locust/cricket	clean	*Lev. 11:22*
lamb/sheep/ram	clean	*Lev. 5:18; 22:23*
ox	clean	*Lev. 4:10; 22:23*
badger	unclean	*Lev. 11:5*
bat	unclean	*Lev. 11:19*
camel (photo above)	unclean	*Lev. 11:4*
crocodile	unclean	*Lev. 11:30*
lizard	unclean	*Lev. 11:30*
mouse/rat	unclean	*Lev. 11:29*
pig	unclean	*Lev. 11:7*
rabbit/hare	unclean	*Lev. 11:6*
weasel	unclean	*Lev. 11:29*

Weasel

Chameleon

Sheep

CLEAN AND UNCLEAN
BIRDS OF LEVITICUS

Birds	Clean or Unclean	Reference
dove	clean	*Lev. 1:14; 12:8*
pigeon	clean	*Lev. 1:14; 12:8*
crow/raven	unclean	*Lev. 11:15*
cuckoo	unclean	*Lev. 11:16*
eagle	unclean	*Lev. 11:13*
falcon	unclean	*Lev. 11:14*
hawk	unclean	*Lev. 11:16*
heron	unclean	*Lev. 11:19*
hoopoe (photo above)	unclean	*Lev. 11:19*
ostrich	unclean	*Lev. 11:16*
owl/nighthawk	unclean	*Lev. 11:16*
pelican	unclean	*Lev. 11:18*
seagull	unclean	*Lev. 11:16*
stork	unclean	*Lev. 11:19*
vulture	unclean	*Lev. 11:13*

Ostrich

CROCODILES, FISH, AND AMPHIBIANS

Name	Description	Reference
crocodile (photo above)	An unclean animal (The crocodile thrived in the Nile and could grow 20 feet in length.)	*Lev. 11:30*
fish	A common food	*Matt. 13:48; 14:17; 17:27; John 21:3–8*
frog	Used by God in plagues	*Exod. 8:2–13; Ps. 105:30; Rev. 16:13*
sponge	Used by someone to give Jesus a drink of sour wine just before He died	*Matt. 27:48; Mark 15:36; John 19:29*
whale	May have been the large fish that swallowed Jonah	*Gen. 1:21; Jon. 1:17; Matt. 12:40*

INSECTS

ant	Portrayed as wise	*Prov. 6:6–8; 30:25*
bee	Mentioned only a few times in scripture, bees get more credit in how many times honey is mentioned.	*Judg. 14:8; Ps. 118:12*
caterpillar/moth/worm	Often referenced symbolically	*Isa. 51:8; Matt. 6:19; Luke 12:33; James 5:2*
fly/gnat/lice	An unclean insect	*Exod. 8:16–18; Eccles. 10:1; Matt. 23:24*
grasshopper/locust/cricket	A clean insect	*Exod. 10:4–19; Lev. 11:22; Num. 13:33; Matt. 3:4*
scorpion	Not technically an insect. Many species of this desert "bug" are deadly poisonous.	*Deut. 8:15; Ezek. 2:6; Luke 11:12*
wasp/hornet	Often sent by God into the enemies' camps	*Exod. 23:28; Deut. 7:20; Josh. 24:12*

Plant	Description	Reference
acacia tree (photo above)	Acacia wood was used to build the ark of the covenant and the first tabernacle.	*Exod. 36:20; 37:1*
almond tree		*Gen. 43:11; Exod. 25:33; Num. 17:8*
aloe	The juice of the aloe plant was used in perfuming garments, beds, and dead bodies, including the body of Jesus.	*Ps. 45:8; Song of Sol. 4:14; John 19:39*
balsam/balm tree	Balm was a valuable ointment that symbolized healing.	*Gen. 37:25; 43:11; Jer. 8:22; 46:11*
barley	A grain with many uses	*Exod. 9:31; Num. 5:15; Judg. 7:13; 1 Kings 4:28*
bitter herbs	Most likely taken with the Passover meal (perhaps endive, chicory, or dandelion)	*Exod. 12:8; Num. 9:11*
bush	Where God appeared to Moses	*Exod. 3:2–4*
cassia	An ingredient in the holy anointing oil	*Exod. 30:24; Ezek. 27:19*
cedar tree	Used in the building of Solomon's temple; also used to make idols	*2 Sam. 5:11; 1 Kings 6:9; Isa. 44:14–15; Ezek. 27:5*
cinnamon		*Exod. 30:23; Prov. 7:17; Song of Sol. 4:14; Rev. 18:13*
coriander		*Exod. 16:31; Num. 11:7*
cucumber vine	The Israelites longed for cucumbers after leaving Egypt.	*Num. 11:5*
cumin	Jesus referenced this spice while instructing the Pharisees.	*Isa. 28:25, 27; Matt. 23:23*
cypress/gopher wood tree	The ark and some idols were built of gopher wood.	*Gen. 6:14; Isa. 44:14*
dill/anise	Jesus referenced this herb while instructing the Pharisees.	*Matt. 23:23*
fig tree	A popular tree discussed throughout the Bible	*Gen. 3:7; Num. 13:23; 1 Sam. 25:18; Mark 11:12–14, 20–21*
fir tree	Wood from fir trees was valued in building.	*2 Sam. 6:5; 1 Kings 6:15; Ezek. 27:5*
flax	Frequently used to make various linens	*Mark 14:51; John 11:44; 13:4–5*

Plant	Description	Reference
frankincense	A popular incense given as a gift to Jesus	*Exod. 30:34; Lev. 2:1; Matt. 2:11*
galbanum	One of the ingredients used in the holy incense	*Exod. 30:34*
gall	A poisonous and bitter herb that was offered along with sour wine to Jesus while He was on the cross	*Jer. 8:14; Matt. 27:34; Acts 8:23*
garlic	One of the spices Israelites yearned for after leaving Egypt	*Num. 11:5*
gourd/vine		*2 Kings 4:39; Jon. 4:6–10*
grape vine	A popular vine mentioned throughout the Bible	*Gen. 9:20; Num. 13:20, 23–24; Judg. 9:27; Matt. 9:17; 21:33; John 15:5*
hyssop	A popular plant used at the Crucifixion to relieve Jesus' thirst	*Exod. 12:22; Lev. 14:4, 6, 51–52; John 19:29; Heb. 9:19*
leek	One of the vegetables the Israelites yearned for after leaving Egypt	*Num. 11:5*
lentil	The dish Jacob used to purchase Esau's birth-right	*Gen. 25:34; 2 Sam. 17:28; 23:11; Ezek. 4:9*
lily	Often mentioned symbolically	*1 Kings 7:19–26; Hosea 14:5; Matt. 6:28–30*
locust tree	Produced beans for food	*2 Kings 6:25; Luke 15:16*
mandrake	Thought to be an aphrodisiac	*Gen. 30:14–16*
melon vine	A food from Egypt that the Israelites longed for	*Num. 11:5; Isa. 1:8; Jer. 10:5*
mint	Jesus referenced this herb while instructing the Pharisees.	*Matt. 23:23; Luke 11:42*
mulberry tree	Jesus referenced this tree when He instructed the apostles on faith.	*Luke 17:6*
mustard	Mustard seeds are only 1–2 mm in diameter.	*Matt. 13:31–32; 17:20; Mark 4:31–32; Luke 13:19; 17:6*
myrrh	Made an appearance both after Jesus' birth and at the Crucifixion	*Exod. 30:23; Esther 2:12; Matt. 2:11*
oak tree		*Gen. 12:6; 13:18; 14:13; 18:1; Judg. 6:11; 2 Sam. 18:9–10; Amos 2:9*
olive tree	A popular tree that produced a fruit with many uses and was made particularly famous by the olive garden called Gethsemane	*Exod. 27:20; Lev. 2:1; Matt. 26:36; Luke 10:34*

Plant	Description	Reference
onion	One of the foods the Israelites longed for in the wilderness	*Num. 11:5*
onycha	An ingredient in the holy anointing oil	*Exod. 30:34*
palm tree	Its branches were waved to welcome Jesus into Jerusalem.	*Exod. 15:27; Neh. 8:15; John 12:13; Rev. 7:9*
papyrus/reed	Used to build Moses' basket and as a staff to mock Jesus	*Exod. 2:3, 5; Isa. 18:2; 19:6; Matt. 11:7; 27:29*
pistachio tree	Jacob told his sons to take pistachios to Joseph as a gift.	*Gen. 43:11*
pomegranate tree	Produced a popular fruit used in holy ceremonies	*Exod. 28:33–34; 39:24–26; Num. 13:23; 20:5; 1 Kings 7:18*
poplar tree		*Gen. 30:37; Hosea 4:13*
spikenard	An expensive oil used to anoint Jesus	*Song of Sol. 1:12; 4:13–14; Mark 14:3; John 12:3*
stacte	A spice used in anointing oil	*Exod. 30:34*
straw	Mixed with clay to make bricks by the Egyptians	*Gen. 24:25; Exod. 5:7; Judg. 19:19; 1 Kings 4:28*
sycamore tree	The tree Zacchaeus climbed to get a better view of Jesus	*1 Kings 10:27; Ps. 78:47; Amos 7:14; Luke 19:4*
tares/weeds	Jesus referenced this poisonous grass that resembles wheat in a parable about evil in the world.	*Matt. 13:25–30, 36–40*
thistles/thorns	Used to fashion a crown for Jesus during the Crucifixion	*Gen. 3:17–18; Matt. 13:7; 27:29; Mark 12:1*
wheat	One of the most important grains mentioned in the Bible	*Gen. 41:5–57; Exod. 29:32; Lev. 23:14; Ruth 2:14; Matt. 12:1; John 12:24*
willow tree	Used to construct the booths for the Festival of Tabernacles	*Lev. 23:40*

Pomegranate

BIBLE LISTS

INTERESTING
BIBLE FACTS

66 Summaries: What Each Book Says

Book	Description
Genesis	God creates the world and chooses a special people.
Exodus	God delivers His people, the Israelites, from slavery in Egypt.
Leviticus	A holy God explains how to worship Him.
Numbers	Faithless Israelites wander forty years in the wilderness of Sinai.
Deuteronomy	Moses reminds the Israelites of their history and God's laws.
Joshua	The Israelites capture and settle the promised land of Canaan.
Judges	Israel goes through cycles of sin, suffering, and salvation.
Ruth	A loyal daughter-in-law offers a picture of God's faithfulness, love, and care.
1 Samuel	Israel's twelve tribes unite under a king.
2 Samuel	David becomes Israel's greatest king, but with major flaws.
1 Kings	Israel divides into rival northern and southern nations.
2 Kings	Both Jewish nations are destroyed for their disobedience to God.
1 Chronicles	King David's reign is detailed and analyzed.
2 Chronicles	Israel's history is presented, from Solomon through division to destruction.
Ezra	Spiritual renewal begins after the Jews return from exile.
Nehemiah	Returning Jewish exiles rebuild the broken walls of Jerusalem.
Esther	A beautiful Jewish girl becomes queen and saves fellow Jews from slaughter.
Job	God allows human suffering for His own purposes.
Psalms	An ancient Jewish songbook showcases prayers, praise, and complaints to God.
Proverbs	Pithy, memorable sayings encourage people to pursue wisdom.
Ecclesiastes	Apart from God, life is empty and unsatisfying.
Song of Solomon	Married love is a beautiful thing worth celebrating.
Isaiah	A coming Messiah will save people from their sins.
Jeremiah	After years of sinful behavior, Judah will be punished.
Lamentations	A despairing author writes a poem about the destruction of Jerusalem.
Ezekiel	Though Israel is in exile, the nation will be restored.

66 Summaries: What Each Book Says (continued)

Book	Description
Daniel	Faithful to God in a challenging setting, Daniel is blessed.
Hosea	A prophet's marriage to a prostitute reflects God's relationship with Israel.
Joel	A locust plague pictures God's judgment on His sinful people.
Amos	Real religion isn't just ritual; it's treating people with justice.
Obadiah	Edom will suffer for participating in Jerusalem's destruction.
Jonah	A reluctant prophet, running from God, is swallowed by a giant fish.
Micah	Israel and Judah will suffer for their idolatry and injustice.
Nahum	Powerful, wicked Nineveh will fall before God's judgment.
Habakkuk	Trust God even when He seems unresponsive or unfair.
Zephaniah	A coming "day of the Lord" promises heavy judgment.
Haggai	Jews returning from exile need to rebuild God's temple.
Zechariah	Jewish exiles should rebuild their temple and anticipate their Messiah.
Malachi	The Jews have become careless in their attitude toward God.
Matthew	Jesus fulfills the Old Testament prophecies of a coming Messiah.
Mark	Jesus is God's Son, a suffering servant of all people.
Luke	Jesus is Savior of all people, whether Jew or Gentile.
John	Jesus is God Himself, the only Savior of the world.
Acts	The Holy Spirit's arrival heralds the beginning of the Christian church.
Romans	Sinners are saved only by faith in Jesus Christ.
1 Corinthians	Paul tackles sin problems in the church at Corinth.

66 Summaries: What
Each Book Says (Continued)

Book	Description
2 Corinthians	Paul defends his ministry to the troubled Corinthian church.
Galatians	Christians are free from restrictive Jewish laws.
Ephesians	Christians are all members of Jesus'"body," the church.
Philippians	Paul writes this "friendship letter" to a beloved church.
Colossians	Jesus Christ is supreme over everyone and everything.
1 Thessalonians	Jesus will return to gather His followers to Him.
2 Thessalonians	Christians should work until Jesus returns.
1 Timothy	Pastors are taught how to conduct their lives and churches.
2 Timothy	The apostle Paul writes final words to a beloved coworker.
Titus	Church leaders are instructed on their lives and teaching.
Philemon	Paul begs mercy for a runaway slave converted to Christianity.
Hebrews	Jesus is better than any Old Testament person or sacrifice.
James	Real Christian faith is shown by one's good works.
1 Peter	Suffering for the sake of Jesus is noble and good.
2 Peter	Beware of false teachers within the church.
1 John	Jesus was a real man, just as He is real God.
2 John	Beware false teachers, who deny Jesus' physical life on earth.
3 John	Church leaders must be humble, not proud.
Jude	Beware of heretical teachers and their dangerous doctrines.
Revelation	God will judge evil and reward His saints.

AUTHORS OF THE BIBLE

Author	Books Written
Moses	Genesis, Exodus, Leviticus, Numbers, Deuteronomy, and one psalm. He may have also written Job.
Joshua	Traditionally credited with Joshua, but some modern scholars dispute this
Samuel	May have written Judges and Ruth. He is also credited with most of 1 and 2 Samuel.
Nathan or Gad	One of these men may have written part of 1 and 2 Samuel.
Jeremiah	Jeremiah and Lamentations. He may have also written 1 and 2 Kings.
Ezra	May have written 1 and 2 Chronicles, Ezra, and Nehemiah
Mordecai	May have written Esther
David	Most of the Psalms
Asaph	Some of the Psalms
Korah	Some of the Psalms
Ethan	One psalm
Herman	One psalm
Solomon	Most of Proverbs, Ecclesiastes, Song of Solomon, and two psalms
Agur	Some of Proverbs
Isaiah	Isaiah. Some scholars believe someone else wrote the second half of the book.
Ezekiel	Ezekiel
Daniel	Daniel. Some scholars dispute this because of the accuracy of his prophecies.

Scroll of Isaiah

AUTHORS OF THE BIBLE (CONTINUED)

Author	Books Written
Hosea	Hosea
Joel	Joel
Amos	Amos
Obadiah	Obadiah
Jonah	Jonah
Micah	Micah
Nahum	Nahum
Habakkuk	Habakkuk
Zephaniah	Zephaniah
Haggai	Haggai
Zechariah	Zechariah
Malachi	Malachi
Matthew the Apostle	Matthew
Mark (John Mark)	Mark
Luke	Luke and Acts
John the Apostle	John; 1, 2, and 3 John; and Revelation
Paul the Apostle	Romans, 1 and 2 Corinthians, Galatians, Ephesians, Philippians, Colossians, 1 and 2 Thessalonians, 1 and 2 Timothy, Philemon, and possibly Hebrews
Barnabas or Apollos	One of these men may have written Hebrews.
James, brother of Jesus	James
Peter the Apostle	1 and 2 Peter
Jude	Jude

Solomon and Sheba

Hosea

Amos

BIBLE FACTS

Bible Facts	Description
Number of books in the Bible	66
Number of books in the Old Testament	39
Number of books in the New Testament	27
Number of chapters in the Bible	1,189
Number of chapters in the Old Testament	929
Number of chapters in the New Testament	260
Number of verses in the Bible	31,101
Number of verses in the Old Testament	23,214
Number of verses in the New Testament	7,959
Number of authors	40
Years spanned	1,500
Longest chapter in the Bible	Psalm 119
Shortest chapter in the Bible	Psalm 117
Longest verse in the Bible	Esther 8:9 (KJV)
Shortest verse in the Bible	John 11:35
Longest book in the Bible	Psalms
Longest book in the New Testament	Luke
Longest book written by one person	Jeremiah
Shortest book in the Bible	3 John
Shortest book in the Old Testament	Obadiah
Number of questions in the Bible	3,294
Number of commands in the Bible	6,468
Number of promises in the Bible	1,260
Number of prophecies in the Bible	more than 8,000
Languages of the Bible	Greek, Hebrew, Aramaic

10 Longest Verses in the KJV Bible

Reference	# of words
Esther 8:9	90
Josh. 8:33	80
Ezek. 48:21	80
Jer. 44:12	80
2 Kings 16:15	79
Dan. 5:23	78
Ezra 3:8	75
Esther 3:12	75
2 Chron. 31:1	72
Rev. 20:4	68

Esther 8:9

Then were the king's scribes called at that time in the third month, that is, the month Sivan, on the three and twentieth day thereof; and it was written according to all that Mordecai commanded unto the Jews, and to the lieutenants, and the deputies and rulers of the provinces which are from India unto Ethiopia, an hundred twenty and seven provinces, unto every province according to the writing thereof, and unto every people after their language, and to the Jews according to their writing, and according to their language.

10 MOST USED WORDS IN THE BIBLE

Word	Approximate Number of Uses *
the	64,040
and	60,382
of	40,029
to	16,372
that	15,778
in	14,482
he	12,425
shall	10,939
for	10,889
unto	10,100

* Actual number depends on translation

OTHER BOOKS MENTIONED IN THE BIBLE

Extra-Biblical Book	Reference
Annals of Jehu	2 Chron. 20:34
Annals of King David	1 Chron. 27:24
Annals of Solomon	1 Kings 11:41
Annals of the kings of Israel	1 Kings 14:19
Annals of the kings of Judah	1 Kings 14:29
Annals of the kings of Media and Persia	Esther 10:2
Book of Jashar	Josh. 10:13; 2 Sam. 1:18
Book of life	Rev. 3:5
Book of the annals	Neh. 12:23; Esther 2:23
Book of the chronicles	Esther 6:1
Book of the Wars of the Lord	Num. 21:14
Book of Truth	Dan. 10:21
First Book of Enoch	Jude 14–15
Letter to Corinth	1 Cor. 5:9
Letter to Laodicea	Col. 4:16
Records of Gad the seer	1 Chron. 29:29
Records of Iddo the seer	2 Chron. 12:15
Records of Nathan the prophet	1 Chron. 29:29
Records of Samuel the seer	1 Chron. 29:29
Records of Shemaiah the prophet	2 Chron. 12:15

Letter to Corinth
Book of Jashar
Book of Truth   Book of the Wars of the Lord   Book of life
Records of Gad the seer
Annals of the kings   Records of Nathan the prophet
Records of Samuel the seer
Records of Shemaiah the prophet   Annals of Solomon
Records of Iddo the seer
Annals of the kings of Israel   Annals of Jehu
Book of the annals
Annals of the kings of Media and Persia   of Judah
Book of the chronicles   Letter to Laodicea
First Book of Enoch
Annals of King David

Solomon

BOOKS OF THE APOCRYPHA

Name	Description
Baruch	Baruch was Jeremiah's secretary. The book was written for Jews who were living in the Hasmonaean period.
Bel and the Dragon	An addition to Daniel. Despite being urged to worship other gods, including Bel and a Dragon, Daniel refused.
Ecclesiasticus (or the All-Virtuous Wisdom of Jesus ben Sira)	A book of wisdom written by Jesus ben Sira
1 & 2 Esdras	A narrative that recounts portions of 2 Chronicles, Ezra, and Nehemiah.
Additions to Esther	Written to better connect Esther to the traditions of Israel's faith
The Epistle of Jeremiah	A sermon against idolatry
Judith	A story about a Jewish woman who was devoted to observing the Law of Moses
1 & 2 Maccabees	Book One is a history of the struggles of the Jews under the leadership of the Hasmonaeans. Book Two is a prequel to the first, focusing on the celebration of Hanukkah.
The Prayer of Azariah and the Song of the Three Young Men	An expansion of the story of Shadrach, Meshach, and Abednego
The Prayer of Manasseh	An addition to 2 Chronicles detailing King Manasseh's repentance
Susanna	An addition to Daniel. Daniel saves a woman from being put to death.
Tobit	A narrative about Tobit, a Jew who was taken captive to Nineveh
The Wisdom of Solomon	A book of wisdom

Seven Maccabean martyrs

Shadrach, Meshach, Abednego

COVENANTS

Covenant	Additional Information	Reference
Noahic Covenant	Sign of the covenant: Rainbow. God promised never again to destroy the world by flood.	*Gen. 6:14–18; 8:20–22; 9:8–13*
Abrahamic Covenant	Sign of the covenant: Circumcision. God promised to give Abraham a multitude of descendants and make them a great nation.	*Gen. 12:1–7; 13:14–18; 15:1–21; 17:1–10; Ps. 105:8–11; Gal. 3:17–18*
Mosaic Covenant	Sign of the covenant: The Sabbath. This was a conditional covenant established with the Israelites. Because God rescued them from Egypt, they were to keep His commandments. If they did, God would prosper them as a nation; if they didn't, they would be punished.	*Exod. 3:12–14; 6:3–8; 31:13–17; Deut. 4:32–34; 31:3, 6*
Davidic Covenant	Sign of the covenant: While no specific sign was indicated, it has been suggested that the sign could be the throne. God promised David that his descendants would always sit on the throne, a promise that reached its fulfillment when Jesus, a descendant of David, was born. He became the last and final King with a reign that lasts forever.	*Gen. 49:10; Num. 24:17; 2 Sam. 7:5–16; 23:5; 1 Kings 11:36; Ps. 89:3–4; Jer. 33:22; Matt. 1:1; Luke 1:32–33*
The New Covenant	Sign of the covenant: Communion, which signifies Christ's death and resurrection. Jesus died on the cross to save the world from sin, giving everlasting life to those who believe in Him.	*Jer. 31:31–39; 32:37–41; Ezek. 36:22–38; 37:1–14; Hosea 2:14–20; Matt. 1:1; 26:26–29; Luke 3:31; 22:20; Heb. 9:11–15*

GENEALOGIES

Description	Reference	Description	Reference
Cain's line	Gen. 4:17–22	Benjamin's line	1 Chron. 7:6–12
From Adam to Noah	Gen. 5:1–32	Naphtali's line	1 Chron. 7:13
Noah's line	Gen. 10:1–32	Manasseh's line	1 Chron. 7:14–19
From Shem to Abraham	Gen. 11:10–26; 1 Chron. 1:24–27	Ephraim's line	1 Chron. 7:20–29
Nahor's line	Gen. 22:20–24	Asher's line	1 Chron. 7:30–40
Abraham's line through Keturah	Gen. 25:1–4; 1 Chron. 1:32–33	Perez's line	Ruth 4:18–22
Abraham's line through Sarah	1 Chron. 1:34	Saul's genealogy	1 Chron. 8:1–40
Ishmael's line	Gen. 25:12–16; 1 Chron. 1:29–31	David's line born in Hebron	2 Sam. 3:2–5; 1 Chron. 3:1–4
Jacob's line	Gen. 35:23–26; 1 Chron. 2:1–2	David's line born in Jerusalem	2 Sam. 5:12–16; 1 Chron. 3:4–9; 14:3–7
Esau's line	Gen. 36:1–43; 1 Chron. 1:35–54	Solomon's governors and officials	1 Kings 4:1–19
Jacob's line who went to Egypt	Gen. 46:8–27; Exod. 6:14–15	Solomon's line	1 Chron. 3:10–24
From Levi to Aaron and Moses	Exod. 6:16–25; Num. 3:17–20; 26:57–60	The temple musicians	1 Chron. 6:33–46
The Israelites who left Egypt	Num. 26:5–51	Aaron's line	1 Chron. 6:50–52
Judah's line	1 Chron. 2:3–55; 4:1–21	Aaron's line who carried the ark	1 Chron. 15:4–10
Simeon's line	1 Chron. 4:24–27, 34–37	The exiles who returned to Jerusalem	Ezra 2:1–61
Reuben's line	1 Chron. 5:3–8	Ezra's genealogy	Ezra 7:1–5
Gad's line	1 Chron. 5:11–15	Those who married foreign women	Ezra 10:18–44
Levi's line	1 Chron. 6:1–30	Jesus' genealogy through Joseph	Matt. 1:1–17
Issachar's line	1 Chron. 7:1–5	Jesus' genealogy through Mary	Luke 3:23–38

31

GOD'S COMMUNICATION METHOD

Way God Communicates in the Bible	Reference
theophany (when God appears to someone)	Gen. 18; Josh. 5:14; Judg. 6:22; Dan. 6:22
voice	Gen. 18:13, 17; Exod. 19:9, 21–24; Isa. 6:8
dreams	Gen. 20:3; 31:10–13; 37:5–9; Matt. 1:20
prophets	Judg. 6:8; 2 Sam. 12:25; Heb. 1:1
signs (writing on the wall)	Judg. 6:36–40; 1 Kings 18:36–38; Dan. 5:5–6
the Holy Spirit	2 Sam. 23:2–3; John 16:12–15; 1 Cor. 2:13
visions	Isa. 1:1; Ezek. 1:1; Dan. 2:19
scripture	Dan. 9:2; Luke 24:27; 1 Cor. 15:3
through Christ	Matt. 5–7; 12:25–37; Heb. 1:2
the church	Acts 3:11–26; 5:1–10; 16:18

Languages Spoken in the Bible

Language	Reference
Arabic	*Acts 2:11*
Aramaic	*2 Kings 18:26*
Ashdod's language	*Neh. 13:24*
Canaan's language	*Isa. 19:18*
Chaldean (Babylonian)	*Dan. 1:4*
Egyptian	*Ps. 114:1*
Greek	*Acts 21:37*
Hebrew	*2 Kings 18:28*
Latin	*John 19:19–20*
Lycaonian	*Acts 14:11*

Codex Arabicus (Arabic)

Codex Frisingensis (Latin)   Papyrus 46 (Greek)

OLD TESTAMENT HIGH PRIESTS

Description	Reference
Aaron	*Exod. 28:1; 29:9; Num. 17; 18:1*
Eleazar	*Num. 20:26, 28; Deut. 10:6*
Phinehas	*Josh. 22:30; 1 Chron. 6:4*
Abishua	*1 Chron. 6:4*
Bukki	*1 Chron. 6:5, 51; Ezra 7:4*
Uzzi	*1 Chron. 6:5, 51; Ezra 7:4*
Zerahiah	*1 Chron. 6:6*
Meraioth	*1 Chron. 6:7*
Amariah	*1 Chron. 6:11; 2 Chron. 19:11*
Eli	*1 Sam. 1:9–18*
Ahitub	*1 Chron. 6:8*
Ahijah	*1 Sam. 14:3*
Ahimelek	*2 Sam. 8:17; 1 Chron. 24:3, 6, 31*
Abiathar	*1 Sam. 23:9*
Zadok	*2 Sam. 8:17; 15:24, 27*
Ahimaaz	*2 Sam. 15:36; 17:17–20*
Azariah	*1 Kings 4:2; 1 Chron. 6:10, 13–14; 2 Chron. 26:17–20*
Johanan	*1 Chron. 6:9–10*
Jehoiarib	*1 Chron. 9:10*
Jehoiada	*2 Kings 11:12–21; 2 Chron. 23*
Uriah	*2 Kings 16:10–16*
Shallum	*1 Chron. 6:13*
Hilkiah	*2 Kings 22:4, 8, 10; 1 Chron. 6:13*
Seraiah	*2 Kings 25:18; 1 Chron. 6:14*
Jehozadak (Josedech/Jozadak)	*1 Chron. 6:14–15; Ezra 3:2*

Artist depictions of high priests

The 10 Commandments

	The 10 Commandments	Reference
1	Have no other gods but the one true God.	*Exod. 20:3; Deut. 5:7; Judg. 2:17; 1 Kings 11:4*
2	Do not create or worship idols.	*Exod. 20:4–6; Deut. 5:8–10; Acts 7:41; 1 Cor. 8:4*
3	Do not disrespect the name of God.	*Exod. 20:7; Deut. 5:11; Ps. 139:20*
4	Observe the Sabbath.	*Exod. 20:8–11; Deut. 5:12–15; Matt. 12:1–8; Mark 6:2; Luke 6:5; John 9:16; Col. 2:16*
5	Honor your parents.	*Exod. 20:12; Deut. 5:16; Matt. 19:19; Eph. 6:1–2; Col. 3:20*
6	Do not commit murder.	*Exod. 20:13; Deut. 5:17; Matt. 5:21; 19:18; Rom. 13:9*
7	Do not commit adultery.	*Exod. 20:14; Deut. 5:18; Matt. 5:27–32; 19:18; John 8:1–11; Rom. 13:9*
8	Do not steal.	*Exod. 20:15; Deut. 5:19; Matt. 19:18; Rom. 2:21; 13:9; Eph. 4:28*
9	Do not testify falsely against your neighbor.	*Exod. 20:16; Deut. 5:20; Prov. 25:18; Matt. 19:18; Mark 14:57*
10	Do not covet anything that belongs to someone else.	*Exod. 20:17; Deut. 5:21; Rom. 7:7; 13:9*

No false witness No murder Honor parents
Commandments
Observe sabbath Don't steal No idols
Ten
No other gods
Don't covet Honor the sabbath No adultery

WEIGHTS AND MEASURES

Measure	Additional Information	Reference
cubit	Approximately 18 inches	*Gen. 6:15; 1 Sam. 17:4; 1 Kings 6:2*
gomed	Approximately 12 inches	*Judg. 3:16*
handbreadth	Approximately 3 inches	*Exod. 25:25; 1 Kings 7:26*
pace/step	Approximately 1 yard	*2 Sam. 6:13*
rod/reed	Approximately 9 feet	*Ezek. 40:3–5; 42:16–19*
span	Approximately 9 inches	*Exod. 28:16; 39:9; Isa. 23:15*
fathom	Approximately 6 feet	*Acts 27:28*
furlong	Approximately 200 yards (also a stadium)	*Rev. 14:20; 21:16*
shekel	Approximately 2/5 of an ounce	*1 Sam. 17:5–7; 2 Kings 7:1*
gerah	Approximately 0.02 ounces; 1/20 of a shekel	*Exod. 30:13; Lev. 27:25*
beka	Approximately 0.2 ounces; ½ of a shekel	*Gen. 24:22; Exod. 38:26*
pim	Approximately 0.3 ounces; 2/3 of a shekel	*1 Sam. 13:21*
mina	Approximately 1¼ pounds; 50 shekels	*Luke 19:16–24*
talent	Approximately 75 pounds; 3000 shekels	*Matt. 25:15–28*
kesitah	A weight measure between ½ and 1 shekel	*Gen. 33:19; Josh. 24:32; Job 42:11*
litra	Approximately 12 ounces	*John 12:3; 19:39*
homer	Approximately 50 gallons (also cor/kor)	*Lev. 27:16; 1 Kings 5:11*
lethek	A dry measure of approximately 25 gallons	*Hosea 3:2*
ephah	A dry measure of approximately 5 gallons	*Ezek. 45:11; Zech. 5:6–10*
seah	A dry measure of approximately 7 quarts	*Gen. 18:6; 1 Sam. 25:18*
omer	A dry measure of approximately 2 quarts	*Exod. 16:22, 36*
cab/kab	A dry measure of approximately 1 quart	*2 Kings 6:25*
choinix	A dry measure of a little more than a quart	*Rev. 6:6*
saton	A dry measure of approximately 6 quarts	*Matt. 13:33; Luke 13:21*
koros	A dry measure of approximately 120 gallons	*Luke 16:7*
bath	Approximately 6 gallons; 1/10 of a homer	*1 Kings 7:23–26*
hin	Approximately 1 gallon; 1/6 of a bath	*Exod. 29:40; Num. 15:4–10*
metretes	Approximately 10 gallons	*John 2:6*
xestes	Approximately 1¼ pints	*Mark 7:4*
tsemed	Approximately ½ an acre (also ma'aneh)	*1 Sam. 14:14; Isa. 5:10*

WHAT THE BIBLE SAYS ABOUT ITSELF

What the Bible Says about Itself	Reference
Jesus validated much of the Old Testament by directly referencing it or by living out its prophecies.	Matt. 5:18; 12:38–41; 19:3–6; Luke 17:26–30; 20:37–38; 24:44; John 6:9
Both the Old Testament and the New Testament were validated by Paul when he quoted Deuteronomy 25:4 and Luke 10:7.	1 Cor. 9:9; 1 Tim. 5:18
It is God-breathed.	2 Tim. 3:16
It is useful for teaching.	2 Tim. 3:16
It is useful for rebuking.	2 Tim. 3:16
It is useful for correcting.	2 Tim. 3:16
It is useful for training in righteousness.	2 Tim. 3:16
It equips us for good works.	2 Tim. 3:17
Scripture was given by God not man.	2 Pet. 1:20
Paul's writings were validated as scripture.	2 Pet. 3:15–16
Paul's words were validated as the Word of God.	1 Thess. 2:13
It is living and active.	Heb. 4:12
It is sharper than a double-edged sword.	Heb. 4:12
It penetrates.	Heb. 4:12
It judges the thoughts and attitudes of the heart.	Heb. 4:12
The book of Revelation is called a prophecy and the Word of God.	Rev. 1:1–3; 22:9–10, 18

BIBLE LISTS

CHARACTERS, HEROES & VILLAINS

BAD WOMEN

Name	Description	Reference
Athaliah	Ahab's daughter, who killed her grandsons and made herself queen.	*2 Kings 11:1–3*
Delilah	Had Samson's hair cut and delivered him to the Philistines	*Judg. 16:1–22*
Herodias	Hated John the Baptist for condemning her relationship with her husband's brother; persuaded her daughter to ask for his head	*Matt. 14:3–6; Mark 6:17–28; Luke 3:19*
Jezebel	King Ahab's wife, who introduced Ahab to Baal and killed God's prophets.	*1 Kings 18:13, 19; 21:5–25*
Job's wife	Advised Job to curse God and die	*Job 2:9–10*
Kozbi	One of the Midianite women who seduced the men of Israel	*Num. 25:14–15*
Maakah	Was deposed as queen mother by Asa because she made an Asherah pole	*1 Kings 15:2–13*
Michal	Showed contempt for David's praise and thus never had children	*1 Sam. 18:20–19:17; 2 Sam. 6:16–23*
Noadiah	A prophet who tried to intimidate Nehemiah	*Neh. 6:14*
Peninnah	Made fun of Hannah for not having a son	*1 Sam. 1:2–7*
Potiphar's wife	Lied that Joseph had tried to seduce her and had him thrown in prison	*Gen. 39:6–23*
Prostitute who stole a baby	Was wisely judged by Solomon and had to give the baby back to his real mother	*1 Kings 3:16–27*
Salome	Asked for the head of John the Baptist (not named in the Bible, but traditionally ascribed this name)	*Matt. 14:3–11*
Sapphira	Ananias's wife. She lied about the money they gave and was struck dead.	*Acts 5:1–10*
Zeresh	Haman's wife. She encouraged Haman to have Mordecai impaled on a pole.	*Esther 5:14*

Samson and Delilah

Samson and Delilah

GENESIS.

CAST OF CHARACTERS: GENESIS THROUGH DEUTERONOMY

40

Name	Description	Reference
Aaron	Moses' brother. Helped deliver Israel out of Egypt.	Exod. 6:20
Abel	Adam and Eve's second son. Was faithful in his offerings. Was killed by his brother Cain.	Gen. 4:2
Abraham	The first patriarch; Isaac's father; founder of the Hebrew nation	Gen. 17:5
Adam	The first person created by God	Gen. 2:20
Balaam	The king of Moab hired him to curse Israel; however, God prevented him from doing so.	Num. 22:5
Balak	King of Moab who wanted Balaam to curse Israel	Num. 22:2
Cain	Adam and Eve's first son. Murdered his brother Abel.	Gen. 4:1
Caleb	One of the twelve Moses sent to explore Canaan. He encouraged the people to go and take possession of the land and was spared from the plague because of his faith.	Num. 13:6
Enoch	Methuselah's father. Walked faithfully with God. Was taken to heaven alive by God.	Gen. 5:22–24
Esau	Isaac and Rachel's son. Sold his birthright to his twin, Jacob, for a bowl of stew.	Gen. 25:25
Eve	Mother of all the living. Was deceived by the serpent.	Gen. 3:20; 4:1
Hagar	Sarah's slave; Abraham's second wife; Ishmael's mother	Gen. 16:1
Isaac	Abraham's son; father of Jacob and Esau	Gen. 25:19–26
Ishmael	Abraham and Hagar's son	Gen. 16:15
Jacob	Abraham's son. Wrestled with God. Father of Israel.	Gen. 32:28
Jethro	Moses' father-in-law. Advised Moses regarding leadership of the Israelites.	Exod. 3:1
Jochebed	Moses' mother	Exod. 2:1–10; 6:20
Joshua	Moses' successor. One of the twelve Moses sent to explore Canaan.	Exod. 17:9
Joseph (Jacob's son)	Was sold into slavery by his brothers and later rescued Egypt and his family from famine	Gen. 37:2–5

Enoch

Adam and Eve

Ishmael banished

Jethro's daughters

CAST OF CHARACTERS: GENESIS THROUGH DEUTERONOMY (CONTINUED)

Name	Description	Reference
Judah	Jacob's son; ancestor of Jesus	Gen. 29:35
Laban	Rachel and Leah's father. Tricked Jacob into working for seven more years.	Gen. 24:29
Leah	Jacob's first wife who bore six of his children	Gen. 29:16
Lot	Abraham's nephew who was delivered from the destruction of Sodom and Gomorrah	Gen. 13:1
Melchizedek	A high priest, a king priest, a priest forever. Resembled the Son of God. Received tithes from Abraham. Blessed Abraham.	Gen. 14:18–20
Miriam	Moses' sister who asked Pharaoh's daughter if she needed a nursemaid, and then brought Moses' mother to her; assisted Moses in delivering Israel; was stricken with leprosy when she rebelled against Moses	Exod. 2:1–10
Moses	Was "more humble than anyone else on the face of the earth." Delivered the Israelites out of Egypt.	Exod. 3:1; Num. 12:3
Noah	Was told to build an ark, and he did. He saved his family from a global flood.	Gen. 6:9
Pharaoh	Enslaved the Israelites in Egypt	Exod. 1:8
Rachel	Jacob's favorite wife; mother of Joseph and Benjamin	Gen. 29–35
Rebekah	Isaac's wife; mother of Esau and Jacob	Gen. 22:23
Sarah	Abraham's wife; Isaac's mother	Gen. 17:15
Seth	Adam and Eve's third son	Gen. 4:25
Shem	Noah's son; Abraham's ancestor	Gen. 11:10
Tamar	A widow who tricked her father-in-law, Judah, into getting her pregnant with twins Perez and Zerah; became an ancestor of Christ	Gen. 38:6

41

Israel in Egypt

CAST OF CHARACTERS: THE HISTORICAL BOOKS

Name	Description	Reference
Abigail	A beautiful and discerning woman who prevented David from killing her husband, Nabal, and his household; later became David's wife.	*1 Sam. 25*
Abner	Saul's uncle. Commander of Saul's army. Defected to David's side after Saul's son offended him.	*1 Sam. 14:50*
Absalom	David's son. Killed his brother Amnon in revenge. Tried to take the throne from David. Famous for his hair, which eventually got him killed.	*2 Sam. 3:3*
King Ahab	Married Jezebel; introduced Baal worship on a national scale	*1 Kings 16:28–34*
Amnon	David's firstborn. Raped his sister and was killed by Absalom.	*2 Sam. 3:2*
Artaxerxes	King of Persia who temporarily stopped the rebuilding of Jerusalem	*Ezra 4:7*
King Asa	Built fortified cities; removed many idols and "did what was right in the eyes of the LORD, as his father David had done"; lacked faith late in life	*1 Kings 15:8–15*
Athaliah	Jezebel's daughter, who killed her grandsons to make herself queen of Judah	*2 Kings 11:1–3*
Bathsheba	David's wife; Solomon's mother	*2 Sam. 11:3*
Boaz	An ancestor of David who married Ruth	*Ruth 2:1*
Cyrus	King of Persia who allowed the Israelites to return to Jerusalem	*Ezra 1:1*
Darius	King of Persia who confirmed Cyrus's decree and helped the Israelites rebuild Jerusalem	*Ezra 6:1*

42

Tomb of Cyrus

Absalom

King Asa

CAST OF CHARACTERS:
THE HISTORICAL BOOKS (CONTINUED)

Name	Description	Reference
David	Second king of Israel. His heart was "fully devoted" to God. His descendants, including Jesus, are called the House of David.	1 Sam. 16:13; 1 Kings 11:4; 15:3
Deborah	Female judge who led the Israelites in their victory over the Canaanites and was called "a mother in Israel"	Judg. 4:4–5
Delilah	Had Samson's hair cut and delivered him to the Philistines	Judg. 16:1–22
Eli	A high priest who cared for young Samuel	1 Sam. 1:9
Elijah	Prophet to King Ahab and King Ahaziah. Was there on Mt. Carmel for the face-off between Baal and Jehovah. Ordered Baal's prophets killed. Was taken to heaven in a whirlwind.	1 Kings 17:1
Elisha	Elijah's successor, who inherited a double portion of Elijah's spirit	1 Kings 19:19
Esther	Jewish queen of Persia. Prevented Haman from killing all the Jews.	Esther
Ezra	A scribe and teacher who led the exiles from Babylon to Jerusalem	Ezra 7:6
Gideon	Tore down the altar to Baal and cut down the Asherah pole; saved Israel from the Midianites and Amalekites	Judg. 6:11
Goliath	A Philistine giant who oppressed the Israelites until he was killed by David	1 Sam. 17:23–50
Haman	Tried unsuccessfully to kill Mordecai and all the Jews	Esther 3:8–15
Hannah	Prayed for a son and gave him to God	1 Sam. 1:10–11, 19–20
King Hezekiah	Restored the temple; reinstituted Passover; prayed for protection from Assyria	2 Kings 16:20
Huldah	A prophet who was consulted when the Book of the Law was found	2 Kings 22:14
Jesse	David's father	1 Sam. 16:1
Jezebel	Ahab's wife, who introduced Ahab to Baal worship and killed God's prophets	1 Kings 18:13, 19
Joab	David's nephew. A commander in David's army. Helped have Uriah killed.	2 Sam. 2:13
Jonathan	King Saul's son; David's good friend	1 Sam. 13:16

Name	Description	Reference
Mordecai	Raised Esther, his cousin, as his own; saved the king from assassination; convinced Esther to save the Jews from extermination	*Esther 2:5–7*
Naaman	An Aram official whom Elisha healed of leprosy	*2 Kings 5:1*
Naomi	Ruth's mother-in-law	*Ruth 1:2*
Nathan	Prophet who advised David during his reign	*2 Sam. 7:2*
Nebuchadnezzar	Powerful king of Babylon. Conquered Jerusalem.	*2 Kings 24:1*
Nehemiah	Cupbearer who received permission to rebuild Jerusalem and became governor	*Neh. 1:1*
Orpah	Naomi's daughter-in-law, who decided to stay in her own land	*Ruth 1:4*
Rahab	A harlot who hid Joshua's spies in her home and was saved when Jericho was destroyed; is included in Jesus' genealogy	*Josh. 2:1–24*
Ruth	Stood by her mother-in-law, Naomi. She is an ancestor of David and Jesus.	*Ruth 1:4*
Samuel	One of Israel's last judges. Lived in the temple from a young age. Installed Saul and David as kings.	1 Sam. 3:1
Saul	Israel's first king, who disqualified himself with repeated disobedience	1 Sam. 11:14–15
Solomon	Israel's wisest king, who had hundreds of wives and worshipped idols in his later years	1 Kings 1:38–39
Queen Vashti	Refused to come to her husband, King Xerxes' party and was deposed for disobedience	*Esther 1:10–12*
Xerxes	King of Persia who took Esther as his wife	*Esther 1:1*

44

Solomon's Sin

Saul Attacking David

CAST OF CHARACTERS: GOSPELS

Name	Description	Reference
Andrew	One of the Twelve; Peter's brother	*Matt. 10:1–4*
Anna	A prophet who never left the temple, but prayed and fasted day and night. When baby Jesus was brought to the temple, she recognized Him as the Messiah.	*Luke 2:36–38*
Annas	Questioned Jesus and then sent Him to the Sanhedrin (who then sent Him to Pilate)	*John 18:13–24*
Bartholomew (Nathanael)	One of the twelve apostles	*Matt. 10:1–4*
Caiaphas	Said, "It is better for you that one man die for the people than that the whole nation perish." He meant to instigate Jesus' murder, but he unknowingly prophesied the purpose of the cross.	*John 11:49–50*
Elizabeth	Zechariah's wife; John the Baptist's mother	*Luke 1:5–6, 24–25*
Gabriel	The angel who announced Jesus and John the Baptist's births	*Luke 1:19, 26*
Herod Antipas	Beheaded John the Baptist.	*Matt. 14:1*
Herodias	Hated John the Baptist for condemning her relationship with her husband's brother. Persuaded her daughter to ask for his head.	*Mark 6:17–28*
Herod the Great	Slaughtered infant boys around the time of Jesus' birth	*Matt. 2:1–12*
James	Brother of the apostle John; member of Jesus' inner circle	*Matt. 4:21*
James son of Alphaeus	One of the Twelve	*Matt. 10:1–4*
Jesus	Son of God. Gave His life on a cross as a ransom for many.	*Matt. 1:1; 20:28*

Madonna and child

Pontius Pilate

Gabriel

Simon the Zealot

CAST OF CHARACTERS: GOSPELS (CONTINUED)

Name	Description	Reference
Joanna	A woman who supported Jesus and who found the empty tomb and told the disciples Jesus had risen.	*Luke 8:3; 24:10*
John the apostle	Apostle in Jesus' inner circle who was charged with the care of Jesus' mother	*Matt. 4:21*
John the Baptist	Jesus' cousin. A prophet. Baptized thousands, including Jesus.	*Matt. 3:1*
Joseph	Raised Jesus as his own son; trusted and obeyed God regarding Mary	*Matt. 1:18*
Judas Iscariot	One of the Twelve. Betrayed Jesus for thirty pieces of silver.	*Matt. 10:1–4*
Lazarus	Brother of Mary and Martha whom Jesus raised from the dead	*John 11:1*
Martha	Sister of Mary and Lazarus who was often anxious and busy	*Luke 10:39–42*
Mary	Jesus' mother	*Matt. 1:16–25*
Mary Magdalene	A close follower of Jesus who was the first to see Him after His resurrection	*John 20:1–2*
Mary of Bethany	Sister of Martha and Lazarus who poured oil on Jesus' feet and wiped them with her hair	*Luke 10:39–42*
Matthew (Levi)	One of the Twelve	*Matt. 10:1–4*
Nicodemus	A member of the Sanhedrin who believed in Jesus and assisted with His burial	*John 3:1*
Philip	One of the Twelve	*Matt. 10:1–4*
Pilate	Governor who consented to Jesus' crucifixion	*Matt. 27:2*
Pilate's wife	Tried to convince Pilate to free Jesus	*Matt. 27:19*
Shepherds	Were told by an angel of Jesus' birth	*Luke 2:8*
Simeon	A righteous man who blessed Jesus when He was brought to the temple as a child	*Luke 2:25*
Simon Peter	Jesus' chief apostle	*Matt. 4:18*
Simon the Zealot	One of the Twelve	*Matt. 10:1–4*
Thaddaeus (Judas)	One of the Twelve	*Matt. 10:1–4*
Thomas	One of the Twelve	*Matt. 10:1–4*
Zechariah	A priest; John the Baptist's father	*Luke 1:5*

46

CAST OF CHARACTERS: ACTS AND THE EPISTLES

Name	Description	Reference
Ananias	Sapphira's husband. Lied about the money they gave and was struck dead.	*Acts 5:1–10*
Ananias	Healed Paul's blindness	*Acts 9:17–19*
Apollos	A preacher taught by Priscilla and Aquila	*Acts 18:24*
Aquila	Priscilla's husband. Lived in Corinth. Traveled with Paul to Ephesus. Risked his life for Paul and the Gentile church.	*Acts 18:2*
Barnabas	Accompanied Paul on his first missionary journey	*Acts 4:36*
Cornelius	A Gentile who was visited by Peter. He and his household were converted.	*Acts 10:1*
Epaphroditus	A leader in the Philippian church	*Phil. 2:25*
Eunice	Timothy's mother, who passed her faith on to him	*2 Tim. 1:5*
Eutychus	Raised from the dead by Paul	*Acts 20:9*
Felix	Governor who heard Paul's defense but refused to take action	*Acts 23:24*
Herod Agrippa I	Ordered the death of the apostle James and persecuted the early church	*Acts 12:1–4*
James	Brother of Jesus. Leader in the church. Wrote the Epistle of James.	*Acts 15:13*
Jason	A believer who took Paul in and was arrested	*Acts 17:5–9*
John Mark	Accompanied Paul and Barnabas. Wrote the Gospel of Mark.	*Acts 12:12*
Jude	Brother of Jesus. Wrote the Epistle of Jude.	*Jude 1*
Lois	Timothy's grandmother, who passed her faith on to him	*2 Tim. 1:5*
Luke	Paul's doctor. Wrote the Gospel of Luke and the Acts of the Apostles.	*Col. 4:14*
Lydia	A dealer in purple cloth from the city of Thyatira. She and her household were baptized by Paul. He then stayed with them awhile.	*Acts 16:14*
Mary	John Mark's mother	*Acts 12:12*
Matthias	Judas's replacement	*Acts 1:26*
Onesimus	Philemon's runaway slave who was converted by Paul and carried Paul's Epistle to Philemon back to Philemon	*Philem. 10*

Cast of Characters:
Acts and the Epistles (continued)

Name	Description	Reference
Paul/Saul	Apostle to the Gentiles. Wrote much of the New Testament.	*Acts 13:9*
Philemon	Paul's fellow worker to whom Paul wrote to make a case for the runaway slave, Onesimus	*Philem. 1*
Philip	A prominent evangelist in the Christian community	*Acts 6:5*
Phoebe	A servant in the church in Cenchreae who assisted Paul and delivered his letter to the Romans	*Rom. 16:1–2*
Porcius Festus	Governor after Felix, who heard Paul's defense and sent him to Caesar for an appeal	*Acts 24:27*
Priscilla	Aquila's wife; a fellow tentmaker whom Paul stayed with in Corinth. She traveled with Paul to Ephesus, helped her husband in instructing Apollos, and also risked her life for Paul and the Gentile church.	*Acts 18:2–4*
Sapphira	Ananias's wife. Lied about the money they gave and was struck dead.	*Acts 5:1–10*
Silas	Joined Paul in his journeys after Barnabas and John Mark left	*Acts 15:40*
Stephen	A deacon who was martyred for the cause of Christ	*Acts 6:5*
Tabitha (Dorcas)	Raised from the dead by Peter	*Acts 9:36*
Timothy	Paul's protégé	*Acts 16:1*
Titus	Paul's protégé	*2 Cor. 2:13*

Roman slaves

Close Friendships

Name	Reference
Judah and Hirah the Adullamite	*Gen. 38:12*
Moses and Joshua	*Num. 11:28*
Naomi and Ruth	*Ruth 1:16–18*
David and Jonathan	*1 Sam. 18:1*
Amnon and Jonadab	*2 Sam. 13:3*
Elijah and Elisha	*2 Kings 2:1–4*
Daniel, Shadrach, Meshach, and Abednego	*Dan. 1:6–7, 19*
Jesus, Lazarus, Mary, and Martha	*John 11:1–3*
Jesus and His disciples	*John 15:13–15*
Paul and Barnabas	*Acts 9:26–27*
Barnabas and John Mark	*Acts 15:39*
Paul and Luke	*Col. 4:14*
Paul and Timothy	*2 Tim. 1:2*

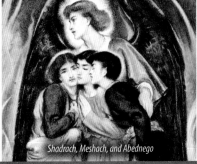

Shadrach, Meshach, and Abednego

DAVID: HIS LAST WORDS

The Last Words of David	Reference
Made Solomon king	1 Kings 1:28–35
Encouraged Solomon to be faithful	1 Kings 2:1–4
Charged Solomon to deal with Joab	1 Kings 2:5–6
Charged Solomon to be kind to the sons of Barzillai of Gilead	1 Kings 2:7
Charged Solomon to deal with Shimei	1 Kings 2:8–9
Gave Solomon the plans for the temple	1 Chron. 28:11–12
Gave Solomon the guidelines for dividing the priests and Levites	1 Chron. 28:13
Gave Solomon the correct weights for the gold articles in the temple	1 Chron. 28:14–18
Charged the people to give toward the work of the temple	1 Chron. 29:1–5
Praised God for the gifts of the temple	1 Chron. 29:10–20

EXAMPLES OF GREAT FAITH

Example of Faith	Reference
Noah building the ark	*Gen. 5–8*
Abraham leaving his home	*Gen. 12:1–4*
Abraham's willingness to sacrifice his son	*Gen. 22:1–19*
Puah and Shiphrah refusing to kill the Hebrew boys	*Exod. 1:15–21*
Moses' mother hiding him after his birth	*Exod. 2:1–4*
Moses and Aaron leading the Israelites out of Egypt	*Exod. 7:6–7*
Caleb and Joshua giving a good report after exploring Canaan	*Num. 13:30*
Rahab protecting the spies	*Josh. 2:1–3*
Joshua and his men destroying Jericho	*Josh. 6*
Gideon defeating the Midianites with only 300 men	*Judg. 7*
Samson killing the Philistines with one blow	*Judg. 16:26–30*
Ruth standing by Naomi rather than remaining in her own land	*Ruth 1:16*
Hannah praying for a son and then giving him to God	*1 Sam. 1*
David slaying Goliath	*1 Sam. 17:45–50*
Jonathan speaking up for David	*1 Sam. 19:1–7*
Elijah during the showdown on Mount Carmel	*1 Kings 18:22–24*
Esther appearing before the king without permission	*Esther 4:15–16*
Nehemiah asking the king to let him return to Jerusalem	*Neh. 2:1–5*
Daniel refusing to eat the king's food	*Dan. 1:8*
Shadrach, Meshach, and Abednego refusing to bow down before the idol	*Dan. 3:16–18*
Daniel praying to God despite the king's orders	*Dan. 6:7–10*

Fall of Jericho

Gideon's victory

Naomi and Ruth

EXAMPLES OF GREAT FAITH (CONTINUED)

Example of Faith	Reference
Joseph taking Mary to be his wife	*Matt. 1:20–24*
The centurion asking Jesus to heal his servant	*Matt. 8:5–10; Luke 7:1–9*
The woman touching Jesus' robe in the crowd	*Matt. 9:20–22; Mark 5:25–34; Luke 8:43–48*
Bartimaeus asking for his sight back	*Matt. 9:27–29; Mark 10:46–52; Luke 18:35–43*
The Canaanite woman asking Jesus to heal her daughter	*Matt. 15:21–28*
The men lowering the paralytic down through the roof	*Mark 2:1–5; Luke 5:17–20*
The woman with the alabaster jar kissing and anointing Jesus' feet	*Luke 7:36–50*
The ten lepers asking to be healed	*Luke 17:12–19*
John believing that Jesus had risen from the dead	*John 20:8*
Stephen dying for the faith	*Acts 6:5; 7:55–59*
Peter going to Cornelius's house	*Acts 10:22–24*
The crippled man at Lystra getting healed by Paul	*Acts 14:8–10*

Jesus heals Bartimaeus

Men lowering the paralytic

Woman with the alabaster jar

FAITHFUL FOLLOWERS

Name	Description	Reference
Abel	Adam and Eve's second son, who was faithful in his offerings	*Gen. 4:1–4*
Abigail	A beautiful and discerning woman who prevented David from killing her husband, Nabal, and his household. She later became David's wife.	*1 Sam. 25*
Abraham	The first patriarch; Isaac's father; founder of the Hebrew nation	*Gen. 17:5*
David	Second king of Israel. His heart was "fully devoted" to God. His descendants, including Jesus, are called the house of David.	*1 Sam. 16:13; 1 Kings 11:4; 15:3*
Enoch	Methuselah's father, who walked faithfully with God and was taken to heaven alive by God.	*Gen. 5:22–24*
Esther	Jewish queen of Persia who prevented Haman from killing all the Jews	*Esther*
Hannah	Prayed for a son and gave him to God	*1 Sam. 1:10–11, 19–20*
Moses	Was "more humble than anyone else on the face of the earth"; delivered the Israelites out of Egypt	*Exod. 3:1; Num. 12:3*
Noah	Was told to build an ark, and he did. He saved his family from a global flood.	*Gen. 6:9*
Ruth	Stood by her mother-in-law Naomi. She is an ancestor of David and Jesus.	*Ruth*

53

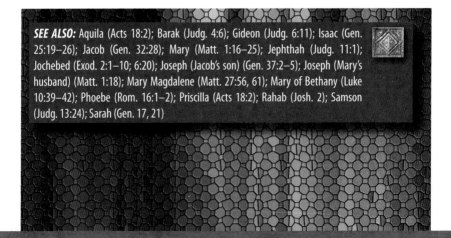

SEE ALSO: Aquila (Acts 18:2); Barak (Judg. 4:6); Gideon (Judg. 6:11); Isaac (Gen. 25:19–26); Jacob (Gen. 32:28); Mary (Matt. 1:16–25); Jephthah (Judg. 11:1); Jochebed (Exod. 2:1–10; 6:20); Joseph (Jacob's son) (Gen. 37:2–5); Joseph (Mary's husband) (Matt. 1:18); Mary Magdalene (Matt. 27:56, 61); Mary of Bethany (Luke 10:39–42); Phoebe (Rom. 16:1–2); Priscilla (Acts 18:2); Rahab (Josh. 2); Samson (Judg. 13:24); Sarah (Gen. 17, 21)

FAMOUS AFRICANS

Name	Description	Reference
Alexander	Son of Simon of Cyrene	*Mark 15:21*
Apollos	Came from Alexandria to teach the gospel, but had to be assisted by Priscilla and Aquila	*Acts 18:24–28*
Asenath	Joseph's wife	*Gen. 41:45*
Candake (Candace)	Queen of the Ethiopians	*Acts 8:27*
Cush	Ham's son	*Gen. 10:6*
Ebed-Melek	Ethiopian treasurer who rescued Jeremiah after he was thrown in a cistern	*Jer. 38:7*
Ethiopian eunuch	Was assisted by Philip as he was trying to understand the Bible; was baptized	*Acts 8:27*
Hagar	Sarah's servant who was given to Abraham and bore Ishmael	*Gen. 16:1*
Ham	Noah's son	*Gen. 10:1*
Jethro	Zipporah's (Moses' wife) father	*Exod. 3:1*
Kedar	A son of Ishmael whose name means "dark-skinned"	*Gen. 25:13*
Lucius of Cyrene	A prophet or teacher at the church in Antioch	*Acts 13:1*
Nimrod	A descendant of Cush who became a mighty warrior. The Tower of Babel was built under his leadership.	*Gen. 10:8–9*
Put	Ham's son	*Gen. 10:6*
Queen of Sheba	Visited Solomon and tested his wisdom; was so impressed with Solomon that she gave him gold, spices, and precious stones	*1 Kings 10:1–13*
Rufus	Son of Simon of Cyrene	*Mark 15:21*
Simeon called Niger	A Christian in Antioch	*Acts 13:1–3*
Simon of Cyrene	Forced to carry Jesus' cross	*Matt. 27:32; Mark 15:21; Luke 23:26*
Tirhakah	A Cushite king of Egypt	*2 Kings 19:9*
Zerah the Cushite	Attacked Judah but was stopped by King Asa and his army	*2 Chron. 14:9–15*
Zipporah	Moses' wife	*Exod. 2:21–22; Num. 12:1*

FAMOUS BROTHERS AND SISTERS

Name	Description	Reference
Abraham and Sarah	Also husband and wife	*Gen. 20:12*
Amram and Jochebed	Moses' parents	*Exod. 6:20*
Moses, Aaron, and Miriam	Worked together to lead the Israelites	*Num. 26:59*
Laban and Rebekah	Laban gave his blessing for Rebekah to marry Isaac.	*Gen. 24:29*
Simeon, Levi, and Dinah	Simeon and Levi killed Shechem and every male in the city because Shechem raped their sister.	*Gen. 34:25*
Absalom, Amnon, and Tamar	Absalom killed Amnon because he raped their sister.	*2 Sam. 13:1*
Jehosheba and Ahaziah	Jehosheba was King Ahaziah's sister. She rescued King Joash.	*2 Kings 11:2*
Lazarus, Mary, and Martha	Close friends of Jesus. Jesus raised Lazarus from the dead.	*John 11:1*

Lazarus, Mary, and Martha

Abraham and Sarah (with Hagar)

Moses and Miriam

FAMOUS COUPLES

Famous Couple	Reference
Adam and Eve	*Gen. 2:20–24*
Abraham and Sarah	*Gen. 11:29*
Nahor and Milkah	*Gen. 11:29*
Abraham and Hagar	*Gen. 16:1–3*
Isaac and Rebekah	*Gen. 24:66–67*
Abraham and Keturah	*Gen. 25:1*
Jacob and Leah	*Gen. 29:22–30; Hosea 12:12*
Jacob and Rachel	*Gen. 29:22–30; Hosea 12:12*
Jacob and Bilhah	*Gen. 30:4*
Jacob and Zilpah	*Gen. 30:9*
Tamar and Er	*Gen. 38:6*
Joseph and Asenath	*Gen. 41:45*
Moses and Zipporah	*Exod. 2:21*
Amram and Jochebed	*Num. 26:59*
Aksah and Othniel	*Josh. 15:16–17; Judg. 1:12–13*
Samson and Philistine woman from Timnah	*Judg. 14:1–10*
Ruth and Boaz	*Ruth 4:13*
Hannah and Elkanah	*1 Sam. 1:1–2*
Merab and Adriel	*1 Sam. 18:18–19*
David and Michal	*1 Sam. 18:27; 2 Sam. 3:14*
David and Abigail	*1 Sam. 25:39–40*
David and Bathsheba	*2 Sam. 11:26–27; 12:24; Matt. 1:6*
Ahab and Jezebel	*1 Kings 16:31; 21:5*
Esther and King Xerxes	*Esther 2:17–18*
Hosea and Gomer	*Hosea 1:2–3; 3:1*
Mary and Joseph	*Matt. 1:24*
Herod and Herodias	*Matt. 14:3–4; Mark 6:17–18; Luke 3:19*
Zechariah and Elizabeth	*Luke 1:5, 13, 24*
Ananias and Sapphira	*Acts 5:1*
Aquila and Priscilla	*Acts 18:1–2*

GOOD AND BAD PARENTS AND CHILDREN

Name	Parent/Child	Reference
Adam and Eve/Abel	good/good	*Gen. 4:2–8*
Adam and Eve/Cain	good/bad	*Gen. 4:8*
Noah/Ham	good/bad	*Gen. 9:21–27*
Abraham and Sarah/Isaac	good/good	*Gen. 21:12*
Isaac/Esau	good/bad	*Gen. 26:34–35*
Jacob/Joseph	good/good	*Gen. 45:9; 46:29*
Jochebed/Moses	good/good	*Exod. 2:2–3*
Manoah/Samson	good/flawed	*Judg. 13:8*
Hannah/Samuel	good/good	*1 Sam. 1:28*
Eli/two sons	bad/bad	*1 Sam. 3:13*
Samuel/his sons	good/bad	*1 Sam. 8:3*
Saul/Jonathan	bad/good	*1 Sam. 20:33*
David/Absalom	good/bad	*2 Sam. 15:10*
Jeroboam/Nadab	bad/bad	*1 Kings 15:25–26*
Hezekiah/Manasseh	good/bad	*2 Kings 21:1–2*
Athaliah/Ahaziah	bad/bad	*2 Chron. 22:2–5*
Manasseh/his sons	bad/unknown	*2 Chron. 33:6*
Herodias/Salome	bad/bad	*Mark 6:24*
Zechariah and Elizabeth/John the Baptist	good/good	*Luke 1:80*
Eunice/Timothy	good/good	*2 Tim. 1:5*

Adam and Eve grieve Abel

Abraham and Isaac

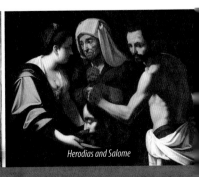

Herodias and Salome

GREAT MEN

Name	Description	Reference
Abraham	The first patriarch; Isaac's father; founder of the Hebrew nation	*Gen. 17:5*
Adam	The first person created by God (photo above)	*Gen. 2:20*
Boaz	An ancestor of David who married Ruth	*Ruth 2:1*
Caleb	One of the twelve Moses sent to explore Canaan. He encouraged the people to go and take possession of the land and was spared from the plague because of his faith.	*Num. 13:1–6, 30; 14:24–38*
Daniel	A prophet who interpreted dreams and survived a lions' den	*Dan. 1:6; 2:24–47; 4:19–27; 6:1–24*
David	Second king of Israel. His heart was "fully devoted" to God. His descendants, including Jesus, are called the house of David.	*1 Sam. 16:13; 1 Kings 11:4; 15:3*
Elijah	Prophet to King Ahab and King Ahaziah. Was on Mount Carmel for the face-off between Baal and Jehovah. Ordered Baal's prophets killed. Was taken to heaven in a whirlwind.	*1 Kings 17:1*
Enoch	Methuselah's father. He walked faithfully with God and was taken to heaven alive by God.	*Gen. 5:22–24*
Ezra	A scribe and teacher who led the exiles from Babylon to Jerusalem	*Ezra 7:6*
Isaiah	A major prophet to four kings of Judah who made several prophecies about Jesus	*Isa. 1:1*
Jacob	Abraham's son who wrestled with God and was the father of Israel	*Gen. 32:28*
Jesus	Son of God. He gave His life on a cross as a ransom for many.	*Matt. 1:1; 20:28*

58

King David

Name	Description	Reference
John the Apostle	Apostle in Jesus' inner circle who was charged with the care of Jesus' mother	*Matt. 4:21*
John the Baptist	Jesus' cousin, a prophet who baptized thousands, including Jesus.	*Matt. 3:1*
Jonathan	King Saul's son; David's good friend	*1 Sam. 13:16*
Joseph (Jacob's son)	Was sold into slavery by his brothers and later rescued Egypt and his family from famine	*Gen. 37:2–5*
Joseph (Mary's husband)	Raised Jesus as his own son; trusted and obeyed God regarding Mary	*Matt. 1:18*
Joshua	Moses' successor. One of the twelve Moses sent to explore Canaan. He brought the Israelites into possession of the promised land.	*Josh. 1:1*
Mordecai	Raised Esther, his cousin, as his own; saved the king from assassination; convinced Esther to save the Jews from extermination.	*Esther 2:5–7*
Moses	Was "more humble than anyone else on the face of the earth"; delivered the Israelites out of Egypt.	*Exod. 3:1; Num. 12:3*
Noah	Was told to build an ark, and he did. He saved his family from a global flood.	*Gen. 6:9*
Paul/Saul	Apostle to the Gentiles who wrote much of the New Testament	*Acts 13:9*
Peter	Jesus' chief apostle	*Matt. 4:18*
Samuel	One of Israel's last judges, who lived in the temple from a young age. He installed Saul and David as kings.	*1 Sam. 3:1*
Solomon	David's son. King of Israel. Built the temple in Jerusalem. Was blessed by God with great wisdom and riches.	*1 Kings 3:5*

59

Moses

Elijah and the woman's son

Daniel in the lions' den

GREAT WOMEN

Name	Description	Reference
Abigail	A discerning woman who prevented David from killing her husband, Nabal, and his household. She later became David's wife.	*1 Sam. 25:3–42*
Anna	A prophet who never left the temple, but prayed and fasted day and night. When baby Jesus was brought to the temple, she recognized Him as the Messiah.	*Luke 2:36–38*
Deborah	Female judge who led the Israelites in their victory over the Canaanites and was called "a mother in Israel"	*Judg. 4:4–5; 5:7*
Elizabeth	Wife of Zechariah and mother of John the Baptist	*Luke 1:5–6, 24–25*
Esther	Jewish queen of Persia who prevented Haman from killing all the Jews	*Esther*
Eunice	Timothy's mother, who passed her faith on to him	*Acts 16:1; 2 Tim. 1:5; 3:14–15*
Eve	Mother of all the living who was deceived by the serpent	*Gen. 3:13, 20; 4:1*
Hannah	Prayed for a son and gave him to God	*1 Sam. 1:10–11, 19–20*
Huldah	A prophet consulted when the Book of the Law was found	*2 Kings 22:14*
Jael	Killed Sisera, commander of the Canaanites	*Judg. 4:18–24*
Jehosheba	Saved Joash's life when Athaliah was murdering the king's heirs	*2 Kings 11:2*
Joanna	A woman who supported Jesus and who found the empty tomb and told the disciples Jesus had risen	*Luke 8:3; 24:10*
Jochebed	Moses' mother	*Exod. 2:1–10; 6:20*
Leah	Jacob's wife who bore six of his children	*Gen. 29–30*
Lois	Timothy's grandmother, who passed her faith on to him	*2 Tim. 1:5*
Lydia	A dealer in purple cloth from the city of Thyatira. She and her household were baptized by Paul. He then stayed with them for a while.	*Acts 16:14*
Martha	Sister of Mary and Lazarus who was often anxious and busy	*Luke 10:39–42; John 11:17–44*
Mary	Jesus' mother (photo above)	*Matt. 1:16–25; Luke 1:26–56*

GREAT WOMEN (CONTINUED)

Name	Description	Reference
Mary Magdalene	A close follower of Jesus who was the first to see Him after His resurrection	*Matt. 27:56, 61; 28:1–11*
Mary of Bethany	Sister of Martha and Lazarus who poured oil on Jesus' feet and wiped them with her hair	*Luke 10:39–42; John 11:28–32; 12:3*
Miriam	Moses' sister who asked Pharaoh's daughter if she needed a nursemaid, and then brought Moses' mother to her. She assisted Moses in delivering Israel; was stricken with leprosy when she rebelled against Moses.	*Exod. 2:1–10; 15:20–21; Num. 12:1–15; 20:1*
Naomi	Ruth's mother-in-law	*Ruth*
Pharaoh's daughter	Rescued Moses from the Nile and raised him as her own son	*Exod. 2:1–10*
Phoebe	A servant in the church in Cenchreae	*Rom. 16:1–2*
Pilate's wife	Tried to convince Pilate to free Jesus	*Matt. 27:19*
Priscilla	Aquila's wife; a fellow tentmaker whom Paul stayed with in Corinth. She traveled with Paul to Ephesus, helped her husband in instructing Apollos, and also risked her life for Paul and the Gentile church.	*Acts 18:2–4, 18–19, 24–26; Rom. 16:3–5; 1 Cor. 16:19; 2 Tim. 4:19*
Puah	Midwife who refused to kill the Hebrew baby boys	*Exod. 1:15–21*
Rachel	Jacob's favorite wife; mother of Joseph and Benjamin	*Gen. 29–35*
Rahab	A harlot who hid Joshua's spies in her home and was saved when Jericho was destroyed; is included in Jesus' genealogy	*Josh. 2; Matt. 1:5*
Rebekah	Isaac's wife; mother of Esau and Jacob	*Gen. 24:15–67; 25:19–28; 26:1–11*
Ruth	Stood by her mother-in-law, Naomi. She is an ancestor of David and Jesus.	*Ruth*
Salome	Zebedee's wife; mother of James and John; witness of the Crucifixion	*Matt. 20:20–23; 27:56; Mark 15:40–41; 16:1*
Sarah	Abraham's wife; Isaac's mother	*Gen. 17, 21*
Shiphrah	Midwife who refused to kill the Hebrew baby boys	*Exod. 1:15–21*
Tamar	A widow who tricked her father-in-law, Judah, into getting her pregnant with twins Perez and Zerah; ancestor of Jesus	*Gen. 38*

Hospitable People

Hospitable People	Person(s) Shown Hospitality	Reference
Abraham	Angels/God	Gen. 18:1–8
Lot	Angels	Gen. 19:4–8
Rebekah and her family	Abraham's servant	Gen. 24:24–25, 31–33
Isaac	Abimelek and his men	Gen. 26:26–31
Jethro (Reuel)	Moses	Exod. 2:18–21
Rahab	The two spies	Josh. 2:1–6
The concubine and her father	The Levite from Ephraim	Judg. 19:1–10
The old man from Gibeah	The Levite from Ephraim	Judg. 19:16–21
Abigail	David and his men	1 Sam. 25:18
The widow at Zarephath	Elijah	1 Kings 17:10–11
The Shunammite woman	Elisha	2 Kings 4:8–10
Elisha	The soldiers from Aram	2 Kings 6:22–23
Simon the leper	Jesus and the disciples	Matt. 26:6
Peter and Andrew	Jesus and the disciples	Mark 1:29
Mary Magdalene, Joanna, Susanna,	Jesus and the disciples	Luke 8:2–3
Mary and Martha	Jesus and the disciples	Luke 10:38; John 12:1–3
Zacchaeus	Jesus	Luke 19:1–10
Simon the tanner	Peter	Acts 10:5–6
Lydia	Paul and his fellow travelers	Acts 16:13–15
Titius Justus	Paul	Acts 18:7
Philip the evangelist	Paul and his fellow travelers	Acts 21:8
Mnason	Paul and his fellow travelers	Acts 21:16
Publius	Paul and his fellow travelers	Acts 28:7

Rebekah and Abraham's servant

Abraham and angels

Rahab and the spies

Zacchaeus

MEMORABLE CONVERSIONS

Name	Description	Reference
Jacob	He wrestled with God.	Gen. 32:22–32
Rahab	She saw what God could do.	Josh. 2:11; Heb. 11:31
Ruth	She chose Naomi's God.	Ruth 1:16
King Saul	God changed his heart.	1 Sam. 10:6–10
Naaman	Elisha cured him of leprosy.	2 Kings 5:15
King Manasseh	He suffered imprisonment and distress.	2 Chron. 33:10–12
King Nebuchadnezzar	God took his authority away and made him live like an animal and eat grass.	Dan. 4:34
King Darius	He witnessed God saving Daniel from the lions' den.	Dan. 6:26
The people of Nineveh	Jonah witnessed to them.	Jon. 3:7–10
Zacchaeus	Jesus visited him.	Luke 19:2–8
The thief on the cross	He witnessed Jesus on the cross while he himself was being crucified.	Luke 23:39–43
Nicodemus	Jesus witnessed to him.	John 3
The Samaritans	The woman at the well witnessed to them.	John 4:42
The man born blind	Jesus opened his eyes.	John 9:35–38
The Jews at Pentecost	Peter preached to them.	Acts 2:22–41
The Samaritans	They heard the message from Philip and saw the signs he performed.	Acts 8:5–25
Simon the sorcerer	He was influenced by Philip.	Acts 8:9–13
The Ethiopian eunuch	Philip helped him understand scripture.	Acts 8:26–40
Paul	Jesus met and blinded him. (Photo above)	Acts 9:1–22
Cornelius	Peter visited his house and shared the gospel with him.	Acts 10
The Gentiles	Peter witnessed to them.	Acts 10:44–48
Lydia	God opened her heart, and Paul shared the gospel with her.	Acts 16:13–15
The Philippian jailer	He witnessed God freeing Paul and Silas from prison.	Acts 16:25–34
Crispus, the synagogue ruler	He was influenced by Paul.	Acts 18:8

NOTABLE FIRSTBORNS

Name	Description	Name	Description
Cain	Son of Adam (Gen. 4:1)	Hanoch	Son of Reuben (Gen. 46:9)
Enoch	Son of Cain (Gen. 4:17)	Jemuel/ Nemuel	Son of Simeon (Gen. 46:10; Exod. 6:15; 1 Chron. 4:24)
Jabal	Son of Lamech (Gen. 4:20)	Gershon	Son of Levi (Gen. 46:11; Exod. 6:16)
Enosh	Son of Seth (Gen. 4:26; 1 Chron. 1:1)	Tola	Son of Issachar (Gen. 46:13)
Enoch	Son of Jared (Gen. 5:18)	Sered	Son of Zebulun (Gen. 46:14)
Methuse-lah	Son of Enoch (Gen. 5:21; 1 Chron. 1:3)	Zephon	Son of Gad (Gen. 46:16)
Lamech	Son of Methuselah (Gen. 5:25; 1 Chron. 1:3)	Imnah	Son of Asher (Gen. 46:17)
Noah	Son of Lamech (Gen. 5:28–29; 1 Chron. 1:3)	Bela	Son of Benjamin (Gen. 46:21)
Japheth	Son of Noah (Gen. 5:32)	Hushim	Son of Dan (Gen. 46:23)
Gomer	Son of Japheth (Gen. 10:2)	Jahziel	Son of Naphtali (Gen. 46:24)
Cush	Son of Ham (Gen. 10:6)	Makir	Son of Manasseh (Gen. 50:23)
Elam	Son of Shem (Gen. 10:22)	Gershom	Son of Moses (Exod. 2:22; 18:2)
Nahor	Son of Serug (Gen. 11:22)	Nadab	Son of Aaron (Exod. 6:23; Num. 3:2)
Terah	Son of Nahor (Gen. 11:24)	Phinehas	Son of Eleazar (a son of Aaron) (Exod. 6:25; 1 Chron. 6:4)
Ishmael	Son of Abraham (Gen. 16:15)	Caleb	Son of Jephunneh (Num. 32:12)
Moab	Son of Lot (Gen. 19:37)	Jonathan	Son of Saul (1 Sam. 14:49–50)
Uz	Son of Nahor (Gen. 22:20–21)	King Jehoiachin	2 Kings 24:6; 1 Chron. 3:16
Nebaioth	Son of Ishmael (Gen. 25:13)	Simon Peter	Matt. 4:18; Mark 1:16; John 1:42
Esau	Son of Isaac (Gen. 25:25)	James	Matt. 4:21; 10:2; Mark 1:19
Reuben	Son of Jacob (Gen. 29:32; 49:3)	Jesus	Matt. 13:55; Mark 6:3; Luke 2:7; 8:19–20; John 7:3–5
Eliphaz	Son of Esau (Gen. 36:4, 10)	Martha of Bethany	Luke 10:38–41; John 11:20; 12:2
Manasseh	Son of Joseph (Gen. 41:51; Josh. 17:1)		

PEOPLE WHO FASTED

Name	Description	Reference
Israel	A means of worship and repentance	*Judg. 20:26;* *1 Sam. 7:5–6*
The people of Jabesh Gilead	A sign of mourning	*1 Sam. 31:13*
David and his men	A sign of mourning	*2 Sam. 1:11–12*
David	David was pleading with God for his son's life.	*2 Sam. 12:16*
Elders and nobles in Naboth's city	Calling a formal fast was one way to prevent a disaster; in this case, it was used manipulatively and dishonestly, and Naboth was killed.	*1 Kings 21:11–12*
Ahab	A way for Ahab to show humility	*1 Kings 21:24, 27*
Ezra and the returning exiles	They were praying for a safe return to Jerusalem.	*Ezra 8:21–23*
Nehemiah	Nehemiah was praying for Jerusalem.	*Neh. 1:1–4*
Esther and Jews in exile	A form of prayer. A way to show humility. Esther needed strength to approach the king.	*Esther 4:16*
Daniel	Daniel fasted and prayed for Jerusalem.	*Dan. 9:1–3*
The people of Nineveh	A way to demonstrate their newfound belief	*Jon. 3:5*
Jesus	Jesus fasted before being tested by the devil in the wilderness.	*Matt. 4:2*
Prophets and teachers at Antioch	A means of praise	*Acts 13:1–3*
Paul and Barnabas	As they committed new elders to the Lord	*Acts 14:23*

Three Temptations of Christ

Vicious Villains

Name	Description	Reference
Abimelek	Killed seventy of his brothers in order to become king	*Judg. 9*
Ahab	King of Israel who married Jezebel and introduced Baal worship on a national scale	*1 Kings 16:28–34*
Athaliah	Ahab's daughter, who killed her grandsons to make herself queen of Judah	*2 Kings 11:1–3*
Cain	Killed his brother Abel, becoming the first murderer	*Gen. 4:1–9*
Delilah	Had Samson's hair cut and delivered him to the Philistines	*Judg. 16:1–22*
Goliath	A Philistine giant who oppressed the Israelites until he was killed by David	*1 Sam. 17:23–50*
Haman	Tried unsuccessfully to kill Mordecai and all the Jews	*Esther 3:8–15*
Herod the Great	Slaughtered infant boys around the time of Jesus' birth	*Matt. 2:1–12*
Jezebel	Ahab's wife, who introduced Ahab to Baal worship and killed God's prophets	*1 Kings 18:13, 19; 21:5–25*
Judas Iscariot	One of the twelve apostles. He betrayed Jesus for thirty pieces of silver.	*Matt. 26:14–25, 47–50; 27:3–10; Acts 1:16–25*
Pharaoh	Enslaved the Israelites and continually refused to let them go free until God forced him to with the ten plagues	*Exod. 5*
Satan	The ultimate enemy who will be defeated at Jesus' return	*Gen. 3:1–14; Job 1:6–12; Rev. 12:9*

Cain and Abel

WOMEN MENTIONED BY PAUL

Name	Description	Reference
Apphia	Allowed the church to meet in her home	*Philem. 2*
Chloe	Informed Paul about arguments in Corinth	*1 Cor. 1:11*
Claudia	A Christian woman in Rome	*2 Tim. 4:21*
Damaris	Became a follower of Christ	*Acts 17:34*
Eunice	Timothy's mother, who passed her faith down to him	*Acts 16:1–3; 2 Tim. 1:5; 3:14–15*
Euodia	An early member of the church at Philippi. Paul pleaded with her to settle her differences with Syntyche.	*Phil. 4:2*
Julia	Recognized by Paul as a saint	*Rom. 16:15*
Junia(s)	Called an apostle by Paul. Junia (Junias in some translations) was in prison with Paul. Scholars disagree about Junia's gender. Junia is a feminine name, but it could also be a form of the masculine Junianus. If Junia was a woman, she was likely the wife of Andronicus.	*Rom. 16:7*
Lois	Timothy's grandmother, who passed down her faith to him	*2 Tim. 1:5*

67

YOUNG PEOPLE

Name	Description	Reference
Abednego	Refused to bow to Nebuchadnezzar's idol	*Dan. 3:16*
Azariah	Became king of Judah at age sixteen	*2 Kings 14:21*
Benjamin	Rachel died while giving birth to him.	*Gen. 35:18*
Daniel	Refused to eat the king's food (photo above)	*Dan. 1:8–16*
David	A shepherd who killed Goliath, played the harp for Saul, and was anointed king	*1 Sam. 16:11; 17:14–15, 50*
David and Bath-sheba's first son	Died as punishment for David's sins	*2 Sam. 12:15–18*
Gershom	God almost killed Moses because he did not circumcise his son Gershom.	*Exod. 2:22; 4:24–26*
Isaac	The promised son born to Abraham. God tested Abraham while Isaac was still a boy.	*Gen. 21:4; 22:12*
Ishmael	Abraham's first son, who was circumcised at age thirteen	*Gen. 16:15; 17:25–26*
Jairus's daughter	Raised from the dead by Jesus	*Mark 5:35, 41–42*
Jehoiachin	Became king of Judah at age eighteen	*2 Kings 24:8*
Jeremiah	Was still young when he was called by God	*Jer. 1:6*
Jesus	Was visited by shepherds and Magi when He was very young. His parents presumed He was lost in Jerusalem when He was twelve but found Him talking with the teachers in the temple.	*Matt. 2:8; Luke 2:8–20, 41–51*
Joash	Was hidden by his aunt so that he wouldn't be killed on orders from his grandmother; became king of Judah at the age of seven	*2 Kings 11:21*

Samson

Sacrifice of Isaac

Moses in a basket

David and Goliath

Name	Description	Reference
John the Baptist	Leaped in Elizabeth's womb when a pregnant Mary visited	*Luke 1:41*
Joseph	Jacob's favorite son who had prophetic dreams and was sold into slavery by his brothers	*Gen. 30:24; 37:3–9, 28*
Josiah	Became king of Judah at age eight	*2 Kings 22:1*
Manasseh	Became king of Judah at age twelve	*2 Kings 21:1*
Mephibosheth	Jonathan's son who became lame in both feet when his nurse accidentally dropped him while fleeing	*2 Sam. 4:4*
Meshach	Refused to bow to Nebuchadnezzar's idol	*Dan. 3:16*
Mika	Son of Mephibosheth	*2 Sam. 9:12*
Moses	Hidden as a baby and then put in a basket and placed in the Nile	*Exod. 2:2–3*
Obed	Son of Ruth and Boaz	*Ruth 4:13–16*
Paul's nephew	Alerted Paul of the plot to kill him	*Acts 23:16*
Samson	His birth was prophesied. His mother was told that he would be a Nazirite and would deliver Israel from the Philistines.	*Judg. 13:5, 24–25*
Samuel	Born as a result of Hannah's prayer and ministered in the temple when he was a boy	*1 Sam. 3:1*
Shadrach	Refused to bow to Nebuchadnezzar's idol	*Dan. 3:16*
Shunammite's son	Raised from the dead by Elisha	*2 Kings 4:32–37*
Solomon	God loved him and had Nathan name him Jedidiah.	*2 Sam. 12:24–25*
Syrophoenician woman's daughter	Jesus cast a demon out of her because of her mother's great faith.	*Mark 7:24–30*
Widow at Zarephath's son	Raised from the dead by Elijah	*1 Kings 17:17–24*

Shadrach, Meshach, and Abednego

BIBLE LISTS

DAILY LIFE
IN BIBLE TIMES

BUILDING MATERIALS

Description	Reference
acacia wood	*Exod. 26:37*
almugwood	*1 Kings 10:12*
bricks	*Gen. 11:3; Exod. 5:7–8, 14; 2 Sam. 12:31; Nah. 3:14*
bronze	*Exod. 26:37*
cedar wood	*1 Kings 7:2; Song of Sol. 1:17*
cypress wood	*Gen. 6:14*
fir wood	*Song of Sol. 1:17*
gold	*1 Kings 6:31–33; 2 Chron. 2:7*
iron	*Gen. 4:22; Deut. 3:11; Josh. 17:18*
juniper wood	*1 Kings 6:34; Ezek. 27:5*
mortar	*Exod. 1:14; Nah. 3:14*
olive wood (photo above)	*1 Kings 6:23*
silver	*Exod. 27:9–11*
stone	*Gen. 11:2–4; 28:22; Isa. 9:10*
tar/pitch	*Gen. 6:14; 11:2–4*

Acacia wood   Juniper tree   Gold   Olive tree

BURIALS

Burial	Burial Place	Reference
Rebekah's nurse Deborah	Under an oak near Bethel	*Gen. 35:8*
Rachel	On the way to Bethlehem	*Gen. 35:19–20*
Abraham, Sarah, Isaac, Rebekah, Leah, and Jacob	In a cave in the field of Machpelah	*Gen. 49:29–33*
Those who complained about eating manna	In Kibroth Hattaavah	*Num. 11:34*
Miriam	In Kadesh in the Desert of Zin	*Num. 20:1*
Aaron	In Moserah	*Deut. 10:6*
Moses	In a valley in Moab across from Beth Peor	*Deut. 34:6*
Achan	Beneath a pile of rocks	*Josh. 7:25–26*
King of Ai	At the entrance to the city gate under a pile of rocks	*Josh. 8:29*
Joshua	At Timnath Serah in the hill country of Ephraim	*Josh. 24:30*
Joseph	At Shechem in the land Jacob had purchased	*Josh. 24:32*
Eleazar	In Gibeah	*Josh. 24:33*
Gideon	In his father Joash's tomb, in Ophrah	*Judg. 8:32*
Jephthah	In Gilead	*Judg. 12:7*
Samson	In his father Manoah's tomb	*Judg. 16:31*
Samuel	At his house in Ramah	*1 Sam. 25:1*
Saul and his sons	Under a tamarisk tree at Jabesh	*1 Sam. 31:12–13*
Abner	In Hebron	*2 Sam. 3:32*
Ish-Bosheth	His head was buried in Abner's tomb	*2 Sam. 4:12*
Absalom	In a pit in a forest under a pile of rocks	*2 Sam. 18:17*
David	In the City of David	*1 Kings 2:10*
Joab	In the desert in his land	*1 Kings 2:34*
Solomon	In the City of David	*1 Kings 11:42–43*
Omri	In Samaria	*1 Kings 16:28*
Ahab	In Samaria	*1 Kings 22:37*

BURIALS (CONTINUED)

Burial	Burial Place	Reference
Jehoram	In Naboth's field	*2 Kings 9:25*
Ahaziah	In the City of David, in his tomb with his fathers	*2 Kings 9:28*
Manasseh	In the garden of Uzza at his palace	*2 Kings 21:18*
Amon	In his tomb in the garden of Uzza	*2 Kings 21:26*
Uzziah	In a burial field for kings	*2 Chron. 26:23*
John the Baptist	(The Bible does not specify, but tradition says Samaria.)	*Matt. 14:12*
Judas	On a potter's field, the "Field of Blood"	*Matt. 27:7; Acts 1:18*
Jesus	In Joseph of Arimathea's tomb	*John 19:38–42*

Rachel's tomb (circa 1930)

Tomb of Abraham (circa 1906)

Tomb of Joseph (circa 1900)

CASTING LOTS

Event Involving the Casting of Lots	Reference
Used by Aaron to decide which goat would be offered and which goat would be a scapegoat	Lev. 16:6–10
Used by the Israelites to determine the distribution of the land	Num. 26:55–56; Josh. 14:2
Used by Joshua to determine who had sinned	Josh. 7:16–18
Used by the Israelites to decide who would go to battle with Gibeah	Judg. 20:9–10
Used by Saul to determine who had sinned	1 Sam. 14:41–42
Used by David to determine ministry functions	1 Chron. 24:3–5; 25:8; 26:12–13
Used by the Israelites to determine who would bring wood to the altar	Neh. 10:34
Used by the Israelites to determine who would live in the newly built Jerusalem	Neh. 11:1
Used by Haman to determine when to kill the Jews	Esther 3:7
Used by sailors to determine who was responsible for the storm	Jon. 1:7
Used by soldiers to determine who would get Jesus' clothes	Matt. 27:35; Mark 15:24; Luke 23:34; John 19:24
Used by priests to determine which priest would burn incense	Luke 1:9
Used by the apostles to determine who would replace Judas	Acts 1:26

Casting lots for Jesus' clothes

Circumcisions

Description	Reference
Every male	*Gen. 17:10, 12*
Ishmael	*Gen. 17:23, 25–26*
Abraham's household	*Gen. 17:23, 27*
Abraham	*Gen. 17:24, 26; Romans 4:9–10, 12*
Isaac	*Gen. 21:4; Acts 7:8*
Every male in Shechem	*Gen. 34:24*
Moses' son	*Exod. 4:24–26*
The Israelite men who had come out of Egypt	*Josh. 5:2–8*
Timothy	*Acts 16:1–3*
Paul	*Phil.3:4–5*
Believers in Christ	*Col. 2:9–11*

Abraham circumcising Ishmael

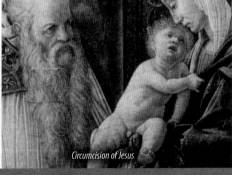

Circumcision of Jesus

CLOTHING

Description	Reference
clothing made of fig leaves	Gen. 3:7
garments of skin made by God Himself	Gen. 3:21
Joseph's lavish robe	Gen. 37:3
veil	Gen. 38:14
cloak	Gen. 39:12
sandals	Exod. 3:5
belt	Exod. 12:11
tunic	Exod. 28:4
breastpiece	Exod. 28:15
sash	Exod. 28:40
cap/headband	Exod. 28:40
linen undergarment	Exod. 28:42
supernatural clothing that did not wear out	Deut. 8:4
robe	1 Sam. 2:19
linen ephod	2 Sam. 6:14
prison clothing	2 Kings 25:29
royal clothing	Esther 8:15
loincloth	Job 12:18
headdress	Isa. 3:20
shawl	Isa. 3:23
sackcloth	Isa. 3:24
belt	Ezek. 23:15
turban	Ezek. 23:15
camel's hair clothing	Mark 1:6
the swaddling clothes baby Jesus was wrapped in	Luke 2:7–12
flowing robes	Luke 20:46–47
grave clothes	John 11:44
Jesus' seamless, woven garment	John 19:23

Fig leaf

Ancient sandal

FOOD

Food	Significance	Reference
wild game	Isaac's favorite	*Gen. 25:28*
lentil stew	Bought by Esau in exchange for his birthright	*Gen. 25:34*
honey, spices, pistachio nuts, almonds	Taken to Joseph as a gift	*Gen. 43:11*
milk and honey	Flowing in Canaan	*Exod. 3:17*
lamb, bitter herbs, unleavened bread	Part of the Passover meal	*Exod. 12:3–8*
locust, katydid, cricket, grasshopper (photo above)	Insects that could be eaten	*Lev. 11:22*
cucumbers, melons, leeks, onions, garlic	Eaten by the Israelites in Egypt	*Num. 11:5*
grain, raisins, figs	Brought to David by Abigail to save her husband's life	*1 Sam. 25:18*
wheat, barley, flour, beans, lentils, honey, curds, cheese	Brought to David and his men	*2 Sam. 17:28–29*
cattle, sheep, goats, deer, gazelles, roebucks, fowl	Solomon's daily provisions	*1 Kings 4:23*
stew made from gourds	Unsafe to eat ("death in the pot") until Elisha added flour	*2 Kings 4:38–41*
vegetables	Daniel's preferred diet	*Dan. 1:12*
locusts and wild honey	John the Baptist's diet	*Matt. 3:4*
fish	Popular Jewish food	*Luke 5:6*

Lentils

Honey

Almonds

GIFTS

Gift	Reference
Abraham's servant gave jewelry and clothing to Rebekah and her family.	*Gen. 24:53*
Jacob gave Esau several herds of animals as a peace offering.	*Gen. 32:13–16*
Jacob sent balm, honey, spices, myrrh, and pistachio nuts to Joseph.	*Gen. 43:11*
Joseph gave new clothing to his brothers.	*Gen. 45:22*
Joseph gave Benjamin three hundred shekels of silver and five sets of clothes.	*Gen. 45:22*
Joseph sent his father ten donkeys loaded with the best things of Egypt.	*Gen. 45:23*
The Israelites gave carts and oxen for the building of the tabernacle.	*Num. 7:3*
God gave the Levites to Aaron and his sons.	*Num. 8:19*
Moses and Eleazar gave 16,750 shekels of gold to God.	*Num. 31:52*
Abigail gave David bread, wine, dressed sheep, roasted grain, raisins, and figs.	*1 Sam. 25:18*
David sent plunder to the elders in Judah.	*1 Sam. 30:26*
Pharaoh gave Gezer to his daughter (Solomon's wife) as a wedding gift.	*1 Kings 9:16*
The queen of Sheba gave Solomon gold, spices, and precious stones.	*1 Kings 10:10*
Solomon's visitors gave him silver, gold, robes, spices, horses, and mules.	*1 Kings 10:25*
King Asa gave King Ben-Hadad silver and gold.	*1 Kings 15:18*
Naaman gave Gehazi two talents of silver and two sets of clothing.	*2 Kings 5:22–23*
King Ben-Hadad sent Elisha the finest wares of Damascus.	*2 Kings 8:9*
King Ahaz gave King Tiglath-Pileser of Assyria silver and gold.	*2 Kings 16:7–8*
King Marduk-Baladan of Babylon sent King Hezekiah of Babylon unknown gifts.	*2 Kings 20:12*
Judah gave unknown gifts to King Jehoshaphat.	*2 Chron. 17:5*
Some Philistines brought gifts and silver to King Jehoshaphat.	*2 Chron. 17:11*
The Arabs brought 7,700 rams and 7,700 goats to King Jehoshaphat.	*2 Chron. 17:11*
King Jehoshaphat gave his sons silver, gold, and fortified cities in Judah.	*2 Chron. 21:3*
Surrounding nations brought valuable gifts to King Hezekiah.	*2 Chron. 32:23*
The Jews gave food to one another and gifts to the poor at Purim.	*Esther 9:22*
King Nebuchadnezzar gave gifts to Daniel.	*Dan. 2:48*
The Magi gave Jesus gold, frankincense, and myrrh.	*Matt. 2:11*
The disciples sent gifts to those living in Judea.	*Acts 11:29–30*
Paul gave gifts to the poor in Jerusalem.	*Acts 24:17*
The church at Philippi sent gifts to Paul through Epaphroditus.	*Phil. 4:18*

IDOLS AND FALSE GODS

Idols and False Gods	Reference
Adrammelek/Adrammelech	2 Kings 17:31
Amon	Jer. 46:25
Anammelek/Anammelech	2 Kings 17:31
Artemis	Acts 19:27
Asherah	Judg. 6:28; 1 Kings 16:33
Ashima	2 Kings 17:30
Ashtoreth/Ishtar	Judg. 2:13; Jer. 44:17–19
Baal (temple in photo above)	Num. 25:5; 1 Kings 16:32
Baal-Zebub	2 Kings 1:2, 16
Bel/Marduk/Bel-Marduk	Isa. 46:1; Jer. 50:2
Bronze snake/Nehushtan	2 Kings 18:4
Chemosh	1 Kings 11:33; 2 Kings 23:13
Dagon	1 Sam. 5:1–5
Golden calfs	Exod. 32:1–6; 1 Kings 12:26–33
Hermes	Acts 14:12
Household gods	Gen. 31:34; Judg. 17:4; 1 Sam. 19:13
Kaiwan/Kiyyun/Saturn	Amos 5:26
Molek	1 Kings 11:5; Zeph. 1:5
Nebo	Isa. 46:1
Nebuchadnezzar's image	Dan. 3:1–6
Nergal	2 Kings 17:30
Nibhaz	2 Kings 17:31
Nisrok/Nisroch	2 Kings 19:37; Isa. 37:38
Rephan	Acts 7:43
Rimmon	2 Kings 5:18
Sakkuth	Amos 5:26
Sukkoth Benoth	2 Kings 17:30
Tammuz	Ezek. 8:14
Tartak	2 Kings 17:31
Zeus	Acts 14:12

JEWISH CALENDAR

Calendar Month	Name(s)	Reference
1st month	Abib/Aviv/Nissan/Nisan	*Exod. 12:2; 13:4*
2nd month	Ziv/Iyyar/Iyar	*1 Kings 6:1, 37*
3rd month	Sivan/Siwan	*Esther 8:9*
4th month	Tammuz/Tamuz	-
5th month	Ab/Av	-
6th month	Elul	*Neh. 6:15*
7th month	Ethanim/Tishri/Tishrei	*1 Kings 8:2*
8th month	Bul/Heshvan/Cheshvan	*1 Kings 6:38*
9th month	Kislev/Chislev/Kislew	*Neh. 1:1*
10th month	Tebeth/Tevet	*Esther 2:16*
11th month	Shebat/Shevat/Shvat	*Zech. 1:7*
12th month	Adar	*Ezra 6:15*
13th month	Veader (Added later to align the calendar with the solar year. It only occurred every three years.)	-

80

Jewish Months and Their Modern Equivalent Months

An additional month named "Second Adar" was added every second or third year to bring the lunar calendar in line with the solar year. Taken from *The QuickView Bible* published by Zondervan. Used by permission.

Jewish Holidays and Festivals

Holiday & Festival	What Is Celebrated	Reference
Festival of Unleavened Bread	Deliverance out of Egypt	Exod. 12:14–17
Passover	Deliverance of Israel's firstborns	Exod. 12:43–49
Festival of Harvest/Weeks (Pentecost)	The giving of firstfruits	Exod. 23:16
Festival of Ingathering/ Tabernacles (Sukkot)	God's provision while in the wilderness	Exod. 23:16; Lev. 23:34
Day of Atonement (Yom Kippur)	Atonement for the entire Israelite nation	Lev. 16
Festival of Trumpets (Rosh Hashanah)	The new year	Lev. 23:23–25
Year of Jubilee	A year of rest and liberation that belonged to God	Lev. 25
Purim	Deliverance of the Jews from Haman's plot to kill them	Esther 9:24–26
Festival of Dedication (Hanukkah)	The victory of the Maccabees and the miracle of the lights	John 10:22

Shofar (trumpet)

Festival of Tabernacles in Jerusalem

Unleavened Bread

Journeys and Modes of Transportation

Journeys and Modes of Transportation	Reference
Noah and his family voyaged by ark.	*Gen. 7:7*
Abraham journeyed to a land he did not know.	*Gen. 12:1*
Hagar and Ishmael wandered in the Desert of Beersheba.	*Gen. 21:4–21*
Abraham rode a donkey to Moriah to sacrifice Isaac.	*Gen. 22:2–3*
Abraham's servant journeyed to find a wife for Isaac.	*Gen. 24:1–14*
A caravan of Ishmaelites (and their camels) took Joseph to Egypt.	*Gen. 37:25–28*
Jacob and his family journeyed to Egypt.	*Gen. 46:26–27*
Moses journeyed to and from Egypt.	*Exod. 2, 4*
The Israelites left Egypt on foot.	*Exod. 12:37–38*
The Israelites journeyed into Canaan across the Jordan.	*Josh. 4:1*
The Danites journeyed to Laish.	*Judg. 18*
The Levite and his concubine tried to journey from Bethlehem to Ephraim.	*Judg. 19*
Ruth and Naomi journeyed from Moab to Bethlehem.	*Ruth 1:6–7*
David went on the run from Saul.	*1 Sam. 18–23*
The queen of Sheba traveled on camels in a caravan to test Solomon.	*1 Kings 10:2*
A whirlwind carried Elijah to heaven.	*2 Kings 2:11–12*
Naaman journeyed to see Elijah.	*2 Kings 5:4–6*
King Solomon rode in a carriage made of wood from Lebanon.	*Song of Sol. 3:9*
Jonah tried to journey to Tarshish by ship. Then he rode around in the belly of a fish. Then he journeyed to Nineveh.	*Jon. 1–3*
The Magi journeyed to Bethlehem to see the young Jesus.	*Matt. 2:1–12*
Jesus journeyed through towns.	*Matt. 9:35*
Mary journeyed to Judea to visit Elizabeth.	*Luke 1:39–40*
Joseph and Mary journeyed to Bethlehem for the census.	*Luke 2:1–5*
The two disciples journeyed to Emmaus.	*Luke 24:13–35*
Jesus made journeys to Jerusalem. On his last journey into Jerusalem, he rode a donkey.	*John 2:13; 5:1; 12:14–15*
Jesus journeyed through Samaria.	*John 4:4–6*
Paul made several missionary journeys, some of which were by ship.	*Acts 13–28*
Paul and soldiers rode on horses.	*Acts 23:23–24*

OLD TESTAMENT LETTERS

Letter Writer	Letter Recipient	Letter Content	Reference
David	Joab	Have Uriah placed in the front lines so that he will be killed.	2 Sam. 11:14–15
Jezebel	Elders in Naboth's city	Kill Naboth.	1 Kings 21:7–11
King of Aram	King of Israel	Heal Naaman of leprosy.	2 Kings 5:4–7
Jehu	Officials of Jezreel	Kill Ahab's descendants.	2 Kings 10:1–7
Sennacherib	King Hezekiah	God cannot deliver you from Assyria.	2 Kings 19:9–14
Marduk-Baladan	King Hezekiah	He is probably offering condolences for Hezekiah's illness.	2 Kings 20:12–13
King Hiram of Tyre	Solomon	He is in agreement to provide building materials for the temple.	2 Chron. 2:11–16
Elijah	King Jehoram	He warns of disobedience.	2 Chron. 21:12–15
King Hezekiah	Israel, Judah, Ephraim, and Manasseh	He gives an invitation to celebrate the Passover at the temple.	2 Chron. 30:1, 6
Men of Trans-Euphrates	King Artaxerxes of Persia	Do not let Jerusalem be rebuilt.	Ezra 4:7–16
King Artaxerxes	Men of Trans-Euphrates	The Jews must stop rebuilding.	Ezra 4:17–23
Men of Trans-Euphrates	King Darius	Please confirm that King Cyrus intended Jerusalem rebuilt.	Ezra 5:6–17
King Darius	Officials of Trans-Euphrates	Let the building continue, and provide assistance.	Ezra 6:1–12
King Artaxerxes	Ezra	Permission to return to Jerusalem.	Ezra 7:12–26
King Artaxerxes	Governors of Trans-Euphrates and Asaph	He grants Nehemiah safe-conduct.	Neh. 2:7–9
Sanballat	Nehemiah	Threatens Nehemiah and the Jews.	Neh. 6:5–7
Tobiah	Nehemiah	Its goal is intimidation.	Neh. 6:19
Mordecai	Jews in King Xerxes's provinces	The letter is an invitation to celebrate Purim.	Esther 9:20–32
Jeremiah	Exiles in Babylon	Expect God to return you to your own land.	Jer. 29:1–23

Precious Metals, Substances, and Stones

Name	Reference	Name	Reference
agate	Exod. 28:19	jacinth	Exod. 28:19
alabaster	Matt. 26:7	jasper	Exod. 28:20
amethyst	Exod. 28:19	lapis lazuli	Exod. 28:18
balm	Ezek. 27:17	lead	Num. 31:22
beryl	Exod. 28:17	marble	1 Chron. 29:2
bronze (brass)	Gen. 4:22	myrrh	Matt. 2:11
carnelian	Exod. 28:17	nard	John 12:3
chrysolite	Exod. 28:17	oil	Luke 7:46
copper	Matt. 10:9	onyx	Exod. 28:20
coral	Job 28:18	pearl	Rev. 21:21
crystal	Job 28:17	ruby	Rev. 21:20
emerald	Exod. 28:18	sapphire	Rev. 21:19
frankincense	Exod. 30:34	silver	Num. 31:22
gold	Num. 31:22	tin	Num. 31:22
incense	Luke 1:10	topaz	Exod. 28:20
iron	Gen. 4:22	turquoise	Exod. 28:18
ivory	1 Kings 10:18		

SIGNIFICANT BUILDINGS

Significant Building	Reference
Tower of Babel	*Gen. 11:4*
tabernacle	*Exod. 26:1–4*
tower of Peniel	*Judg. 8:17*
temple	*1 Kings 6*
Solomon's Palace	*1 Kings 7:1–12*
rebuilt temple	*Ezra 2:68*
rebuilt Jerusalem wall	*Neh. 6:1*
synagogue	*Matt. 4:23*
Herod's temple	*Luke 21:5*
theater at Ephesus	*Acts 19:31*

Theater at Ephesus

Tower of Babel

Model of the tabernacle

WEAPONS

Weapon	Reference
battering ram	*Ezek. 4:2; 21:22; 26:9*
bows and arrows	*2 Kings 9:24; 13:15; 1 Chron. 12:2*
club	*Jer. 51:20*
javelins	*Josh. 8:18; 1 Sam. 17:6; 2 Sam. 18:14*
jawbone of a donkey	*Judg. 15:15–16*
shields	*1 Kings 10:17; 2 Chron. 11:12; 14:8*
sling-shots	*Judg. 20:16; 1 Sam.17:40; 1 Chron. 12:2*
spears	*Num. 25:7; Judg. 5:8; 1 Sam. 13:19; 17:7*
swords	*Gen. 34:25; Josh. 10:11; Judg. 8:10*

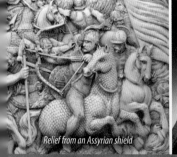
Relief from an Assyrian shield

Bronze weapon

Arrowheads from the Iron Age

WINE

Event Involving Wine	Reference
Noah became drunk and his son saw him naked.	*Gen. 9:21*
Melchizedek gave bread and wine to Abraham.	*Gen. 14:18*
Lot's daughters got him drunk so that he would get them pregnant.	*Gen. 19:32*
Jacob brought Isaac wine when he took Esau's blessing.	*Gen. 27:25*
Wine was served as a drink offering.	*Exod. 29:40*
Wine was forbidden for Aaron and his sons to drink when entering the tent of meeting.	*Lev. 10:9*
Nazirites were not allowed to drink wine.	*Num. 6:1–4*
Abigail brought wine to David.	*1 Sam. 25:18*
Absalom waited until Amnon was drunk to kill him.	*2 Sam. 13:28*
Nehemiah was responsible for serving wine to the king.	*Neh. 2:1*
King Xerxes gave a banquet and served wine generously.	*Esther 1:7–8*
Daniel refused the wine in the king's court.	*Dan. 1:8*
A hand wrote on the wall while Belshazzar and his officials drank wine.	*Dan. 5:1–5*
Jesus was offered wine mixed with gall.	*Matt. 27:34*
Jesus was offered wine vinegar from a sponge on a stick.	*Matt. 27:48*
John the Baptist was forbidden to drink wine.	*Luke 1:15*
Jesus changed water into wine.	*John 2:3–10*
When the disciples spoke in tongues, people thought they were drunk.	*Acts 2:13*
Paul instructed the Ephesians not to get drunk.	*Eph. 5:18*
Paul wrote that deacons should not indulge in wine.	*1 Tim. 3:8*
Wine could be used to cure stomach problems.	*1 Tim. 5:23*

Belshazzar's feast

Melchizedek and Abraham

Abigail meets David

BIBLE LISTS

THE DARKER
SIDE OF
THE STORY

7 Deadly Sins

Deadly Sin	Reference
anger	*Gen. 4:5; Num. 22:27; 1 Sam. 18:8*
covetousness	*Josh. 7:21; 1 Kings 21:2–4; 2 Kings 5:20–24*
envy	*Gen. 4:3–7; 37:3–4; Num. 12:1–3*
gluttony	*Exod. 16:19–20; 1 Sam. 2:12–17; 1 Cor. 11:20–22*
lust	*Gen. 34:1–4; 2 Sam. 11:2–4; 13:10–14*
pride	*2 Chron. 32:25; Esther 3:5; Dan. 5:20*
sloth	*Isa. 56:10; Acts 17:21; 2 Thess. 3:11; Heb. 6:12*

CITIES OF REFUGE

City of Refuge	Location	Reference
Bezer	Desert near the tribe of Reuben	*Josh. 20:8*
Golan	Bashan near the tribe of Manasseh	*Josh. 20:8*
Hebron/Kiriath Arba	Hill country of Judah	*Josh. 20:7*
Kedesh	Galilee	*Josh. 20:7*
Ramoth	Gilead near the tribe of Gad	*Josh. 20:8*
Shechem	Hill country of Ephraim	*Josh. 20:7*

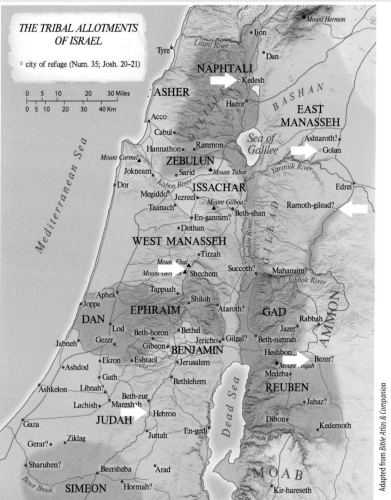

THE TRIBAL ALLOTMENTS OF ISRAEL

○ city of refuge (Num. 35; Josh. 20–21)

0   5   10   20   30 Miles
0 5 10   20   30   40 Km

Adapted from *Bible Atlas & Companion*

CONSEQUENCES OF SIN

Sinner/Sin	Result of Sin	Reference
Noah's drunkenness	Noah's son saw him naked.	Gen. 9:20–23
Lot's daughters' incestuous pregnancies	Their descendants became hostile to Israel.	Gen. 19:35–38
Abraham and Sarah's decision to have a son without God	Ishmael's descendants were hostile to Israel.	Gen. 25:17–18
Jacob's theft of Esau's blessing	We can assume that Jacob never saw his mother alive again.	Gen. 35:29
Judah's failure to keep his promise to Tamar	He had children with his daughter-in-law.	Gen. 38:15–30
Samson's failure to keep his secret	He lost his strength and was captured and tortured by the Philistines.	Judg. 16:21
Samuel's sons' disobedience	The Israelites decided they wanted a king to rule them.	1 Sam. 8:4–5
Saul's disobedience	Jonathan never became king.	1 Sam. 15:26–29
Peter's denial of Christ	He suffered grief and lack of confidence.	Matt. 26:75; John 21:15–17
Judas's betrayal of Christ	He committed suicide.	Matt. 27:3–5

Noah becomes drunk

Lot and his daughters

DISEASES AND AFFLICTIONS

Description	Reference
blindness	*Acts 9:8*
boils	*Exod. 9:9–10*
consumption	*Deut. 28:22*
deformities	*Lev. 21:20*
dropsy (swelling)	*Luke 14:1–4*
dysentery	*Acts 28:8*
eczema	*Lev. 21:20*
epilepsy	*Mark 9:17–29*
fever	*Luke 4:38–39*
gangrene	*2 Tim. 2:17*
gout	*2 Chron. 16:12*
hemorrhage	*Luke 8:43–48*
inflammation	*Deut. 28:22*
insanity	*Dan. 4:33*
itch	*Deut. 28:27*
lameness	*2 Sam. 4:4*
leprosy	*Luke 5:12–13*
muteness	*Ezek. 33:22*
paralysis	*Mark 2:1–12*
plague	*2 Sam. 24:15*
tumor	*Deut. 28:27*
worms	*Acts 12:23*

Healing of the blind man

DESTROYED CITIES AND PLACES

Destroyed Place	Reference
Ai	*Josh. 8:28*
Ar	*Isa. 15:1*
Babylon	*Jer. 50:23*
Debir	*Josh. 10:38*
Eglon	*Josh. 10:34*
Gomorrah	*Gen. 19:28*
Hazor	*Josh. 11:10*
Hebron	*Josh. 10:36*
Heshbon	*Num. 21:27–28*
Jericho	*Josh. 6:26*
Jerusalem	*Ezra 4:15*
Kedar	*Jer. 49:28*
Kir	*Isa. 15:1*
Lachish	*Josh. 10:31*
Libnah	*Josh. 10:29*
Makkedah	*Josh. 10:28*
Shechem	*Judg. 9:38–45*
Sodom	*Gen. 19:28*
Tyre	*Ezek. 26:15–19*
Zephath	*Judg. 1:17*
Ziklag	*1 Sam. 30:3*

Lot leaving Sodom

Roman troops ransack temple

EVIL ALLIANCES

Alliances	Description	Reference
Joseph's brothers	Plotted to kill Joseph, and then changed their minds and sold him	*Gen. 37:18*
Israel and the Gibeonites	The Gibeonites tricked Israel into a treaty.	*Josh. 9*
Canaanite kings	Joined forces to battle against Israel	*Josh. 9:1–2*
Northern kings	Joined forces to battle against Israel	*Josh. 11:1–5*
Solomon and Pharaoh	Solomon married Pharaoh's daughter.	*1 Kings 3:1*
Solomon and other nations	Solomon married women from nations that God had forbidden him to.	*1 Kings 11:1–4*
King Asa and Ben-Hadad	Asa gave Ben-Hadad temple treasures to keep peace.	*1 Kings 15:18–20*
King Ahaz and Tiglath-Pileser, king of Assyria	Joined forces to battle against Syria and Israel	*2 Kings 16:7–9*
Israel and Egypt	The Israelites fled to Egypt to escape the Babylonians.	*2 Kings 25:26; Isa. 30:1–3*
King Ahab and King Jehoshaphat	Joined forces to battle against Ramoth Gilead	*2 Chron. 18:1–4*
King Ahaziah and King Joram	Joined forces to battle against Ramoth Gilead	*2 Chron. 22:1–5*
King Joash and Judah	Plotted against and stoned Zechariah	*2 Chron. 24:20–22*
King Joash's officials	Conspired against and killed Joash in his bed	*2 Chron. 24:25–26*
Sanballat, Tobiah, the Arabs, the Ammonites, and the people of Ashdod	Conspired to stop the rebuilding of the wall	*Neh. 4:7–8*
Bigthana and Teresh	Plotted to kill King Xerxes	*Esther 2:21*
Haman and the royal officials	Plotted to kill the Jews	*Esther 3:2–7*
King Pekah of Israel and King Rezin of Aram	Joined forces to battle against King Ahaz of Judah	*Isa. 7:1–9*
The Pharisees	Plotted to kill Jesus	*Matt. 12:14*
Judas and the Jewish leaders	Judas agreed to deliver Jesus to the chief priests.	*Matt. 26:14–16*
The Pharisees and Herodians	Plotted to kill Jesus	*Mark 3:6*
Some Gentiles and Jews	Plotted to kill Barnabas and Paul	*Acts 14:5*
More than forty men	Plotted to kill Paul	*Acts 23:13–15*

GOD'S DISCIPLINE FOR SIN

Sinner/Sin	God's Discipline	Reference
Miriam was jealous of Moses.	She was afflicted with leprosy.	*Num. 12:10*
Moses did not trust God when he struck the rock for water.	He and Aaron did not bring their people into the promised land.	*Num. 20:10–12*
Israelites complained and lacked faith.	Snakes bit the Israelites, and many of them died.	*Num. 21:4–6*
Saul continually disobeyed.	He was dethroned.	*1 Sam. 16:1*
David had an affair with Bathsheba.	Their son died.	*2 Sam. 12:13–14*
David took a census.	God sent a plague and seventy thousand people died.	*2 Sam. 24:13–15*
The people of Israel and Judah were disobedient.	They were exiled.	*2 Kings 17:23; 1 Chron. 6:15*
Jonah refused to go to Nineveh.	He was thrown off a ship and swallowed by a giant fish.	*Jon. 2:1–9*
Zechariah had a lack of faith about John the Baptist's birth.	He was unable to speak until his son's birth.	*Luke 1:19–20*
Ananias and Sapphira lied to God.	They were struck dead.	*Acts 5:1–11*
Paul persecuted Christians.	He was struck blind.	*Acts 9:7–9*

Jonah

David and Saul

Moses and the bronze snake

INSTANCES OF REVENGE

Instance of Revenge	Reference
Cain against Abel	Gen. 4:1–16
Simeon and Levi against the men of Shechem	Gen. 34:25
Potiphar's wife against Joseph	Gen. 39:6–20
Joseph against his brothers	Gen. 42:9–24
Moses against an Egyptian	Exod. 2:11–12
The Israelites against the Midianites	Num. 31:2–3
Adoni-Zedek against Gibeon	Josh. 10:1–4
Samson against the men of Ashkelon	Judg. 14:10–19
Samson against the Philistines	Judg. 15:4–8; 16:28–30
The Israelites against the Benjamites	Judg. 20
The Israelites against the Amalekites	1 Sam. 15:2–3
Saul against the priests	1 Sam. 22:11–19
Joab against Abner	2 Sam. 3:22–34
Absalom against Amnon	2 Sam. 13:23–29
Jezebel against Elijah	1 Kings 19:2
Ahab against Micaiah	1 Kings 22:26–27
Haman against Mordecai	Esther 3:8–15
The Philistines against Judah	Ezek. 25:15–17
Herodias against John the Baptist	Mark 6:19–24
The Jews against Stephen	Acts 7:54, 59

Beheading of John the Baptist

Cain and Abel

The stoning of Stephen

MURDERED AND MARTYRED

Murdered/Martyred	Murderer	Reference
Abel	Cain	*Gen. 4:8*
Seventy brothers	Abimelek, Gideon's son	*Judg. 9:4–5*
Levite's concubine	Men of Gibeah	*Judg. 20:4–5*
Ahimelek, other priests, and inhabitants of Nob	Doeg (ordered by King Saul)	*1 Sam. 22:18–19*
Abner	Joab and his brother Abishai	*2 Sam. 3:30*
Ish-Bosheth, Saul's son	Rekab and Baanah	*2 Sam. 4:5–6*
Uriah	David	*2 Sam. 12:9*
Amnon, David's son	Absalom's men	*2 Sam. 13:28–29*
King Nadab and King Jeroboam's family	Baasha	*1 Kings 15:28–29*
King Elah and King Baasha's whole family	Zimri	*1 Kings 16:9–12*
God's prophets	Jezebel	*1 Kings 18:4*
Naboth	Jezebel	*1 Kings 21:7–14*
King Joash	Jozabad and Jehozabad	*2 Kings 12:19–21*
King Pekahiah, Argob, and Arieh	Pekah	*2 Kings 15:24–25*
King Amon	His officials	*2 Kings 21:23*
King Ahaziah's family	Athaliah, Ahaziah's mother	*2 Chron. 22:10*
Zechariah, son of priest Jehoiada	King Joash	*2 Chron. 24:20*
Uriah	King Jehoiakim	*Jer. 26:21–23*
John the Baptist	Herod Antipas	*Mark 6:17–29*
Jesus	Jewish leaders/Romans	*Mark 14:1*
Stephen	The Jews	*Acts 7:59*
James, the apostle	Herod Agrippa I	*Acts 12:1–2*
Christians	Paul	*Acts 26:10*

Killing and burial of Stephen

PEOPLE PUT IN PRISON

Inmate	Reference
Apostles	*Acts 5:18*
Aristarchus	*Col. 4:10*
Christians	*Acts 8:3*
Epaphras	*Philem. 23*
Hanani the seer	*2 Chron. 16:7–10*
Hoshea	*2 Kings 17:4*
Jehoiachin	*2 Kings 25:27*
Jeremiah	*Jer. 37:15–16*
John	*Acts 4:3*
John the Baptist	*Mark 6:17*
Joseph	*Gen. 39:20*
Manasseh	*2 Chron. 33:11*
Paul	*Acts 16:22–23; 24:27*
Peter	*Acts 4:3; 12:1–3*
Samson	*Judg. 16:21*
Silas	*Acts 16:22–23*

An apostle of Christ

Joseph

John the Baptist

STRUCK DEAD BY GOD

Victim	Reference
Er, son of Judah	*Gen. 38:6–7*
Onan, son of Judah	*Gen. 38:8–10*
Egypt's firstborns	*Exod. 12:30*
Abihu and Nadab	*Lev. 10:1–2*
Korah, Dathan, Abiram, and their households	*Num. 16:26–32*
Two hundred and fifty of Korah's followers	*Num. 26:10*
Seventy men of Beth Shemesh	*1 Sam. 6:19*
Nabal	*1 Sam. 25:36–38*
Uzzah	*2 Sam. 6:6–7*
Ananias and Sapphira	*Acts 5:1–11*

Death of Pharaoh's firstborn son

The death of Ananias

TITLES AND NAMES OF SATAN

Title and Name of Satan	Reference
Abaddon/Apollyon (Destroyer)	*Rev. 9:11*
accuser	*Rev. 12:10*
angel of the Abyss	*Rev. 9:11*
Beelzebul	*Matt. 12:24*
Belial	*2 Cor. 6:15*
devil	*Matt. 25:41*
dragon	*Rev. 13:2*
enemy/adversary	*1 Pet. 5:8*
evil one	*Matt. 13:19*
father of lies	*John 8:44*
god of this age/world	*2 Cor. 4:4*
liar	*John 8:44*
morning star (Lucifer in some translations. Scholars debate whether this name was meant to represent Satan or the king of Babylon.)	*Isa. 14:12*
murderer	*John 8:44*
prince of demons	*Matt. 12:24*
prince of this world	*John 14:30*
roaring lion	*1 Pet. 5:8*
ruler of the kingdom of the air	*Eph. 2:2*
Satan	*Job 1:6*
serpent	*Gen. 3:1*
tempter	*Matt. 4:3*
wolf	*John 10:12*

Artist depictions of Satan

VIOLATIONS: 10 COMMANDMENTS

Commandment	Famous Violation	Reference
1. Have no other gods but the one true God.	Solomon was led by his many wives to worship other gods.	*1 Kings 11:1–8*
2. Do not create or worship idols.	The golden calf	*Exod. 32:1–7*
3. Do not disrespect the name of God.	God commanded the Israelites to stone a blasphemer.	*Lev. 24:10–16*
4. Observe the Sabbath.	Merchants who were trying to sell wine and other goods in Jerusalem on the Sabbath were kicked out of the city.	*Neh. 13:15–22*
5. Honor your parents.	Absalom conspired against his father, King David.	*2 Sam. 15*
6. Do not commit murder.	Cain murdered his brother, Abel.	*Gen. 4:8*
7. Do not commit adultery.	David and Bathsheba	*2 Sam. 11*
8. Do not steal.	Rachel stole her father's household gods.	*Gen. 31:19*
9. Do not testify falsely against your neighbor.	Evil men falsely accuse Naboth so that he is executed.	*1 Kings 21*
10. Do not covet anything that belongs to someone else.	Judas Iscariot coveted money.	*Matt. 26:14–16*

Worship of the golden calf

Cain and Abel

Judas betrays Jesus

BIBLE LISTS

FUN &
FASCINATING FACTS

Baskets

Event Involving a Basket	Reference
Joseph's fellow prisoner dreamed of baskets of bread.	*Gen. 40:16*
Moses was put into a basket as a child. (Photo above)	*Exod. 2:1–6*
Worship laws included baskets of bread	*Lev. 8:26, 31*
To carry heads of men	*2 Kings 10:7*
Hebrew prophets used baskets in their prophecies.	*Jer. 24:2; Amos 8:1–2; Zech. 5*
Jesus used baskets as a teaching illustration.	*Matt. 5:15–25*
Leftover bread was picked up in a basket after Jesus' miraculous provision.	*Matt. 15:37*
Paul escaped from a city in basket.	*Acts 9:20–31*

Joseph interprets dreams

Paul's escape

Finding of Moses

Greetings

Greetings	Reference
A bow	*Gen. 19:1*
"God be gracious to you, my son."	*Gen. 43:29*
A bow and a kiss	*Exod. 18:7*
"The Lᴏʀᴅ be with you!"	*Ruth 2:4*
"Long life to you! Good health to you and your household! And good health to all that is yours!"	*1 Sam. 25:6*
"Greetings!"	*Matt 26:49; 28:9; James 1:1*
A kiss	*Matt. 26:49; Rom. 16:16*
"Greetings, you who are highly favored! The Lord is with you."	*Luke 1:28*
"Peace be with you!"	*John 20:21*
"The God of peace be with you all."	*Rom. 15:33*
"Grace and peace to you from God our Father and the Lord Jesus Christ."	*1 Cor. 1:3*
"The churches in the province of Asia send you greetings. Aquila and Priscilla greet you warmly in the Lord, and so does the church that meets at their house. All the brothers and sisters here send you greetings."	*1 Cor. 16:19–20*
"The grace of the Lord Jesus be with you."	*1 Cor. 16:23*
"The grace of the Lord Jesus Christ be with your spirit."	*Phil. 4:23*
"I pray that you may enjoy good health and that all may go well with you, even as your soul is getting along well."	*3 John 2*
"Peace to you."	*3 John 14*

EPISODES OF LAUGHTER

Description	Reference
Abraham fell facedown laughing when he found out he and Sarah would have a son.	*Gen. 17:17*
Sarah laughed at the thought of conceiving at her age.	*Gen. 18:12*
Isaac's name means "he laughs."	*Gen. 21:3–7*
Eliphaz mentioned laughter in his speech to Job.	*Job 5:22*
God told Job that the donkey laughs at the commotion in the town, the ostrich laughs at horse and rider, the horse laughs at fear, and the Leviathan laughs at the rattling of the lance.	*Job 39:7, 18, 22; 41:29*
God laughs at people's vain plots.	*Ps. 2:4*
God laughs at the wicked.	*Ps. 37:13; 59:8*
The righteous will laugh at the wicked.	*Ps. 52:6*
Wisdom will laugh when disaster strikes those who refuse to listen.	*Prov. 1:26*
Even in laughter, the heart may ache.	*Prov. 14:13*
The "Proverbs 31" woman can laugh at the days to come.	*Prov. 31:25*
Laughter is madness.	*Eccles. 2:2*
There is a time to laugh.	*Eccles. 3:4*
Frustration is better than laughter.	*Eccles. 7:3, 6*
The Lord mentioned laughter in relation to judging Babylon.	*Jer. 51:39*
The enemies of Jerusalem laughed at her destruction.	*Lam. 1:7*
The Babylonians laughed at fortified cities.	*Hab. 1:10*
The mourners laughed when Jesus said the girl was not dead.	*Matt. 9:24*
Those who wept will laugh. Those who laughed will mourn and weep.	*Luke 6:21, 25*
James wrote that believers should change their laughter to mourning.	*James 4:9*

LOST AND FOUND

Lost and Found	Reference
Saul's donkeys	*1 Sam. 9:20*
Shimei's slaves	*1 Kings 2:38*
Book of the Law	*2 Kings 22:8*
King Ahaziah	*2 Chron. 22:9*
Parable: Treasure in a Field	*Matt. 13:44*
Parable: Pearls	*Matt. 13:45–46*
Jesus in Jerusalem	*Luke 2:48–49*
Parable: sheep	*Luke 15:3–7*
Parable: coin	*Luke 15:8–10*
Parable: son (the prodigal son)	*Luke 15:11–32*

Parable of the pearl

Treasure in a field

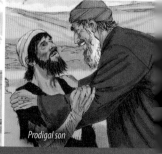
Prodigal son

SARCASTIC COMMENTS

Comment Made	Spoken by	Reference
"Am I my brother's keeper?"	Cain to God	*Gen. 4:9*
"Here comes that dreamer!"	Joseph's brothers	*Gen. 37:19*
"Was it because there were no graves in Egypt that you brought us to the desert to die?"	Israelites to Moses	*Exod. 14:11*
"Go and cry out to the gods you have chosen. Let them save you when you are in trouble!"	God to Israel	*Judg. 10:14*
"If you had not plowed with my heifer, you would not have solved my riddle."	Samson to his thirty companions	*Judg. 14:18*
"Am I a dog, that you come at me with sticks?"	Goliath to David	*1 Sam. 17:43*
"Am I so short of madmen that you have to bring this fellow here to carry on like this in front of me?"	King Achish of Gath	*1 Sam. 21:15*
"You're a man, aren't you? And who is like you in Israel? Why didn't you guard your lord the king?"	David to Abner	*1 Sam. 26:15*
"How the king of Israel has distinguished himself today, going around half-naked in full view of the slave girls of his servants as any vulgar fellow would!"	Michal to David	*2 Sam. 6:20*
"Shout louder! . . . Surely he is a god! Perhaps he is deep in thought, or busy, or traveling. Maybe he is sleeping and must be awakened."	Elijah to Baal's prophets	*1 Kings 18:27*
"One who puts on his armor should not boast like one who takes it off."	King Ahab to Ben-Hadad	*1 Kings 20:11*
"I will give you two thousand horses—if you can put riders on them!"	The Assyrian king to King Hezekiah	*2 Kings 18:23*
"How you have helped the powerless! How you have saved the arm that is feeble! What advice you have offered to one without wisdom! And what great insight you have displayed! Who has helped you utter these words? And whose spirit spoke from your mouth?"	Job to his "friend"	*Job 26:2–4*
"Where were you when I laid the earth's foundation? Tell me, if you understand. Who marked off its dimensions? Surely you know!"	God to Job	*Job 38:4–5*
"What is the way to the abode of light? And where does darkness reside? Can you take them to their places? Do you know the paths to their dwellings? Surely you know, for you were already born! You have lived so many years!"	God to Job	*Job 38:19–21*

Comment Made	Spoken by	Reference
"What are those feeble Jews doing? Will they restore their wall? Will they offer sacrifices? Will they finish in a day? Can they bring the stones back to life from those heaps of rubble—burned as they are?"	Sanballat to Jews	*Neh. 4:2*
"Like a scarecrow in a cucumber field, their idols cannot speak; they must be carried because they cannot walk. Do not fear them; they can do no harm nor can they do any good."	God to Israel	*Jer. 10:5*
"You have not obeyed me; you have not proclaimed freedom to your own people. So I now proclaim 'freedom' for you, declares the Lord—'freedom' to fall by the sword, plague and famine."	God to Israel	*Jer. 34:17*
"Go up to Gilead and get balm, Virgin Daughter Egypt. But you try many medicines in vain; there is no healing for you."	God to Israel	*Jer. 46:11*
"Hail, king of the Jews!"	Those who mocked Jesus	*Matt. 27:29*
"Already you have all you want! Already you have become rich! You have begun to reign—and that without us! How I wish that you really had begun to reign so that we might reign with you!"	Paul to Corinth	*1 Cor. 4:8*
"You gladly put up with fools since you are so wise!"	Paul to Corinth	*2 Cor. 11:19*
"How were you inferior to the other churches, except that I was never a burden to you? Forgive me this wrong!"	Paul to Corinth	*2 Cor. 12:13*

108

Job's comforters

Jesus mocked

Goliath taunts David

SECOND CHANCES

Second Chance	Reference
Abraham and Sarah after orchestrating Ishmael's birth	*Gen. 17:18–21*
Joseph's brothers after selling him into slavery	*Gen. 42–45*
Pharaoh after abusing Israel and holding Israelites in slavery	*Exod. 7–11*
The Israelites after worshipping the golden calf	*Exod. 32:7–14*
The Israelites after complaining	*Num. 11:1–2*
The Israelites after multiple instances of disobedience	*Judg. 1–18*
Samson after telling Delilah the secret of his strength	*Judg. 16:28–30*
David after seducing Bathsheba and having Uriah killed	*2 Sam. 12:13*
King Ahab after he worshipped Baal and tried to kill Elijah	*1 Kings 21:29*
David after taking the census	*1 Chron. 21:1–27*
King Rehoboam after he abandoned the law and God	*2 Chron. 12:5–12*
King Hezekiah and Judah after Hezekiah's pride	*2 Chron. 32:24–26*
King Manasseh after leading Judah into sin	*2 Chron. 33:10–19*
King Nebuchadnezzar after taking Jerusalem and killing many people	*Dan. 4:31–37*
Jonah after he disobeyed and ran away from God	*Jon. 2:10–3:3*
Nineveh after much wickedness	*Jon. 3:4–10*
Peter after denying Christ	*John 21:15–17*

Peter denies Christ

Joseph greets his father

Samson's final victory

THE SIGNIFICANCE OF WATER

The Significance of Water	Reference
Before the earth was formed, the Spirit of God was moving over the surface of the waters.	Gen. 1:1–2; 2 Pet. 3:5–6
Four rivers flowed from the Garden of Eden: Pishon, Gihon, Tigris, and Euphrates.	Gen. 2:6, 10–14
God used water as a means of judgment, but Noah and his family were saved by their faith.	Gen. 7:11; 1 Pet. 3:20–21
God demonstrated His power to Pharaoh by turning the Nile into blood.	Exod. 7:17–21
God saved the Israelites by allowing them dry passage across the Red Sea and the Jordan.	Exod. 14:15–22, 29–31; Josh. 3:14–17
The Egyptians drowned while pursuing the Israelites.	Exod. 14:23–28
God gave the people of Israel water from a rock.	Exod. 17:6; Num. 20:7–11
Water was used to rid uncleanness.	Exod. 29:4; 30:18–21; Lev. 8:6; 11:40; 16:4, 24, 26; Num. 8:7; 19:1–10; Luke 11:37–41
Water serves as a symbol of the Holy Spirit.	Isa. 44:3; John 7:37–38
God called Himself a spring of living water.	Jer. 2:13; 17:13
Rain was withheld as a sign of God's judgment.	1 Kings 8:35; Amos 4:7
God proved that He, not Baal, was responsible for sending rain.	1 Kings 18:16–46; Ps. 29:3; Jer. 10:13; Zech. 10:1
Jonah was enveloped in water.	Jon. 2:5–6
Jesus showed that He is God's Son by walking on water.	Matt. 14:22–33
Jesus told Nicodemus that a person has to be born of water and the Spirit.	John 3:5
Jesus offers Himself as living water.	John 4:7–15; 7:37–38; Rev. 21:6; 22:17
Baptism symbolizes death, burial, and resurrection.	Rom. 6:3–4; Col. 2:12

Noah's ark

Moses strikes the rock

UNUSUAL CREATURES

Creature	Reference
Behemoth	*Job 40:15–24*
Leviathan	*Job 41:1*
Ezekiel's four living creatures	*Ezek. 1:4–28*
Daniel's four beasts	*Dan. 7–8*
Revelation's four living creatures (photo above)	*Rev. 4:6–9*
slain Lamb	*Rev. 5:6*
dragon	*Rev. 12:3*
creature like a leopard	*Rev. 13:1–2*
lamb-dragon	*Rev. 13:11*
scarlet beast	*Rev. 17*

Leviathan

Worship before God's throne

Ezekiel's vision

BIBLE LISTS

GEOGRAPHY &
PEOPLE GROUPS

DESERTS

Desert	Description	Reference
Arabian	Large desert that bordered Canaan	*Exod. 23:31*
Beersheba	Desert where Hagar and Ishmael wandered	*Gen. 21:14; 1 Kings 19:3–4*
Beth Aven	Near Benjamin's border	*Josh. 18:12*
Damascus	Where Elijah anointed Hazael, Jehu, and Elisha	*1 Kings 19:15–16*
Edom	Desert through which King Joram and King Jehoshaphat went to battle with Moab	*2 Kings 3:8*
En Gedi	Where David hid from Saul	*1 Sam. 24:1*
Gibeon	Where Joab pursued Abner	*2 Sam. 2:24*
Jeruel	Where God told the Israelites they could find the armies of Ammon and Moab	*2 Chron. 20:16*
Judea	Where John the Baptist preached	*Matt. 3:1*
Kedemoth	The place from where Moses sent messengers offering peace to the Edomites	*Deut. 2:26*
Maon	Where David and his men camped	*1 Sam. 23:24–25*
Paran	Where Ishmael lived	*Gen. 21:21; Num. 10:12*
Red Sea Desert	Where God led the Israelites to the Red Sea (photo above)	*Exod. 13:18*
Shur	Where the angel found Hagar and Ishmael	*Gen. 16:7*
Sin	Where Israel camped and complained that they had no food; where God provided manna	*Exod. 16:1*
Sinai	Where the Israelites camped, near Mount Sinai	*Exod. 19:1–2; Num. 33:16*
Zin	Where Moses got water from a rock; where Miriam died and was buried	*Num. 20:1–11*
Ziph	Where David and his men hid from Saul	*1 Sam. 23:14–15*

Desert in southern Judah

EGYPT

Egypt Mentioned in the Bible	Reference
Ham's descendants through his son Egypt settled there.	Gen. 10:6, 13–14
People went there for food during a famine.	Gen. 12:10; 41:57
Egyptians often intermarried with people from other nations.	Gen. 21:21; 1 Kings 3:1; 11:19
It was the place of the Israelites' captivity.	Exod. 1:8–22
Moses was raised there.	Exod. 2:5–10
Egyptians were visited by plagues.	Exod. 7–10
It was known for tasty foods.	Num. 11:5
The climate was dry.	Deut. 11:10–11
Egyptians were known for wisdom.	1 Kings 4:30; Acts 7:22
People often fled there.	1 Kings 11:18; Matt. 2:12–13
Egyptians dabbled in the occult.	Isa. 19:3
Its destruction was prophesied.	Isa. 19:5–10; Jer. 46:2–12; Ezek. 30:14–18
Egyptians were considered proud and arrogant.	Ezek. 29:3
It had great wealth.	Heb. 11:26

Egyptian pyramids

King Tut's mask

Carved owl in the Temple of Karnak

ENEMIES OF ISRAEL

Enemy	Reference
Amalekites	*Num. 13:29*
Ammonites	*Gen. 19:38; Num. 21:24; Deut. 2:19–21*
Amorites	*Gen. 15:21; Exod. 3:8, 17; 23:23; 33:2; 34:11; Josh. 9:1; 12:8; Judg. 3:5*
Canaanites	*Gen. 15:21; Exod. 3:8, 17; 23:23; Deut. 20:17; Josh. 9:1; 12:8; Judg. 3:5*
Edomites	*2 Sam. 8:13–14*
Girgashites	*Gen. 15:18–21; Deut. 7:1; Josh. 3:10*
Hittites (photo above)	*Gen. 15:20; Exod. 3:8, 17; 23:23; 33:2; 34:11; Josh. 9:1; 12:8; Judg. 3:5*
Jebusites	*Gen. 15:21; Exod. 3:8, 17; 34:11; Deut. 20:17; Josh. 9:1; 12:8; Judg. 3:5*
Kadmonites	*Gen. 15:19*
Kenites (Midianites)	*Gen. 15:19; 1 Sam. 27:10*
Kenizzites	*Gen. 15:19*
Moabites	*Josh. 24:9; Judg. 3:12; 2 Sam. 8:2; 2 Kings 3:7; 1 Chron. 18:2; 2 Chron. 20:1*
Perizzites	*Gen. 15:20; Exod. 3:8, 17; 23:23; 33:2; 34:11; Josh. 9:1; 12:8; Judg. 3:5*
Philistines	*Judg. 3:3, 31; 1 Sam. 4:1*
Rekabites	*Neh. 3:14; Jer. 35*
Rephaites	*Gen. 15:20*

Samson defeats the Philistines

Map of Israel's Enemies

Hittites
Assyrians
Arameans

ISRAEL

Ammonites

Philistines

Edomites

Moabites

King Saul falls in battle

ISLANDS

Island	Description	Reference
Cauda/Clauda	Off the southwest coast of Crete. Paul passed by here on his way to Rome.	*Acts 27:16*
Cos/Coos/Kos	Paul spent a night here.	*Acts 21:1*
Crete (possibly Caphtor)	Paul visited this large island on the way to Rome.	*Jer. 47:4; Acts 27:12*
Cyprus	Barnabas's hometown. Where Paul began his missionary efforts.	*Acts 11:19*
Elishah	This island is part of the Peloponnesus.	*Ezek. 27:7*
Kios/Chios	Paul anchored offshore here on his way to Jerusalem.	*Acts 20:15*
Malta	Paul and his shipwrecked crew swam ashore here.	*Acts 28:1–9*
Patmos	John was exiled here. (Photo above)	*Rev. 1:9*
Rhodes	Paul probably visited here on his way from Greece to Syria.	*Acts 21:1*
Samos	Paul sailed past this island on his way to Miletus.	*Acts 20:15*
Samothrace	Paul spent the night here on his way to Philippi.	*Acts 16:11*
Syracuse	Paul stayed here three days on his way to Rome.	*Acts 28:12*
Tyre	This small island was part of the city of Tyre.	*Isa. 23:1–2*

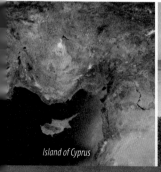

Island of Cyprus

Crete

Malta

LAKES AND SEAS

Body of Water	Additional Information	Reference
Adriatic Sea	A sea across which Paul and his crew sailed	*Acts 27:27*
Sea of Galilee/Kinnereth/Lake Tiberias	Popular sea during Jesus' time; largest freshwater lake in Israel (photo above)	*Num. 34:11;* *Matt. 4:18*
Sea of Jazer	A sea near Jazer (possibly the Dead Sea)	*Jer. 48:32*
Mediterranean/Great Sea/Sea of the Philistines	An important route for travelers during biblical times	*Ezek. 47:10*
Red Sea	Sea through which the Israelites crossed on dry land	*Exod. 10:19*
Salt Sea/Dead sea	A saltwater lake near the Valley of Siddim	*Gen. 14:3*

Images from the Dead Sea

Mountains

Mountain	Description	Reference
Abarim	Located near Nebo	*Num. 33:47–48*
Ararat	Where the ark went aground	*Gen. 8:4*
Bashan	Located northeast of the Sea of Galilee	*Ps. 68:15*
Carmel	Where Elijah's and Baal's prophets had their showdown	*1 Kings 18:19*
Ebal	Where the Israelites pronounced curses (photo above, left)	*Deut. 27:13*
Gaash	Joshua was buried north of this mountain.	*Judg. 2:9*
Gerizim	Where the Israelites pronounced blessings (photo above, right)	*Deut. 11:29*
Gilboa	Mountain on which King Saul was killed	*2 Sam. 21:12*
Hakilah	Located south of Jeshimon	*1 Sam. 23:19*
Hermon	Located near the Valley of Lebanon	*Josh. 13:11*
Hor	The Israelites' camp after wandering for forty years	*Num. 34:7–8*
Horeb/Sinai	Where the Ten Commandments were given to Moses	*Exod. 3:1; 19:2*
Lebanon	Mountain range near Tyre	*Deut. 3:25*
Moreh	The Midians camped near this mountain.	*Judg. 7:1*
Moriah	Where Abraham was going to sacrifice Isaac	*Gen. 22:2*
Nebo	Moses viewed Canaan from this mountain.	*Deut. 34:1*
Olives	Where Jesus and His disciples often met	*Matt. 24:3*
Perazim	Located near where the Philistines were defeated	*Isa. 28:21*
Tabor	Where Barak camped	*Judg. 4:6*
Zion	The temple was built on this mountain.	*2 Sam. 5:7; 2 Kings 19:31*

Ararat (Armenia)

Mt Carmel (Israel)

Mt. Sinai (Sinai Peninsula)

Names for Jerusalem

Name for Jerusalem	Reference
City of David	2 Sam. 5:7
City of God	Ps. 46:4
City of Judah	2 Chron. 25:28
City of Righteousness	Isa. 1:26
City of the Great King	Ps. 48:2
City of the Lord	Isa. 60:14
Faithful City	Isa. 1:26
Holy city	Neh. 11:1
Jebus	Judg. 19:10
Jerusalem	Judg. 19:10
Salem	Gen. 14:18
Throne of the Lord	Jer. 3:17
Zion	2 Sam. 5:7

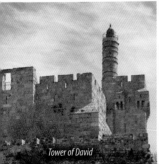
Tower of David

Children walking in Jerusalem

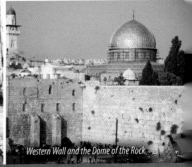
Western Wall and the Dome of the Rock

People Group	More Information	Reference	People Group	More Information	Reference
Ammonites		Gen. 19:38	Hittites	A Canaanite nation	Gen. 15:20
Amorites	A Canaanite nation	Deut. 7:1	Israelites	Nation created by God	Exod. 1:1–7
Arabs		2 Chron. 21:16	Jebusites	A Canaanite nation	Deut. 7:1
Arameans		1 Kings 10:29	Lydians		Jer. 46:9
Assyrians	Took Israel into exile	2 Kings 17:23	Maonites		Judg. 10:12
Babylonians	Took Judah into exile	2 Kings 25:1	Medes	Rulers during the exile	Dan. 5:28–31
Canaanites	God gave their land to the Israelites.	Gen. 12:6	Meunites		1 Chron. 4:41
Chaldeans	Abraham's people	Gen. 11:28	Moabites	Descendants of Lot	Gen. 19:37
Cretans		Acts 2:11	Parthians		Acts 2:9
Edomites	Descendants of Esau	Num. 20:14	Perizzites		Gen. 15:20
Egyptians	Israel's slave masters	Exod. 1:8	Persians	Rulers during the exile	Dan. 6:8
Elamites		Acts 2:9	Philistines	Major Israelite enemy	Judg. 13:1
Ethiopians		Acts 8:27	Phoenicians		Acts 11:19
Girgashites	A Canaanite nation	Deut. 7:1	Rephaites	A Canaanite nation	Gen. 15:20
Greeks		John 12:20	Romans	Rulers during the time of Christ	Luke 2:1
Hamites		1 Chron. 4:41			

PERSIAN KINGS

Persian King Mentioned in the Bible	Reference
Artaxerxes I	*Ezra 7–10; Neh. 1–13*
Cyrus	*Ezra 1–3; Isa. 45; Dan. 10:1*
Darius the Great	*Ezra 5–6*
Xerxes	*Esther 1:10*

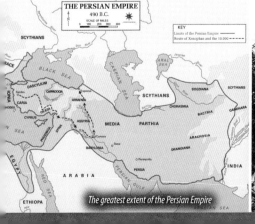

The greatest extent of the Persian Empire

Cyrus the Great

Xerxes

THE PROMISED LAND

Name and Attribute of the Promised Land	Reference
Boundaries: from the river of Egypt to the great river, the Euphrates	Gen. 15:18
Land of the Kenites, Kenizzites, Kadmonites, Hittites, Perizzites, Rephaites, Amorites, Canaanites, Girgashites, Hivites, and Jebusites	Gen. 15:19–21; Exod. 3:17
Land flowing with milk and honey	Exod. 3:8
A possession	Exod. 6:8
Land of Canaan	Lev. 14:34
"A land with brooks, streams, and deep springs gushing out into the valleys and hills; a land with wheat and barley, vines and fig trees, pomegranates, olive oil and honey; a land where bread will not be scarce and you will lack nothing; a land where the rocks are iron and you can dig copper out of the hills."	Deut. 8:7–9
"Not like the land of Egypt. . .where you planted your seed and irrigated it by foot as in a vegetable garden. But the land you are crossing the Jordan to take possession of is a land of mountains and valleys that drinks rain from heaven. It is a land the Lord your God cares for; the eyes of the Lord your God are continually on it from the beginning of the year to its end."	Deut. 11:10–12
Hittite country	Josh. 1:4
Land of Israel	1 Sam. 13:19
Israel	1 Kings 4:7
Land of Judah	Isa. 26:1
Beulah	Isa. 62:4
The Lord's land	Hosea 9:3
Holy land	Zech. 2:12
Country of the Jews	Acts 10:39
Promised land	Heb. 11:9

Artist depictions of Moses viewing the Promised Land

RIVERS

River	Description	Reference
Abana	In Damascus	*2 Kings 5:12*
Arnon	From Gilead to the Dead Sea	*Deut. 2:36*
Euphrates	From Eden	*Gen. 2:14*
Gihon	From Eden through Cush	*Gen. 2:13*
Habor	In Gozan	*2 Kings 17:6*
Jabbok	Near the Jordan	*Deut. 2:37*
Jordan	From Hermon through the Sea of Galilee to the Dead Sea	*Gen. 13:10–11; Josh. 1:2; 2 Kings 2:13–14; 5:14; Matt. 3:5–13*
Kanah Ravine	Bordered the Ephraimites' land	*Josh. 16:8*
Kebar/Chebar	A canal off the Euphrates	*Ezek. 1:1*
Kishon	In the Jezreel Valley	*Judg. 5:21*
Nile	Through Egypt	*Exod. 1:22*
Pharpar	In Damascus	*2 Kings 5:12*
Pishon	From Eden through Havilah	*Gen. 2:10–11*
Tigris	From Eden through Ashur	*Gen. 2:14*
Ulai	East of Susa	*Dan. 8:16*

Nile River

Tigris River

SIGNIFICANT CITIES

City	Reference
Antioch	*Acts 6:5; 11:19; 14:19*
Ashkelon	*Judg. 1:18; 14:19; 1 Sam. 6:17*
Babel	*Gen. 11:1–9*
Babylon	*Gen. 10:10; 2 Kings 20:14*
Beersheba	*Gen. 21:32; 26:23*
Bethlehem	*Josh. 19:15; Judg. 12:10; Ruth 1:19; Luke 2:4*
Caesarea (photo above)	*Matt. 16:13; Mark 8:27*
Damascus	*Gen. 14:15; 15:2; Acts 9*
Dan	*Gen. 14:14; Josh. 19:47; Judg. 18:29*
Harran	*Gen. 11:31; Acts 7:4*
Hazor	*Josh. 11:1–12*
Hebron	*Gen. 23:17–21; Josh. 21:13; Judg. 16:3*
Jericho	*Num. 22:1; 26:3; 31:12; Matt. 20:29*
Jerusalem	*Josh. 10:1; 15:8, 63; Song of Sol. 6:4; John 12:12*
Jezreel	*1 Kings 21; 2 Kings 9:30–37*
Joppa	*2 Chron. 2:16; Ezra 3:7; Jon. 1:3*
Lachish	*Josh. 10:5, 32; 2 Kings 14:19*
Megiddo	*Josh. 12:21; 17:11; Judg. 1:27*
Nazareth	*Matt. 2:23; 4:13*
Samaria	*1 Kings 16:29, 32*
Shechem	*Gen. 12:6; 33:18; Josh. 21:21*
Tyre	*Josh. 19:29; 2 Sam. 5:11; Acts 21:4–7*
Ur	*Gen. 11:28, 31; Neh. 9:7*

Roman theater, Caesarea, Israel

VALLEYS

Valley	Description	Reference
Achor	Where the Israelites stoned Achan	*Josh. 7:24*
Aijalon	Where the sun stood still	*Josh. 10:12*
Baca/Baka	Where pilgrims traveled through to reach Jerusalem	*Ps. 84:6*
Ben Hinnom	Where children were sacrificed	*2 Chron. 28:3*
Berakah	Where King Jehoshaphat and his army praised God	*2 Chron. 20:26*
Beth Peor	Located in Moab; where Moses was buried	*Deut. 34:6*
Bokim	Where the angel of the Lord appeared	*Judg. 2:5*
Elah	Where the Israelites camped to meet the Philistines	*1 Sam. 17:2*
Eshkol	Valley from which the spies viewed Canaan	*Num. 32:9*
Ge Harashim	Means "valley of skilled workers"	*1 Chron. 4:14*
Gerar	Where Isaac lived	*Gen. 26:17*
Gibeon	Where David defeated the Philistines	*1 Chron. 14:13–16*
Hamon Gog	Where Gog would be buried	*Ezek. 39:11*
Hebron	Where Joseph searched for his brothers	*Gen. 37:14*
Iphtah El	Bordered Zebulun's land	*Josh. 19:14*
Jehoshaphat	Where Israel would be judged	*Joel 3:2, 14*
Jericho	One of the valleys that Moses viewed from Nebo	*Deut. 34:3*
Jezreel	Where Israel's enemies camped	*Judg. 6:33*
Lebanon	Valley that Joshua captured	*Josh. 11:17*
Megiddo	Where King Josiah was killed	*2 Chron. 35:22*
Rephaim	Where David defeated the Philistines	*2 Sam. 5:18*
Salt	Where David killed 18,000 Edomites	*2 Sam. 8:13*
Shaveh/King's Valley	Where the king of Sodom met Abraham	*Gen. 14:17*
Shittim/Acacias	Located just north of the Dead Sea (photo above)	*Joel 3:18*
Siddim	Where five kings joined forces for battle	*Gen. 14:3–8*
Sorek	Where Delilah lived	*Judg. 16:4*
Sukkoth	Located east of the Jordan	*Ps. 60:6*
Zeboyim	Where the Philistines sent detachments	*1 Sam. 13:18*
Zephathah	Where King Asa and Zerah fought a battle	*2 Chron. 14:9–10*
Zered	Where the Israelites camped	*Num. 21:12*

BIBLE LISTS

FATHER, SON &
THE HOLY SPIRIT

DIVINE TRAITS OF JESUS

Divine Trait of Jesus	Reference
He has authority to forgive sins.	*Matt. 9:2, 6; Luke 7:48*
He is omnipotent (possessing unlimited authority).	*Matt. 11:27; 28:18; John 5:21–22; 10:18*
He has the right to receive praise and worship.	*Matt. 21:16*
He is omniscient (all-knowing).	*John 1:48; 2:25*
He is preexistent.	*John 8:23, 58; 17:5, 24*
He is one with God.	*John 10:30–33; 12:45; 14:9, 23*
He has authority to answer prayers.	*John 14:13–14; Acts 7:59*

At the well

Jesus with children

Temptation of Christ

Transfiguration

The "I Am" Sayings of Jesus

Words of Jesus	Reference
"I am the bread of life."	*John 6:35*
"I am the light of the world."	*John 8:12*
"I am the gate for the sheep."	*John 10:7*
"I am the good shepherd."	*John 10:11*
"I am the resurrection and the life."	*John 11:25*
"I am the way and the truth and the life."	*John 14:6*
"I am the true vine."	*John 15:1*

THE LAMB OF GOD

The Lamb of God	Reference
God provided a ram (a male sheep) to take Isaac's place.	Gen. 22:6–8, 13; Rom. 3:25; Heb. 2:17; 1 John 2:2; 4:10
A lamb was slain for Passover, its blood placed on the doorpost as a substitute for the firstborn of the household.	Exod. 12:1–13; 2 Chron. 30:15–17; Mark 14:12; Luke 22:7; Eph. 1:7; Heb. 9:22
A lamb was used as a sin offering.	Lev. 4:32–33; 14:12–25; 2 Chron. 29:21–22; John 1:29
The lamb was to be slain only at a prescribed location. (Jesus had to go to Jerusalem.)	Lev. 17:2–4; Matt. 16:21
Blood makes atonement for sins because life is in it.	Lev. 17:10; Heb. 9:22; 1 John 1:7
A lamb had to be a male without defect. (Jesus was without defect/sin.)	Exod. 12:5; Num. 6:14; Ezek. 46:6; Heb. 4:15; 1 Pet. 1:19
The lamb had to be sacrificed whole. (None of Jesus' bones were broken.)	Exod. 12:9; Ps. 34:20; John 19:36
It was prophesied that Jesus would be slaughtered like the Passover lamb.	Isa. 53:7; Acts 8:32; 1 Cor. 5:7
Jesus was called the Lamb of God.	John 1:29, 36; Rev. 5:6–13; 21:14, 27; 22:1–3
Unlike the lambs, Jesus was the final sacrifice, sufficient for all.	Heb. 10:1–3
Both Passover and Communion are commemorations of events: Passover commemorates the sparing of the firstborn. Communion commemorates the sparing of the world.	Exod. 12:27; Matt. 26:28
Both Passover and Communion celebrate deliverance from bondage: The Jews were delivered from the bondage of the Egyptians. Christians are delivered from the bondage of sin.	Deut. 16:1; John 6:54
In Genesis the lamb was slain for the individual. In Exodus the lamb was slain for the family (house). In Leviticus the lamb was slain for the nation. In the New Testament the Lamb was slain for the world.	Gen. 22:7–8, 10–13; Exod. 12:3–4; Lev. 16:23–24; John 1:29; 11:50–52

Jesus' Words from the Cross

Words from the Cross	Reference
"Father, forgive them, for they do not know what they are doing."	*Luke 23:34*
"Truly I tell you, today you will be with me in paradise."	*Luke 23:43*
"Woman, here is your son. . . . Here is your mother."	*John 19:26–27*
"Eli, Eli, lema sabachthani?" (which means, "My God, my God, why have you forsaken me?")	*Matt. 27:46*
"I am thirsty."	*John 19:28*
"It is finished."	*John 19:30*
"Father, into your hands I commit my spirit."	*Luke 23:46*

Christ on the Cross

Miracles of Jesus

Miracle	Reference
Healed a man with leprosy	Mark 1:40–45
Healed the centurion's servant	Matt. 8:5–13
Healed Peter's mother-in-law	Matt. 8:14–15
Cast "Legion" out of a man and into pigs	Mark 5:1–13
Healed a paralytic	Luke 5:18–26
Healed a woman's bleeding	Mark 5:25–34
Calmed a storm	Matt. 8:23–27
Healed two blind men	Matt. 9:27–31
Cast a demon out of a man who could not talk	Matt. 9:32–35
Healed a shriveled hand	Luke 6:6–10
Healed a demon-possessed man who could not see or speak	Matt. 12:22
Walked on the water	Matt. 14:22–33
Cast a demon out of a Canaanite woman's daughter	Matt. 15:21–28
Fed four thousand people with seven loaves of bread and a few small fish	Matt. 15:30–38
Put the coin in the fish's mouth	Matt. 17:24–27
Cursed the fig tree	Matt. 21:17–22
Cast a demon out of a boy	Mark 9:14–29
Healed Bartimaeus and another blind man	Matt. 20:29–34
Healed a man who was deaf and could not speak well	Mark 7:31–37
Cast a demon out of a man	Mark 1:21–28

Catch of fish

Loaves and fishes

Walking on water

Miracle	Reference
Healed a blind man	*Mark 8:22–26*
Provided a net full of fish	*Luke 5:1–11*
Raised the widow's son from the dead	*Luke 7:11–17*
Raised Jairus's daughter from the dead	*Luke 8:41–56*
Healed a crippled woman	*Luke 13:10–17*
Healed a man with abnormal swelling	*Luke 14:1–6*
Healed ten men with leprosy	*Luke 17:11–19*
Turned water into wine	*John 2:1–11*
Healed the official's son	*John 4:46–54*
Healed a disabled man at Bethesda Pool	*John 5:1–18*
Fed five thousand people with five loaves of bread and two small fish	*John 6:1–14*
Healed a blind man	*John 9*
Raised Lazarus from the dead	*John 11*
Provided a net full of fish	*John 21:1–14*
Healed Malchus's ear	*Matt. 26:51–56*
Rose from the dead	*Luke 24:1–8*
Ascended into heaven	*Acts 1:9–11*

Widow's son   *Jairus's daughter*   *Lazarus*

THE PARABLES OF JESUS

Parable	Reference
Bearing Fruit: Grace and Time	*Luke 13:6*
Character: Salt Without Taste	*Luke 14:34–35*
Discipleship: Being Watchful	*Luke 12:35–40*
Discipleship: Guests of the Bridegroom	*Mark 2:18–20*
Discipleship: Servant's Duty	*Luke 17:7–10*
Discipleship: Unprepared Builder	*Luke 14:28–30*
Discipleship: War Plans	*Luke 14:31–33*
Discipleship: Wise Builder	*Luke 6:47–49*
Discipleship: Wise Servant	*Matt. 24:45–51*
Discipleship: Wise Steward	*Luke 12:42–48*
Evangelism: Being Light	*Mark 4:21–23*
Evangelism: Growing Seed	*Mark 4:26–29*
Evangelism: Lost Coin	*Luke 15:8–10*
Evangelism: Lost Sheep	*Luke 15:4–7*
Forgiveness: Two Debtors	*Luke 7:41–43*
God: The Landowner	*Mark 12:1–12*
God: Loving Father and the Prodigal Son	*Luke 15:11–32*
God: Vine and Branches	*John 15:1–17*
Heaven: Rich Man and Lazarus	*Luke 16:19–31*
Heaven: Sheep and Goats	*Matt. 25:31–46*
Humility: Children	*Matt. 11:16–19; Luke 7:31–35*
Humility: Honored Guests	*Luke 14:7–11*
Jesus: The Bread of life	*John 6:31–38*
Jesus: The Good Shepherd	*John 10:1–18*
Jesus: The Great Physician	*Matt. 9:10–13*
Jesus: The Sign of Jonah	*Matt. 12:38–42*
Jesus' Return: Being Alert	*Mark 13:33–37*
Jesus' Return: The Fig Tree	*Mark 13:28–32*
Kingdom of God: A Banquet	*Luke 14:15–24*

THE PARABLES OF JESUS (CONTINUED)

Parable	Reference
Kingdom of God: The Farmer (Part 1)	*Mark 4:3–20*
Kingdom of God: The Farmer (Part 2)	*Matt. 13:18–23*
Kingdom of God: The Great Pearl	*Matt. 13:45–46*
Kingdom of God: Hidden Treasure	*Matt. 13:44*
Kingdom of God: Large Net of Fish	*Matt. 13:47–50*
Kingdom of God: Mustard Seed	*Matt. 13:31–32*
Kingdom of God: New Cloth	*Matt. 9:16*
Kingdom of God: New Wine	*Luke 5:37–39*
Kingdom of God: Old and New	*Matt. 13:52*
Kingdom of God: Ten Bags of Gold	*Matt. 25:14–30*
Kingdom of God: Ten Bridesmaids	*Matt. 25:1–13*
Kingdom of God: Ten Minas	*Luke 19:11–27*
Kingdom of God: Undivided Kingdom	*Matt. 12:24–30*
Kingdom of God: The Unmerciful Servant	*Matt. 18:21–35*
Kingdom of God: Wedding Banquet	*Matt. 22:1–14*
Kingdom of God: Weeds in a Field (Part 1)	*Matt. 13:24–30*
Kingdom of God: Weeds in a Field (Part 2)	*Matt. 13:36–43*
Kingdom of God: Workers in the Vineyard	*Matt. 20:1–16*
Kingdom of God: Working Sons	*Matt. 21:28–32*
Kingdom of God: Yeast	*Matt. 13:33; Luke 13:20–21*
Loving Others: Banquet Invitations	*Luke 14:12–14*
Loving Others: Good Samaritan	*Luke 10:25–37*
Money: Rich Fool	*Luke 12:16–21*
Money: Unjust Steward	*Luke 16:1–13*
Prayer: Friend at Midnight	*Luke 11:5–13*
Prayer: God the Just Judge	*Luke 18:1–8*
Prayer: Pharisee and Tax Collector	*Luke 18:9–14*
Spiritual Warfare: Unclean Spirit	*Luke 11:24–26*

JESUS

TITLES AND NAMES OF CHRIST

Title or Name	Reference	Title or Name	Reference
The Almighty	Rev. 1:8	Light of the World	John 8:12
Alpha and Omega	Rev. 1:8	Lord	John 20:28
The Amen	Rev. 3:14	The Lord Our Righteous Savior	Jer. 23:6
Branch	Isa. 11:1	Mediator	Heb. 9:15
Bread of Life	John 6:35	Messiah	Matt. 1:16
Bright Morning Star	Rev. 22:16	Mighty God	Isa. 9:6
Christ	John 1:41	Pioneer and Perfecter of Faith	Heb. 12:2
Cornerstone	Eph. 2:20	Prince of Peace	Isa. 9:6
Everlasting Father	Isa. 9:6	Rabbi	John 1:38
Faithful One/Holy One	Ps. 16:10	Redeemer	Gal. 3:13
God	John 1:1	The Resurrection and the Life	John 11:25
Good Shepherd	John 10:11	Rock	1 Cor. 10:4
High Priest	Heb. 4:14	Root and the Offspring of David	Rev. 22:16
I Am	John 8:58	Root of Jesse	Isa. 11:10
Immanuel	Matt. 1:23	Savior	Eph. 5:23
Jesus	Matt. 1:1	Son of David	Matt. 12:23
Jesus of Nazareth	Matt. 26:71	Son of God	John 1:49
Judge	2 Tim. 4:8	Son of Man	Matt. 12:8
King of Glory	Ps. 24:7	Vine	John 15:1
King of Kings and Lord of Lords	Rev. 19:16	Wonderful Counselor	Isa. 9:6
Lamb of God	John 1:29	The Word	John 1:1

TITLES AND NAMES OF GOD

Title or Name	Reference	Title or Name	Reference
Abba (Father)	Mark 14:36	I Am	Exod. 3:14
Ancient of Days	Dan. 7:9	Judge	Gen. 18:25
Consuming Fire	Deut. 4:24	King of Glory	Ps. 24:7–10
Creator	Gen. 14:19	Lamp	2 Sam. 22:29
Deliverer	2 Sam. 22:2	Light	Ps. 27:1
El-Shaddai	Exod. 6:3	Living God	2 Kings 19:15–16
Eternal God	Gen. 21:33	Lord	Gen. 15:2
Everlasting God	Isa. 40:28	Lord Almighty/Lord of Hosts	1 Sam. 1:3
Everlasting King	Jer. 10:10	Lord God	Gen. 2:4
Faithful God	Ps. 31:5	Lord Is Peace	Judg. 6:22–24
Father	Isa. 63:16	Lord Our Banner	Exod. 17:15
Fortress	2 Sam. 22:2	Lord Our Provider	Gen. 22:14
Gardener	John 15:1	Lord Our Righteous Savior	Jer. 23:6
God Almighty	Gen. 17:1	Lord Who Heals	Exod. 15:25–26
God/Elohim	Gen. 1:1	Potter	Isa. 64:8
God in Heaven	Josh. 2:11	Redeemer	Isa. 54:8
God Most High	Gen. 14:18–19	Refuge	Ps. 9:9
God of Abraham, Isaac, and Jacob	Exod. 3:16	Rock	2 Sam. 22:2
God of Israel	Exod. 5:1	Savior	Isa. 45:21
Helper	Ps. 27:9	Shepherd	Ps. 23
Hiding Place	Ps. 32:7	Shield	Prov. 30:5
Holy One	Isa. 5:24	Strong Tower	Ps. 61:3
Husband	Isa. 54:5		

Titles and Names of the Spirit

Title or Name	Reference
Advocate/Counselor/Comforter	John 14:16, 26
Eternal Spirit	Heb. 9:14
Holy Spirit/Ghost	Matt. 1:18
Power of the Most High	Luke 1:35
Seal	Eph. 1:13
Spirit of Adoption	Rom. 8:15
Spirit of Christ	Rom. 8:9
Spirit of Counsel and of Might	Isa. 11:2
Spirit of Glory	1 Pet. 4:14
Spirit of God	Gen. 1:2
Spirit of Grace	Heb. 10:29
Spirit of Holiness	Rom. 1:4
Spirit of Knowledge and Fear of the Lord	Isa. 11:2
Spirit of Life	Rom. 8:2
Spirit of the Father	Matt. 10:20
Spirit of the Lord	Luke 4:18
Spirit of the Son of God	Gal. 4:6
Spirit of Truth	John 14:17
Spirit of Wisdom and of Understanding	Isa. 11:2
Symbol: Dove	Luke 3:22
Symbol: Fire	Acts 2:3
Symbol: Water	John 7:37–39
Symbol: Wind	John 3:8

OLD TESTAMENT PROPHECIES
FULFILLED BY JESUS

Old Testament Prophecy	What the Prophecy Reveals	New Testament Fulfillment
Gen. 3:15	He will defeat Satan.	*Gal. 4:4–5; Rev. 12:11*
Gen. 12:1–3	He will be a descendant of Abraham.	*Matt. 1:1, 17; Gal. 3:16*
Exod. 12:46	He will not have any of His bones broken.	*John 19:33, 36*
Deut. 18:15–18	He will be a prophet like Moses.	*Acts 3:20–22*
Ps. 2:1–2, 6–7	He will be opposed by both Jews and Gentiles. He will be King of Zion and the Son of God.	*Luke 1:32, 35; 23:10–12; John 18:33–37; Acts 4:27*
Ps. 16:10	His body will not decay in the grave.	*Luke 24:6, 31, 34; Acts 2:31*
Ps. 22:1–18	He will be forsaken by God, mocked by people, and have His clothing divided by the casting of dice.	*Matt. 27:39–44, 46; Luke 22:63–65; John 19:18–20, 23–24; Rom. 15:3*
Ps. 41:9	He will be betrayed by a friend.	*Matt. 26:14–16; Mark 14:10–11*
Ps. 47:5	He will ascend into heaven.	*Luke 24:51; Acts 1:9*
Ps. 69:4	He will be rejected and hated.	*Matt. 13:57; Mark 6:4; Luke 4:24*
Ps. 69:9	He will have great love for God's house.	*John 2:17*
Ps. 69:21	He will be offered gall and vinegar to drink.	*Matt. 27:34; John 19:29–30*
Ps. 72:10–11	He will be adored by great people. He will have universal dominion.	*Matt. 2:1–11; Phil. 2:9, 11*
Ps. 78:2	He will preach in parables.	*Matt. 13:34–35; Mark 4:33–34*
Ps. 110:1, 4	He will sit at the right hand of God. He will serve in Melchizedek's order of priests.	*Col. 3:1; Heb. 1:3; 5:5–6*
Ps. 118:22	He will be rejected by Jewish rulers.	*Matt. 21:42; 1 Pet. 2:4–7*
Isa. 7:14	He will be born of a virgin.	*Matt. 1:21–23; Luke 1:34–35; 2:7*
Isa. 8:14	He will be a stumbling block.	*Luke 2:34; Rom. 9:32–33; 1 Pet. 2:8*
Isa. 9:1–2, 7	He will have a ministry that begins in Galilee. He will have an everlasting kingdom.	*Matt. 4:12–16, 23; Luke 1:32–33*
Isa. 11:10; 42:1	He will have Gentile followers.	*John 10:16; Acts 10:34–35, 45, 47*
Isa. 28:16	He will be the chief cornerstone.	*1 Pet. 2:6–7*
Isa. 35:5–6	He will perform miracles.	*Matt. 11:4–6; John 9:6–7*
Isa. 40:3 (see also Mal. 3:1)	He will be preceded by an anointed messenger.	*Matt. 3:13; Mark 1:2–3; Luke 1:17, 76–77; 3:3–6; John 1:23*

OLD TESTAMENT PROPHECIES
FULFILLED BY JESUS (CONTINUED)

Old Testament Prophecy	What the Prophecy Reveals	New Testament Fulfillment
Isa. 42:1–6	He will be meek and speak out for justice.	*Matt. 12:15–21*
Isa. 50:6	He will be spat on and beaten.	*Matt. 26:67; Mark 14:65; 15:19; Luke 22:63; John 19:1–5*
Isa. 53:1–12	He will be condemned as a sinner and will suffer. He will be silent before His accusers (and later intercede for them) and be buried with the rich.	*Matt. 26:62–63; 27:11–14, 27–50, 57–60; Mark 15:4–5, 21–37, 42–46; Luke 23:6–9, 32–46, 50–54; John 19:16–30, 38–42; 1 Pet. 2:22–23*
Isa. 61:1	He will be anointed by the Spirit of God.	*Matt. 3:16; Mark 1:10; Luke 3:22; 4:16–19; John 3:34; 5:30; Acts 10:38; Rev. 19:11*
Isa. 61:1–2	He will enter public ministry.	*Luke 4:16–21, 43*
Jer. 23:5–6; 33:14–16	He will be a descendant of David.	*Matt. 1:1, 17; Acts 13:22–23; Rom. 1:3*
Jer. 31:15	He will be alive during the slaughter of Bethlehem's children.	*Matt. 2:16–18*
Hosea 11:1	He will be called out of Egypt.	*Matt. 2:15*
Mic. 5:2–5	He will be born in Bethlehem.	*Matt. 2:1–6; Luke 2:4–7*
Zech. 9:9	He will enter Jerusalem by riding a donkey.	*Matt. 21:1–5*
Zech. 11:12–13	He will be betrayed for thirty pieces of silver, which will later buy a potter's field.	*Matt. 26:15; 27:7*
Zech. 12:10	He will be pierced.	*John 19:34, 37*
Zech. 13:7	He will be forsaken by His disciples.	*Matt. 26:31, 56; Mark 14:27, 50*
Mal. 3:1	He will arrive at Jerusalem's temple.	*Matt. 21:12; Mark 11:11; Luke 19:45–48; John 2:13–16*

POST-RESURRECTION APPEARANCES

Appearance	Reference
The women on the road	*Matt. 28:1–10*
The disciples on a mountain in Galilee. This meeting is often called "The Great Commission." There were at least eleven disciples there, but probably more. This could be the same event Paul refers to when he speaks of more than 500 disciples.	*Matt. 28:16–20*
Mary Magdalene at the tomb	*Mark 16:9; John 20:10–16*
Cleopas and an unnamed disciple on the road to Emmaus	*Mark 16:12–13; Luke 24:13–35*
The eleven disciples in the upper room	*Mark 16:14; Luke 24:36–49*
Peter	*Luke 24:34; 1 Cor. 15:5*
The eleven disciples, except for Thomas	*John 20:19–20*
The eleven disciples, including Thomas	*John 20:24–28*
Peter, Thomas, Nathanael, James, John, and two other disciples at the Sea of Galilee	*John 21:1–7*
Paul on the road to Damascus	*Acts 9:1–5; 1 Cor. 15:8*
More than 500 disciples	*1 Cor. 15:6*
James, brother of Jesus	*1 Cor. 15:7*

Road to Emmaus

BIBLE LISTS

MIRACLES &
STRANGE EVENTS

ACTS OF NATURE

Event	Description	Reference
earthquake	Occurred at Mount Sinai when God gave the Law to Moses	*Exod. 19:18*
earthquake	Destroyed Korah and his followers	*Num. 16:31–33*
earthquake	Confused the Philistines	*1 Sam. 14:15*
earthquake	Sent to Elijah after he killed the prophets of Baal and fled from Jezebel	*1 Kings 19:11–12*
earthquake	Occurred during the reign of King Uzziah	*Amos 1:1*
earthquake	Mentioned in connection with the Day of the Lord	*Zech. 14:4–5*
earthquake	Occurred at Jesus' death	*Matt. 27:51–54*
earthquake	Occurred at Jesus' resurrection	*Matt. 28:2*
earthquake	Occurred at Philippi while Paul and Silas were in jail	*Acts 16:26*
earthquake	Occurred in John's revelations	*Rev. 6:12–24; 11:19; 16:18*
fire/sulfur	Used to destroy Sodom and Gomorrah	*Gen. 19:23–25; Luke 17:29*
fire/sulfur	Used by God to answer Elijah's request	*1 Kings 18:36–38*
fire/sulfur	Sent to Elijah after he killed the prophets of Baal and fled from Jezebel	*1 Kings 19:11–12*
fire/sulfur	Consumed King Ahaziah's men	*2 Kings 1*
fire/sulfur	Consumed the burnt offering during the dedication of the temple	*2 Chron. 7:1–3*
fire/sulfur	Killed Job's sheep and servants	*Job 1:16*
flood	Used by God as a worldwide judgment	*Gen. 6–9; 10:1, 32; 11:10;*
hail	One of the plagues against Egypt	*Exod. 9:19–34; Ps. 78:47–48*
hail	Killed the Amorites	*Josh. 10:11*
storm	Used by God to speak to Job	*Job 38:1; 40:6*
storm	Sent by God to chastise Jonah	*Jon. 1:4–12*
storm	Calmed by Jesus	*Matt. 8:23–27; Luke 8:24*
storm	Caused Paul's shipwreck	*Acts 27:14–20*

Angelic Appearances

Appearance	Reference	Appearance	Reference
Guarded the tree of life	Gen. 3:24	Instructed Joseph to marry	Matt. 1:20–23
To Abraham	Gen. 18:1–10	Warned Joseph of Danger	Matt. 2:13
Escorted Lot out of Sodom	Gen. 19:1, 13–16	Gave guidance to Joseph	Matt. 2:19–23
Provided water for Hagar	Gen. 21:14–20	Strengthened Jesus when tempted	Matt. 4:11; Mark 1:13
Saved Issac from sacrifice	Gen. 22:10–12	Rolled away a gravestone	Matt. 28:2–4
Jacob's dream and ladder	Gen. 28:11–15	Appeared to Zechariah	Luke 1:11–21
Told Jacob to return home	Gen. 31:10–13	Gabriel appeared to Mary	Luke 1:26–38
Killed Egypt's firstborn	Exod. 12:21–27	Told shepherds about Jesus	Luke 2:12
Traveled with Israel's army	Exod. 14:19	Praised God at Jesus' birth	Luke 2:13–14
Sent ahead of Israel	Exod. 23:20–23	Strengthened Jesus in the Garden of Gethsemane	Luke 22:43
Visited Samson's parents	Judg. 13:1–17	Appeared to the women at the tomb	Luke 24:4
Struck Israel with plague	2 Sam. 24:15–17	Appeared to Mary Magdalene at Jesus' tomb	John 20:10–13
Fed Elijah	1 Kings 19:3–7	Visited disciples	Acts 1:10–11
Killed 185,000 Assyrians.	2 Kings 19:35; 2 Chron. 32:21	Released the apostles	Acts 5:17–20
Appeared before God	Job 1:6–12	Spoke to Moses on Sinai	Acts 7:37–38
Appeared in Isaiah's vision	Isa. 6:1–8	Guided Philip	Acts 8:26–29
Protected men in furnace	Dan. 3:24–28	Told Cornelius to send men for Peter	Acts 10:1–3
Visited Daniel	Dan. 8:16; 9:21	Rescued Peter after arrest	Acts 12:7–11
Explained vision to Daniel	Dan. 10:4–5	Killed Herod Agrippa	Acts 12:21–23
Assisted each other	Dan. 10:13, 21	Encouraged Paul in storm	Acts 27:21–25
Will appear in end times	Dan. 12:1	Argued with the devil	Jude 9
Appeared to Zechariah	Zech. 2:1–3	In John's visions	Rev. 5:11; 8–9; 12:7–9; 15

DREAMS

Dream	Reference
God appeared to Abimelek to tell him that Sarah was married to Abraham.	Gen. 20:3–6
Jacob saw a stairway to heaven with angels ascending and descending.	Gen. 28:10–14
God blessed Jacob with Laban's flock and told him to go home.	Gen. 31:10–12
God appeared to Laban and told him not to harm Jacob.	Gen. 31:24
Joseph dreamed that his parents and brothers would bow down to him.	Gen. 37:5–10
The chief cupbearer dreamed he would be restored in three days.	Gen. 40:9–13, 21
The chief baker dreamed that he would be hanged in three days.	Gen. 40:16–19, 22
Pharaoh dreamed of seven years of plenty and seven years of famine.	Gen. 41:1–7, 17–30
A friend of Gideon dreamed that they would defeat the Midianites.	Judg. 7:13–15
God asked Solomon what he wanted most. Solomon chose wisdom.	1 Kings 3:5–15
King Nebuchadnezzar dreamed about the various kingdoms that would rule after him.	Dan. 2:28–40; 4:3
Daniel dreamed of the four kingdoms that would rule the earth during that time period, and of the end times.	Dan. 7:1–28
An angel of the Lord told Joseph to take Mary as his wife because she was pregnant with God's Son.	Matt. 1:20
God warned the Magi not to bring news back to Herod. (Photo above)	Matt. 2:12
An angel of the Lord told Joseph to take his family to Egypt because Herod wanted to kill Jesus.	Matt. 2:13
An angel of the Lord told Joseph that it was safe to return to Israel.	Matt. 2:19–21
Joseph was told in a dream to go live in Nazareth in Galilee.	Matt. 2:22–23
Pilate's wife was tortured by dreams of Jesus, and she wanted Pilate to set Him free.	Matt. 27:19

Joseph (son of Jacob) dreams

Dream of Jesus' earthly father

Jacob's ladder

Events of the Passion Week

Event	Day of the Week	Reference
Jesus arrives at Bethany and has dinner with Martha, Mary, and Lazarus. Mary anoints Him with oil.	Friday/ Saturday	*John 11:55–12:1*
Jesus is welcomed into Jerusalem.	Sunday	*Matt. 21:1–9; Mark 11:1–11; Luke 19:28–44; John 12:12–19*
The temple is cleansed and the fig tree is cursed. Jesus foretells His death.	Monday	*Matt. 21:10–19; Mark 11:12–18; Luke 19:45–48; John 12:20–50*
The disciples notice the withered fig tree. Jesus is challenged in various ways by the religious leaders and praises the widow's offering. Jesus discusses signs of the end with His disciples and tells them that He will be handed over for crucifixion in two days. The religious leaders plot to arrest Jesus. Jesus is anointed in Simon's house. Judas agrees to betray Jesus.	Tuesday/ Wednesday	*Matt. 21:20– 26:16; Mark 11:19–14:12; Luke 20:1–21:26; 22:1–6*
Jesus eats the Passover with His disciples, predicts Judas's betrayal, washes the disciples' feet, and institutes communion. Jesus talks to His disciples on the way to Gethsemane. Jesus predicts Peter's denial, agonizes in the garden, and is arrested.	Thursday	*Matt. 26:17–71; Mark 14:12–72; Luke 22:7–65; John 13–17; 18:12–25*
Jesus is taken to Pilate. Judas hangs himself. Jesus is crucified, dies, and is buried.	Friday	*Matt. 27:1–61; Mark 15 Luke 22:66–23:55; John 18:26–19:42*
Pilate allows the Jewish leaders to place a guard at the tomb. The women rested on the Sabbath after preparing the spices for Jesus.	Saturday	*Matt. 27:62–66; Luke 23:56*
Jesus is resurrected and commissions the disciples.	Sunday	*Matt. 28; Mark 16; Luke 24; John 20:1–23*

145

Stations of the Cross

FAMOUS BATTLES

Battle	Reference
The war of the kings and Abraham's rescue of Lot	*Gen. 14*
Israel's victory over Egypt at the Red Sea	*Exod. 14:23–31*
Israel defeats the army of Amalek while Moses keeps his arms raised	*Exod. 17:5–13*
The battle against the Amalekites and Canaanites (Israel defeated)	*Num. 14:40–45*
Moses' battle against the Midianites	*Num. 31*
Joshua's victory over Jericho	*Josh. 6:1–20*
The 1st battle against Ai (Israel defeated)	*Josh. 7:1–5*
The 2nd battle against Ai	*Josh. 8:18–29*
The victory over the Amorite kings of Jerusalem, Hebron, Jarmuth, Lachish, and Eglon (the sun stands still)	*Josh. 10:5–43*
Joshua's victory over the northern kings	*Josh. 11*
Othniel's victory over Aram	*Judg. 3:7–11*
Ehud's victory over Moab	*Judg. 3:28–30*
Deborah and Barak's victory over Hazor and its commander Sisera	*Judg. 4*
Gideon and 300 men achieve victory over the Canaanites.	*Judg. 6:33–35; 7:5–8, 19–25*
The battle between Abimelek and Shechem	*Judg. 9:39–57*
Jephthah's victory over the Ammonites	*Judg. 11:30–39*
Jephthah's victory over Ephraim	*Judg. 12:1–6*
Samson's victory over the Philistines	*Judg. 16:23–32*
The Danites' victory over Laish	*Judg. 18:27–29*

Moses

Fall of Jericho

David and Goliath

Famous Battles (CONTINUED)

Battle	Reference
The civil war between Benjamin and the other tribes	*Judg. 20*
Israel's battle against the Philistines under Samuel (the ark is captured)	*1 Sam. 4*
Saul and Jonathan's victory over the Philistines	*1 Sam. 13–14*
Saul's battle against the Amalekites	*1 Sam. 15:4–11*
David's battle against Goliath	*1 Sam. 17:34–54*
David's battle against the Philistines	*1 Sam. 23:1–6*
David's victory over the Amalekites	*1 Sam. 30*
Saul's final battle against the Philistines	*1 Sam. 31*
The battle between the house of David and the house of Saul	*2 Sam. 2:8–23*
David's battle against the Arameans and the Ammonites	*2 Sam. 10*
David's battle against the Ammonites (Uriah killed)	*2 Sam. 11:1, 14–16*
The battle between Absalom and David's men (Absalom killed)	*2 Sam. 18:1–18*
David and Joab's victory over Sheba the Benjamite	*2 Sam. 20:1–10*
David's battles against the Philistines	*2 Sam. 21:15–22*
King Ahab's battle against the Arameans	*1 Kings 20:13–34*
King Ahab and King Jehoshaphat's battle against Ramoth Gilead (Ahab dies)	*1 Kings 22:1–38*
King Jehu's victory over King Joram	*2 Kings 9:24*
King Jehu's victory over the house of Ahab	*2 Kings 10:10–11*
King Jehoash's victory over King Amaziah	*2 Kings 14:11–14*
Babylon's capture of Judah	*2 Kings 25:1–21; Jer. 37:1–10*
The battle between King Abijah and King Jeroboam (Jeroboam killed)	*2 Chron. 13:1–20*
King Asa's victory over the Cushites	*2 Chron. 14:9–15*
King Jehoshaphat's battle against Ammon, Moab, and Mount Seir	*2 Chron. 20:22–23*
King Uzziah's victory over the Philistines and the Ammonites	*2 Chron. 26:6–8*
Hezekiah's battle against Assyria (photo p. 146)	*2 Chron. 32*

Taking of Jericho

Rescue of Lot

HEALINGS

Healing	Reference
Miriam was healed of leprosy.	*Num. 12:13–15*
King Jeroboam's withered hand was healed.	*1 Kings 13:6*
Naaman was healed of leprosy.	*2 Kings 5:9–14*
King Hezekiah was healed of his illness.	*2 Kings 20:1–7*
Job was healed from his sores.	*Job 2:7; 42:16–17*
King Nebuchadnezzar was healed of his madness.	*Dan. 4:34*
The masses were healed.	*Matt. 4:23–24*
The centurion's servant was healed.	*Matt. 8:5–13*
Peter's mother-in-law was healed.	*Matt. 8:14–15*
Two blind men received their sight.	*Matt. 9:27–31*
Bartimaeus and another blind man were healed.	*Matt. 20:29–34*
Malchus's ear was healed.	*Matt. 26:51–56*
A woman was healed of her bleeding.	*Mark 5:25–34*
A man who could not hear and could not speak well was healed.	*Mark 7:31–37*
A blind man was healed.	*Mark 8:22–26*
A paralyzed man was healed.	*Luke 5:18–26*
A shriveled hand was healed.	*Luke 6:6–10*
A crippled woman was healed.	*Luke 13:10–17*
A man was healed of abnormal swelling.	*Luke 14:1–6*
Ten men were cured of leprosy.	*Luke 17:11–19*
An official's son was healed.	*John 4:46–54*
A disabled man was healed at Bethesda Pool.	*John 5:1–18*
A man who was born blind was made to see.	*John 9*
A crippled beggar was healed.	*Acts 3:1–10*
The masses were healed.	*Acts 5:15–16*
Paul's sight was restored.	*Acts 9:17–18*
Aeneas, a paralytic, was healed.	*Acts 9:32–34*
A man with crippled feet was healed.	*Acts 14:8–20*
Publius's father was healed.	*Acts 28:7–10*

MIRACLES OF MOSES AND AARON

Miracle	Reference
Moses' rod into a snake	*Exod. 4:2–3*
Nile turned to blood	*Exod. 7:19–21*
Plague of frogs	*Exod. 8:5–6*
Plague of gnats	*Exod. 8:16–17*
Plague of flies	*Exod. 8:21–24*
Plague of boils	*Exod. 8:21–24*
Plague of hail	*Exod. 9:22–24*
Plague of locusts	*Exod. 10:12–13*
Plague of darkness	*Exod. 10:21–22*
Parting of the Red Sea	*Exod. 14:21–29*
Bitter water turned to sweet	*Exod. 15:22–25*
Water from a rock at Horeb	*Exod. 17:5–6*
Victory over the Amalekites	*Exod. 17:8–13*
Buds on Aaron's staff	*Num. 17:6–9*
Water from a rock at Kadesh	*Num. 20:6–11*

African bull frog

Hail

Miracles of the Prophets

Miracle	Reference
Elijah stopped the rain.	*1 Kings 17:1*
Elijah provided for a widow and her son.	*1 Kings 17:13–15*
Elijah raised the widow's son from the dead.	*1 Kings 17:19–21*
Elijah ended the drought	*1 Kings 18:1, 41–46*
Elijah called down fire at Mount Carmel.	*1 Kings 18:19–40*
Elijah called down fire to kill the soldiers of Moab.	*2 Kings 1:9–10*
Elijah divided the Jordan River.	*2 Kings 2:8*
Elisha divided the Jordan River.	*2 Kings 2:14*
Elisha made poisonous water good.	*2 Kings 2:19–22*
Elisha increased the widow's oil.	*2 Kings 4:1–7*
Elisha raised the widow's son from the dead.	*2 Kings 4:32–37*
Elisha made poisonous food good.	*2 Kings 4:38–41*
Elisha fed a hundred men with twenty loaves of bread.	*2 Kings 4:42–44*
Elisha healed Naaman of leprosy.	*2 Kings 5:9–14*
Elisha rescued an axhead by making it float.	*2 Kings 6:1–7*
Elisha opened his servant's spiritual eyes.	*2 Kings 6:15–17*
Elisha struck the Aramean army blind.	*2 Kings 6:18*

Elijah

Elisha

MIRACLES OF THE APOSTLES

Miracle	Reference
Peter and John healed a crippled beggar. (Photo above)	*Acts 3:1–10*
Peter judged Ananias and Sapphira.	*Acts 5:1–11*
Peter healed Aeneas, who was paralyzed.	*Acts 9:32–34*
Peter raised Tabitha from the dead.	*Acts 9:36–43*
Paul blinded the sorcerer, Elymas.	*Acts 13:9–11*
Paul healed a man with crippled feet.	*Acts 14:8–20*
Paul cast a demon out of a slave girl.	*Acts 16:16–40*
Paul raised Eutychus from the dead.	*Acts 20:7–12*
Paul healed Publius's father.	*Acts 28:7–10*

Peter and John heal a lame man

Peter's shadow heals a man

Paul before the Proconsul

MIRACULOUS FOOD

Miracle	Reference
God provides manna and quail.	Exod. 16:1–36
Moses hits the rock and water flows.	Exod. 17:1–17; Num. 20:1–13
God brings quail to the Israelite camp.	Num. 11:31–35
Elijah fed by ravens	1 Kings 17:1–6
Widow's flour and oil multiplied	1 Kings 17:7–16
Curing of poisoned food	2 Kings 4:38–41
Elisha multiplies bread.	2 Kings 4:42–44
Jesus feeds 5,000.	Matt. 14:13–21
Jesus feeds 4,000.	Mark 8:1–9
Jesus turns water into wine.	John 2:1–10

Manna

Water from a rock

A widow's oil

MIRACULOUS PREGNANCIES

Mother	Miraculous Child(ren)	Reference
Sarah	Isaac	*Gen. 21:1–5*
Rebekah	Esau and Jacob	*Gen. 25:21–26*
Rachel	Joseph and Benjamin	*Gen. 30:22–24*
Manoah's wife	Samson	*Judg. 13:2–5*
Hannah	Samuel	*1 Sam. 1:19–20*
The Shunammite woman	son's name unknown	*2 Kings 4:13–17*
Mary	Jesus	*Matt. 1:18–20; Luke 1:31, 35*
Elizabeth	John the Baptist	*Luke 1:7, 11–13, 24–25*

153

Manoah and wife

Mary and Joseph

Jacob and Rachel

Mary visits Elizabeth

THE 10 PLAGUES OF EGYPT

	Plague	Reference
1	Nile into blood	*Exod. 7:20*
2	frogs	*Exod. 8:6*
3	gnats/lice	*Exod. 8:17*
4	flies	*Exod. 8:24*
5	death of livestock	*Exod. 9:3*
6	boils	*Exod. 9:9*
7	hail	*Exod. 9:24*
8	locusts	*Exod. 10:13*
9	darkness	*Exod. 10:22*
10	death of the Egyptians' firstborns	*Exod. 12:29*

Water turned to blood
7:19

Infestation of frogs
8:5

Influx of gnats
8:16

Masses of flies
8:24

Livestock died
9:6

Outbreak of boils
9:10

Pounding hailstorm
9:22

Swarms of locusts
10:12

Overwhelming darkness
10:21

Death of the firstborn
12:29

Taken from *The QuickView Bible* by Zondervan. Used by permission.

VISIONS

Vision	Reference
God appeared to Abraham and promised him a son and numerous descendants.	*Gen. 15:1–5*
God appeared to Jacob to tell him to take his family to Egypt.	*Gen. 46:1–4*
God appeared to Samuel to inform him of Eli's fate.	*1 Sam. 3:10–15*
Isaiah had a vision about the fates of Judah and Jerusalem.	*Isa. 1:1; 2:1–4:6*
Isaiah had a vision in which God called him to be His prophet.	*Isa. 6:1–13*
Ezekiel had a vision when God called him to be His prophet.	*Ezek. 1:1–2:3*
God appeared to Ezekiel to warn him about the punishment to come.	*Ezek. 8:1–11:25*
Ezekiel and the dry bones followed by plans for rebuilding of the temple. (Photo above)	*Ezek. 37:1–48:35*
God revealed King Nebuchadnezzar's dream to Daniel in a vision.	*Dan. 2:19, 45*
Daniel had visions/dreams about the four kingdoms that would rule the world and about the end times.	*Dan. 7*
Daniel had another vision about the four kingdoms and about an evil ruler who would rise up from one of them.	*Dan. 8*
Gabriel revealed to Daniel when the Messiah would arrive.	*Dan. 9*
Daniel was given more detail about the kingdoms that would rule.	*Dan. 10:1–12:13*
Obadiah had a vision about Edom's judgment.	*Obad. 1–21*
Micah had a vision about Samaria and Jerusalem's judgment.	*Mic. 1:1–16*
Nahum had a vision about Nineveh's judgment.	*Nah. 1–3*
God appeared to Zechariah the prophet and assured him the temple would be rebuilt.	*Zech. 1:8–6:8*
God appeared to Zechariah the priest and told him he would have a son named John.	*Luke 1:5–22*
Jesus appeared to Paul, blinded him, and converted him.	*Acts 9:3–6; 26:12–18*
God appeared to Ananias and sent him to heal Saul.	*Acts 9:10–12*
God appeared to Saul to tell him Ananias would come to heal him.	*Acts 9:12*
God appeared to Cornelius and sent him to get Peter from Joppa.	*Acts 10:1–6*
God appeared to Peter to prepare him to accept the Gentiles.	*Acts 10:9–16; 11:5*
Paul had a vision of a man from Macedonia asking for help.	*Acts 16:9–10*
God appeared to Paul to let him know that he would be safe from harm.	*Acts 18:9–10*
God gave John a vision regarding the end times.	*Rev. 1–22*

BIBLE LISTS

MYSTERIES,
SECRETS &
THE AFTERLIFE

ATTRIBUTES OF THE KINGDOM OF GOD/HEAVEN

Attribute	Reference
We should repent because it is near.	Matt. 3:2
It belongs to those who are poor in spirit.	Matt. 5:3
It belongs to those who are persecuted because of righteousness.	Matt. 5:10
It is pressing ahead relentlessly.	Matt. 11:12
Many people will reject its message. Its secrets are given only to the select.	Matt. 13:1–23
Believers and unbelievers will coexist together until the end, at which time they will be separated.	Matt. 13:24–30, 36–43, 47
Though it starts out small, it will grow.	Matt. 13:31–33
It is a treasure, and people will give up all they have to enter into it.	Matt. 13:44–46
Those without a childlike faith will never enter it.	Matt. 18:3
Everyone will be judged according to his or her ability to forgive.	Matt. 18:23–35
It is hard for the rich to enter it.	Matt. 19:23–24
The last will be first, and the first will be last. A person who finds Christ at the end of his or her life will enjoy the same heaven as the person who spends an entire life in Christ's service.	Matt. 20:1–16
It will be taken away from those who do not produce fruit.	Matt. 21:43
It is important to be prepared for it.	Matt. 22:1–14
It is important to be ready for it when it comes.	Matt. 25:1–13
Jesus was sent to preach its good news.	Luke 4:43
Those who begin to serve and then look back are not fit for its service.	Luke 9:62
Its coming is not something that can be observed.	Luke 17:20
It is inside of us.	Luke 17:21
Those who leave everything for it will receive a reward.	Luke 18:29–30
It will not appear immediately.	Luke 19:11
No one can enter it unless they are born again.	John 3:3–5
It has nothing to do with what you eat or drink.	Rom. 14:17
The wicked will not inherit it.	1 Cor. 6:9
Flesh and blood cannot inherit it.	1 Cor. 15:50
Jesus will welcome us into it.	2 Pet. 1:11
Jesus will reign there forever.	Rev. 12:10

DEPICTIONS OF HEAVEN

Description of Heaven	Reference
Abraham's bosom/Abraham's side	Luke 16:22–23
Father's house	John 14:2
heaven	Matt. 3:17
heavenly country	Heb. 11:16
the Holy City/new Jerusalem	Rev. 21:2
home of righteousness	2 Pet. 3:13
kingdom	Matt. 25:34
kingdom of Christ and God	Eph. 5:5
kingdom of heaven	Matt. 23:13
new heaven and new earth	2 Pet. 3:13
paradise	Luke 23:43; 2 Cor. 12:4
a Sabbath-rest	Heb. 4:9
throne of God	Rev. 7:15

DEPICTIONS OF HELL

Description of Hell	Reference
burning sulfur/fire and brimstone	*Rev. 14:10*
consuming fire	*Isa. 33:14*
darkness	*Matt. 8:12*
death	*Prov. 5:5; 23:14*
eternal fire	*Matt. 25:41*
eternal punishment	*Matt. 25:46*
everlasting burning	*Isa. 33:14*
everlasting destruction	*2 Thess. 1:9*
fiery furnace	*Matt. 13:42*
fiery lake of burning sulfur	*Rev. 19:20*
the fire	*Jude 23*
gates of Hades	*Matt. 16:18*
gloomy dungeons	*2 Pet. 2:4*
the grave	*Ps. 9:17; Prov. 15:24*
hell	*2 Pet. 2:4*
lake of fire	*Rev. 20:15*
prison	*1 Pet. 3:19*
unquenchable fire	*Matt. 3:12*
wine of God's fury	*Rev. 14:10*

DISGUISES

The Disguised	Additional Information	Reference
Jacob	Disguised himself as Esau to trick Isaac	*Gen. 27:15–17*
Tamar	Disguised herself as a prostitute to trick Judah	*Gen. 38:14*
The people of Gibeon	Disguised themselves as poor travelers to trick Joshua	*Josh. 9:3–6*
Michal	Disguised an idol as David, using clothes and goat hair, to trick Saul's men	*1 Sam. 19:13*
Saul	Disguised himself to consult a medium	*1 Sam. 28:8*
Jeroboam's wife	Disguised herself so that Ahijah the prophet would not recognize her	*1 Kings 14:2*
An unknown prophet	Disguised himself with a headband so King Ahab would not recognize him	*1 Kings 20:38*
Ahab	Disguised himself to go into battle	*1 Kings 22:30*
Josiah	Disguised himself to go into battle	*2 Chron. 35:22*

Isaac blessing Jacob

Tamar and Judah

GREAT ESCAPES

The Escapees	Rescued By	Rescued From	Reference
Noah and his family	God	The flood	*Gen. 7:7*
Lot	Abraham	Captivity	*Gen. 14:15–16*
Lot and his daughters	Angels	Sodom and Gomorrah	*Gen. 19:15–26*
Jacob	Rebekah	Esau	*Gen. 27:41–45*
Joseph	Reuben	His brothers	*Gen. 37:19–24*
Moses	His mother	Pharaoh	*Exod. 2:1–14*
Jethro's daughters	Moses	Shepherds	*Exod. 2:18–19*
Moses	Zipporah	God	*Exod. 4:24–26*
Israelites	Moses and Aaron	Egypt	*Exod. 12:40–42*
Israelites	God	Egyptian army	*Exod. 14:29–31*
The two spies	Rahab	Men of the city	*Josh. 2:1–7*
Rahab	Joshua	Jerusalem	*Josh. 6:17, 22–23*
Jotham	A hiding spot	Abimelek	*Judg. 9:4–5*
Jonathan	Saul's men	Saul	*1 Sam. 14:43–45*
David	Michal	Saul	*1 Sam. 19:11–16*
David	Jonathan	Saul	*1 Sam. 20:18–42*
Jonathan and Ahimaaz	A man and wife	Absalom's men	*2 Sam. 17:17–20*
David	Abishai	Ishbi-Benob	*2 Sam. 21:15–17*
King Rehoboam	His chariot	All Israel	*1 Kings 12:18*
King Xerxes	Mordecai	Bigthana and Teresh	*Esther 2:21–23*
The Jews in Persia	Esther	Haman	*Esther 4:12–17*
Ishmael and eight men	Ammonites	Johanan	*Jer. 41:14–15*
Shadrach, Meshach, and Abednego	An angel (or possibly Jesus)	The fiery furnace	*Dan. 3:21–27*
Daniel	God's angel	The lions' den	*Dan. 6:16–23*
Jonah	God	The belly of the big fish	*Jon. 1:15–2:10*
Jesus	Joseph	Herod	*Matt. 2:13–16*
The apostles	An angel	Jewish leaders	*Acts 5:17–19*
Paul	His followers	The Jews	*Acts 9:23–25*
Peter	An angel	Herod	*Acts 12:6–11*

MYSTERIOUS DEATHS

Person or Group	Type of Death	Reference
Er, son of Judah	Struck down by God	*Gen. 38:6–7*
Onan, son of Judah	Struck down by God	*Gen. 38:8–10*
Egypt's firstborns	Struck down by God	*Exod. 12:30*
Egyptian soldiers	Drowned in the Red Sea	*Exod. 14:27–28*
Korah, Dathan, Abiram, and their households	Swallowed by the earth	*Num. 16:26–32*
14,700 Israelites	Killed by plague	*Num. 16:49*
Many Israelites	Killed by snakes	*Num. 21:6*
24,000 Israelites	Killed by plague	*Num. 25:8–9*
250 of Korah's followers	Devoured by fire	*Num. 26:10*
Nadab and Abihu	Struck down by God	*Num. 26:61*
Amorites	Killed by hail	*Josh. 10:11–12*
Philistines	Killed by tumors	*1 Sam. 5:8–12*
Seventy men	Struck down by God in Beth Shemesh	*1 Sam. 6:19*
Uzzah	Struck down by God	*2 Sam. 6:6–7*
David's first son with Bathsheba	Became ill and died	*2 Sam. 12:15–18*
Man of God from Judah	Killed by a lion	*1 Kings 13:23–24*
An officer of the king	Trampled by people at the gate	*2 Kings 7:17*
Foreigners brought to Samaria	Killed by lions	*2 Kings 17:24–26*
185,000 Assyrian soldiers	Killed by the angel of the Lord	*2 Kings 19:35*
Job's sons and daughters	Crushed when wind collapsed the house on top of them	*Job 1:18–19*
Ananias and Saphirra	Dropped dead after lying	*Acts 5:1–11*
King Herod	Eaten by worms	*Acts 12:23*

Death of Uzzah

The Assyrian army

Nadab and Abihu

STRANGE EVENTS

Unexplainable Event	Reference
God taking Enoch from earth	Gen. 5:24
Lot's wife turning to a pillar of salt	Gen. 19:26
The burning bush	Exod. 3:2–6
Fire consuming Nadab and Abihu	Lev. 10:1–7
Miriam's sudden case of leprosy	Num. 12:9–10
The earth splitting and swallowing Korah	Num. 16:31–32
Balaam's donkey's speech	Num. 22:22–30
The collapsing of Jericho's walls	Josh. 6:20
The sun standing still	Josh. 10:12–14
Fire from a rock	Judg. 6:19–21
The outbreak of tumors	1 Sam. 5:9
King Jeroboam's withered hand	1 Kings 13:4–6
Elijah going to heaven in a whirlwind	2 Kings 2:11–13
Fire from heaven consuming sacrifices	2 Chron. 7:1
The fiery furnace that did not burn	Dan. 3:19–27
The wonders at Pentecost	Acts 2
Apostles being freed from prison	Acts 5:17–26
Saul's conversion	Acts 9:1–20
Peter being freed from prison	Acts 12:3–10
Herod Agrippa's death	Acts 12:23

Pentecost

Men in a fiery furnace

Balaam's talking donkey

SECRET JOURNEYS

Secret Journey	Reference
Jacob ran away from Laban without telling him.	*Gen. 31:20–21*
Baby Moses floated down the Nile in a basket.	*Exod. 2:3–5*
Moses fled to Midian.	*Exod. 2:15*
Two spies snuck around Canaan.	*Josh. 2:1*
Jonathan traveled to the Philistine outpost.	*1 Sam. 14:1*
Samuel traveled to anoint David as king.	*1 Sam. 16:1–3*
David snuck out through a window and fled.	*1 Sam. 19:12*
David traveled to Nob to flee from Saul.	*1 Sam. 21:1–2*
Saul went to visit the medium.	*1 Sam. 28:8*
Messengers went throughout the tribes of Israel to proclaim Absalom king.	*2 Sam. 15:10*
The people of Jabesh Gilead stole Saul and his sons' bones from Beth Shan.	*2 Sam. 21:12*
Jeroboam's wife traveled to Shiloh to consult the prophet Ahijah.	*1 Kings 14:1–4*
Jonah tried to run away to Tarshish. (Photo above)	*Jon. 1:3*
Herod sent the Magi to Bethlehem to find Jesus so that Herod could kill Him.	*Matt. 2:7–8*
Jesus passed through Galilee.	*Mark 9:30*
Judas went to meet with the chief priests and the officers of the temple guard to arrange Jesus' betrayal.	*Luke 22:3–6*
Nicodemus visited Jesus at night.	*John 3:1–2*
Jesus went to the Festival of Tabernacles.	*John 7:10*
Jesus stopped moving around publicly and went to Ephraim.	*John 11:54*

Israeli spies

David escapes through a window

Magi journey to Jesus

TOP SECRET

SECRETS KEPT

Secret	Reference
Adam and Eve tried to keep their sin a secret from God.	*Gen. 3:8–10*
Rebekah secretly planned for Jacob to steal Esau's blessing.	*Gen. 27:5–10*
Laban secretly replaced Rachel with Leah.	*Gen. 29:25*
Jacob's sons secretly planned to kill Shechem and his men.	*Gen. 34:13*
Reuben and his brothers kept the secret that Joseph was still alive.	*Gen. 37:29–33*
Potiphar's wife kept the secret that Joseph had not actually touched her.	*Gen. 39:16–20*
Moses' mother kept him a secret for three months.	*Exod. 2:1–2*
The Gibeonites pretended to be from a far-off land.	*Josh. 9:22*
Judge Ehud pretended to have a secret message for King Eglon of Moab.	*Judg. 3:16–19*
Delilah convinced Samson to share the secret of his strength.	*Judg. 16:15–17*
Doeg, Saul's shepherd, told him that David had been at Nob with Ahimelek.	*1 Sam. 22:9–10*
Joab kept David's secret regarding Uriah.	*2 Sam. 11:14–18*
A young man told Absalom that Jonathan and Ahimaaz were at En Rogel.	*2 Sam. 17:17–18*
Elisha continuously told the king of Israel all of King Ben-Hadad's secrets.	*2 Kings 6:9–12*
Esther and Mordecai kept her nationality a secret.	*Esther 2:20*
King Zedekiah secretly swore not to let anyone kill Jeremiah.	*Jer. 38:16*
Daniel kept his vision a secret.	*Dan. 7:28*
Jesus' disciples didn't tell anyone that He was the Messiah.	*Matt. 16:20*
The disciples kept Jesus' transfiguration a secret.	*Matt. 17:9*
The time of Jesus' return is kept secret.	*Matt. 24:36–37*
Jesus tried to keep His presence in Tyre secret.	*Mark 7:24–25*
Joseph of Arimathea was secretly a disciple of Jesus.	*John 19:38*
Some Jews secretly persuaded men to lie about Stephen.	*Acts 6:9–11*

Samson and Delilah

Delilah cuts Samson's hair

Samson's final victory

Verses about the Afterlife

Scripture	Reference
"Be afraid of the One who can destroy both soul and body in hell."	Matt. 10:28
"But I tell you that everyone will have to give account on the day of judgment for every empty word they have spoken...."	Matt. 12:36–37
"For the Son of Man is going to come in his Father's glory with his angels, and then he will reward each person according to what they have done."	Matt. 16:27
"All the peoples of the earth will mourn when they see the Son of Man coming on the clouds of heaven, with power and great glory. And he will send his angels with a loud trumpet call, and they will gather his elect from the four winds, from one end of the heavens to the other."	Matt. 24:30–31
"When the Son of Man comes in his glory, and all the angels with him, he will sit on his glorious throne. All the nations will be gathered before him, and he will separate the people one from another as a shepherd separates the sheep from the goats. He will put the sheep on his right and the goats on his left...."	Matt. 25:31–36
"For God so loved the world that he gave his one and only Son, that whoever believes in him shall not perish but have eternal life."	John 3:16
"Very truly I tell you, whoever hears my word and believes him who sent me has eternal life and will not be judged but has crossed over from death to life. Very truly I tell you, a time is coming and has now come when the dead will hear the voice of the Son of God and those who hear will live."	John 5:24–25
"Jesus said to her, 'Your brother will rise again.' Martha answered, 'I know he will rise again in the resurrection at the last day.' Jesus said to her, 'I am the resurrection and the life. The one who believes in me will live, even though they die; and whoever lives by believing in me will never die. Do you believe this?'"	John 11:23–26
"My Father's house has many rooms; if that were not so, would I have told you that I am going there to prepare a place for you?"	John 14:2
"For if we have been united with him in a death like his, we will certainly also be united with him in a resurrection like his."	Rom. 6:5
"For the wages of sin is death, but the gift of God is eternal life in Christ Jesus our Lord."	Rom. 6:23
"For as in Adam all die, so in Christ all will be made alive.... For he must reign until he has put all his enemies under his feet. The last enemy to be destroyed is death."	1 Cor. 15:22–26
"So will it be with the resurrection of the dead. The body that is sown is perishable, it is raised imperishable;... If there is a natural body, there is also a spiritual body."	1 Cor. 15:42–44

VERSES ABOUT THE AFTERLIFE (CONTINUED)

Scripture	Reference
"Listen, I tell you a mystery: We will not all sleep, but we will all be changed—in a flash, in the twinkling of an eye, at the last trumpet. For the trumpet will sound, the dead will be raised imperishable, and we will be changed. For the perishable must clothe itself with the imperishable, and the mortal with immortality. When the perishable has been clothed with the imperishable, and the mortal with immortality, then the saying that is written will come true: 'Death has been swallowed up in victory. Where, O death, is your victory? Where, O death, is your sting?'"	*1 Cor. 15:51–55*
"For to me, to live is Christ and to die is gain. If I am to go on living in the body, this will mean fruitful labor for me. Yet what shall I choose? I do not know! I am torn between the two: I desire to depart and be with Christ, which is better by far; but it is more necessary for you that I remain in the body."	*Phil. 1:21–24*
"Since, then, you have been raised with Christ, set your hearts on things above, where Christ is, seated at the right hand of God. Set your minds on things above, not on earthly things. For you died, and your life is now hidden with Christ in God. When Christ, who is your life, appears, then you also will appear with him in glory."	*Col. 3:1–4*
". . .we who are still alive and are left will be caught up together with them in the clouds to meet the Lord in the air. And so we will be with the Lord forever."	*1 Thess. 4:13–17*
"Now there is in store for me the crown of righteousness, which the Lord, the righteous Judge, will award to me on that day—and not only to me, but also to all who have longed for his appearing."	*2 Tim. 4:8*
"I am the Living One; I was dead, and now look, I am alive for ever and ever! And I hold the keys of death and Hades."	*Rev. 1:18*
"To the one who is victorious, I will give the right to sit with me on my throne, just as I was victorious and sat down with my Father on his throne."	*Rev. 3:21*
"The sea gave up the dead that were in it, and death and Hades gave up the dead that were in them, and each person was judged according to what they had done. Then death and Hades were thrown into the lake of fire. The lake of fire is the second death. Anyone whose name was not found written in the book of life was thrown into the lake of fire."	*Rev. 20:13–15*
"But the cowardly, the unbelieving, the vile, the murderers, the sexually immoral, those who practice magic arts, the idolaters and all liars—they will be consigned to the fiery lake of burning sulfur. This is the second death."	*Rev. 21:8*
"Look, I am coming soon! My reward is with me, and I will give to each person according to what they have done."	*Rev. 22:12*

SEE ALSO: *Ps. 139:8; Dan. 12:1–2; Matt. 18:9; Mark 12:24–25; Rom. 4:17; 1 Cor. 9:25; 2 Cor. 4:10–11; 2 Cor. 5:6–10; Eph. 2:6; 1 Thess. 5:9–10; 2 Thess. 1:9; Heb. 9:27–28; 1 Pet. 1:3; 1 John 1:2; Rev. 2:11; Rev. 14:9–10; Rev. 19:20; Rev. 20:4–6*

BIBLE LISTS

WHAT'S IN
A NAME?

BABIES NAMED BY GOD

Baby	Reference
Isaac	*Gen. 17:19*
Ishmael	*Gen. 16:11*
Jesus	*Matt. 1:21*
Jezreel	*Hosea 1:4*
John (the Baptist)	*Luke 1:13*
Lo-Ammi	*Hosea 1:9*
Lo-Ruhamah	*Hosea 1:6*
Maher-Shalal-Hash-Baz	*Isa. 8:1–3*
Solomon/Jedidiah	*1 Chron. 22:9; 2 Sam. 12:25*

THE MANY HERODS

The Herods	Description	Reference
Herod the Great	Governor of Galilee who ordered all the male children in Bethlehem killed	*Matt. 2:16*
Herod Archelaus	Herod the Great's son who ruled Judea after his father's death	*Matt. 2:21–22*
Herod Antipas	Herod the Great's son who ruled Galilee and Peraea. Beheaded John the Baptist. Pilate sent Jesus to him after finding Him guilty of no crime. (Photo above)	*Matt. 14:3–12; Luke 23:6–12*
Herod Philip I	Herod the Great's son. Lost his wife, Herodias, to his brother Herod Antipas.	*Matt. 14:3–12*
Philip the Tetrarch (Herod Philip II)	Herod the Great's son. Ruled Iturea, Batanea, Auranitis, and Traconitis.	*Luke 3:1*
Herod Agrippa I	Herodias's brother. Killed the apostle James and put Peter in prison.	*Acts 12:1–19*
Herod Agrippa II	Asked by Festus to hear Paul's case. Found no fault in Paul, but refused to convert to Christianity.	*Acts 25:13–26:31*

Salome (Movie, 1918)

Herod Agrippa

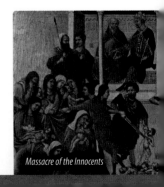

Massacre of the Innocents

MEN NAMED JOSHUA

Person	Reference
Moses' assistant and Israel's leader into Canaan (photo above)	Num. 27:18–21
Man of Beth Shemesh in whose field the ark of the covenant stopped	1 Sam. 6:13–14
Governor during the time of King Josiah	2 Kings 23:8
A high priest whom Satan tried to accuse	Zech. 3:1–9
Eliezer's son, an ancestor of Jesus	Luke 3:29

The name Jesus is a Greek form of the Hebrew name Joshua.

NAMES SHARED BY MEN AND WOMEN

Name	Information and Reference
Abihail	Leader of the Levites in the wilderness (Num. 3:35); Abishur's wife (1 Chron. 2:29); descendant of Gad (1 Chron. 5:14); David's niece and King Rehoboam's mother-in-law (2 Chron. 11:18); Esther's father, Mordecai's uncle (Esther 2:15)
Abijah	Samuel's son who was corrupt (1 Sam. 8:2); son of Jeroboam I (1 Kings 14:1–18); King Ahaz's wife, King Hezekiah's mother (2 Kings 18:2); descendant of Benjamin (1 Chron. 7:8); head of Levite priests during David's reign (1 Chron. 24:10); head of a priestly family during Ezra and Nehemiah's time (Neh. 10:7); head of a priestly family who returned to Jerusalem with Zerubbabel (Neh. 12:4); king of Judah, also known as Abijam (Matt. 1:7)
Ahlai	Descendant of Judah (1 Chron. 2:31, 34); Zabad's father (1 Chron. 11:41)
Athaliah	King Ahab's daughter who became queen (2 Kings 11:1–3); one of Jehoram's sons (1 Chron. 8:26); one of the descendants of Elam who returned with Ezra (Ezra 8:7)
Ephah	Descendant of Abraham through Keturah (Gen. 25:4); Caleb's concubine (1 Chron. 2:46); descendant of Judah (1 Chron. 2:47)
Gomer	Japheth's son (Gen. 10:2); prostitute God told Hosea to marry (Hosea 1:2–3)
Hushim	Son of Dan (Gen. 46:23); Benjaminite whose husband divorced her (1 Chron. 8:8)
Maakah	One of Nahor's sons (Gen. 22:24); David's wife, Absalom's mother (2 Sam. 3:3); father of King Achish of Gath (1 Kings 2:39); Caleb's concubine (1 Chron. 2:48); Makir's wife (1 Chron. 7:15–16); ancestor of King Saul, wife of Jeiel (1 Chron. 9:35); Hanan's (one of David's mighty men) father (1 Chron. 11:43); Shephatiah's (one of David's chief officers) father (1 Chron. 27:16); Absalom's daughter, Abijah's mother (2 Chron. 11:20–22)
Miriam	Moses and Aaron's sister (Exod. 15:20); descendant of Judah, Mered and Bithiah's son (1 Chron. 4:17–18)
Noadiah	Levite present when the temple treasure was returned to Jerusalem (Ezra 8:33); prophet who tried to stop Nehemiah from rebuilding (Neh. 6:14)
Noah	Righteous man who built the ark (Gen. 6:9); a daughter of Zelophehad (Num. 26:33)
Oholiba-mah	One of Esau's wives (Gen. 36:2); chief of an Edomite clan (Gen. 36:41)
Puah	Hebrew midwife who refused to kill the Hebrew boys (Exod. 1:15); Judge Tola's father (Judg. 10:1); Issachar's son (1 Chron. 7:1)
Shelomith	Mother of a man (from the tribe of Dan) who was stoned for blasphemy (Lev. 24:11); descendant of David (1 Chron. 3:19); descendant of the Kohathites (1 Chron. 23:18); descendant of Moses who was in charge of the temple treasury (1 Chron. 26:25–28); Rehoboam and Maakah's son (2 Chron. 11:20); Ezra's companion (Ezra 8:10)
Timna	Concubine for one of Esau's sons (Gen. 36:12); chief descended from Esau (Gen. 36:40)

PEOPLE WHO HAD THEIR NAMES CHANGED

Old Name	New Name	Reference
Abram	Abraham	*Gen. 17:5*
Azariah	Abednego	*Dan. 1:6–7*
Ben-Oni	Benjamin	*Gen. 35:18*
Daniel	Belteshazzar	*Dan. 1:6–7*
Gideon	Jerub-Baal	*Judg. 6:32*
Hadassah	Esther	*Esther 2:7*
Hananiah	Shadrach	*Dan. 1:6–7*
Hoshea	Joshua	*Num. 13:16*
Jacob	Israel	*Gen. 32:28; 35:10*
Joseph	Zaphenath-Paneah	*Gen. 41:45*
Mishael	Meshach	*Dan. 1:6–7*
Pashhur	Magor-Missabib (or Terror on Every Side)	*Jer. 20:3*
Sarai	Sarah	*Gen. 17:15*
Saul	Paul	*Acts 13:9*
Simon	Peter	*John 1:42*

Hello
my name is

PEOPLE WHO SHARED A NAME

Name	Information and Reference
Abigail	Wife of Nabal and David (1 Sam. 25:39–42); Joab's aunt (2 Sam. 17:25)
Abimelek	King of Gerar during the time of Abraham (Gen. 20:1–2); king of Gerar during the time of Isaac (Gen. 26:1); Gideon's son who killed his seventy brothers (Judg. 9:1–5); Abimelek/Achish King of Gath whom David fled to (1 Sam. 21:10; Ps. 34)
Adah	One of Lamech's two wives (Gen. 4:19); one of Esau's Canaanite wives (Gen. 36:2)
Ahinoam	Saul's wife (1 Sam. 14:50); one of David's wives, Amnon's mother (1 Sam. 25:43)
Anah	Zibeon the Hivite's son, Oholibamah's father (Gen. 36:2); Seir the Horite's son (Gen. 36:20); Zibeon's son, found hot springs in the desert (Gen. 36:24)
Ananias	Was struck dead for lying (Acts 5:1–5); restored Paul's sight after the Damascus experience (Acts 9:17–19); high priest who testified against Paul (Acts 24:1)
Azariah	King of Judah known frequently as Uzziah (2 Kings 14:21); chief priest from Zadok's family (2 Chron. 31:10); assisted Ezra in teaching the law (Neh. 8:7); Daniel's friend whose name was changed to Abednego (Dan. 1:6–7); approximately twenty others
Deborah	Rebekah's nurse (Gen. 35:8); judge and prophet (Judg. 4:4)
Eleazar	Aaron's son, chief of the Levites (Num. 3:32); Abinadad's son, guarded the ark of the covenant (1 Sam. 7:1); one of David's three mighty men (2 Sam. 23:9); Phinehas's son (Ezra 8:33); four others
Herod	See separate chart—"The Many Herods"
James	Apostle, Alphaeus's son, possibly Matthew's brother (Matt. 10:3); prominent apostle, John's brother, Zebedee's son (Mark 1:19); James the younger, Joses/Joseph's brother, Mary's son (Mark 15:40); apostle Judas/Thaddaeus's father (Luke 6:16); Jesus' brother (Gal. 1:19)
Jehoshaphat	An official in Solomon's court (1 Kings 4:3); king of Judah (1 Kings 22:41); King Jehu's father (2 Kings 9:2)
Joel	Samuel's oldest son, who was corrupt (1 Sam. 8:2–5); one of David's mighty men (1 Chron. 11:38); prophet (Joel 1:1); eight others
John	The apostle, Zebedee's son, James's brother (Matt. 4:21); John the Baptist, Jesus' forerunner (Mark 1:4); Peter and Andrew's father (John 1:42); member of the high priest's family (Acts 4:6); John Mark, Barnabas's cousin, Paul's companion (Col. 4:10)
Jonathan	Saul's son, David's best friend (1 Sam. 13:16); one of David's nephews (2 Sam. 21:21); priest, prophet Zechariah's father (Neh. 12:35); approximately ten others
Joseph	Jacob's favorite son who ruled Egypt (Gen. 30:22–24); Jesus' adoptive father (Matt. 1:16); one of Jesus' brothers (Matt. 13:55); Joseph of Arimathea, who gave his own tomb to Jesus (Mark 15:43); Joseph Barsabbas/Justus, a candidate to replace Judas (Acts 1:23); six others

PEOPLE WHO SHARED A NAME (CONTINUED)

Name	Information and Reference
Joshua	See separate chart—"Men Named Joshua"
Judas	One of the Twelve, also known as Thaddaeus (Matt. 10:3; Luke 6:16); Iscariot, apostle who betrayed Jesus (Matt. 10:4); one of Jesus' brothers, also known as Jude (Matt. 13:55; Jude 1); a Galilean who started a revolt (Acts 5:37); host to Paul (Acts 9:11); Judas Barsabbas who was paired with Silas (Acts 15:22)
Levi	Jacob's son, from whom the priests descended (Gen. 29:34); apostle also known as Matthew (Mark 2:14); an ancestor of Jesus (Luke 3:24); Simeon's son, an ancestor of Jesus (Luke 3:29)
Mary	See separate chart—"Women Named Mary"
Micah	Man from Ephraim who made idols and hired a Levite (Judg. 17–18); Mephibosheth's son (1 Chron. 8:34); prophet (Mic. 1:1)
Michael	Father of one of the twelve spies (Num. 13:13); one of King Jehoshaphat's sons (2 Chron. 21:2); archangel (Dan. 10:13); six others
Milkah	Nahor's wife, Bethuel's father (Gen. 22:21–23); one of Zelophehad's daughters (Num. 26:33)
Naamah	Tubal-Cain's sister (Gen. 4:22); King Rehoboam's mother (1 Kings 14:21)
Nathan	One of David and Bathsheba's sons (2 Sam. 5:14); prophet who advised David (2 Sam. 7:1–3); one of David's thirty men (2 Sam. 23:36); seven others
Obadiah	King Ahab's official who worshipped God and hid the prophets (1 Kings 18:3); commander in David's army (1 Chron. 12:8–9); prophet (Obad. 1:1); approximately ten others
Philip	The apostle (Matt. 10:3); Herod, who lost his wife Herodias to his brother Antipas (Matt. 14:3–12); tetrarch who ruled Iturea and Traconitis (Luke 3:1); evangelist (Acts 21:8)
Saul	King of Edom (Gen. 36:37); Israel's first king (1 Sam. 9:17); apostle whose name was changed to Paul (Acts 13:9)
Simon	One of Jesus' brothers (Matt. 13:55); a former leper at whose house Jesus ate (Matt. 26:6); Simon of Cyrene, who carried Jesus' cross (Matt. 27:32); Simon the Zealot, one of the Twelve (Luke 6:15); Simon Peter, Andrew's brother, Jesus' chief disciple (John 1:42); Judas Iscariot's father (John 6:71); magician who tried to pay to receive the Holy Spirit (Acts 8:18–19); tanner whom Peter stayed with (Acts 9:43)
Tamar	Judah's daughter-in-law, bore twins to Judah (Gen. 38:6); David's daughter, Absalom's sister whom Amnon raped (2 Sam. 13:22); Absalom's daughter (2 Sam. 14:27)
Zadok	A priest of David (2 Sam. 15:24); King Jotham's grandfather (2 Kings 15:32–33); brave soldier in David's army (1 Chron. 12:28); six others
Zechariah	King of Israel (2 Kings 14:29); one of King Jehoshaphat's sons (2 Chron. 21:2); prophet and priest (Neh. 12:16; Zech. 1:1); John the Baptist's father, a priest (Luke 1:13); priest who was killed (Luke 11:51); approximately twenty others

TITLES AND NAMES OF CHRISTIANS

Title or Name	Reference
believers	Acts 5:12
body of Christ	Eph. 1:22–23
branches	John 15:5
brothers and sisters	James 2:15
Christians	Acts 11:26
church	Matt. 16:18
disciples	John 8:31
elect	2 Tim. 2:10
flock	Acts 20:28
friends	John 15:15
God's children	Luke 20:36
heirs	Gal. 4:7
light of the world	Matt. 5:14
priesthood	1 Pet. 2:5, 9
righteous	1 Pet. 3:12
saints/holy people	Rom. 1:7
servants	Acts 4:29
sheep/lambs	John 21:15–17
slaves	1 Cor. 7:22
the Way	Acts 19:9

WOMEN NAMED MARY

Person	Reference
Mother of Jesus (photo above)	Matt. 1:16
Mother of James the younger and Joses/Joseph	Mark 15:40
Mary Magdalene, the first to see the risen Lord	Mark 16:9
Mary of Bethany, Lazarus and Martha's sister who sat at Jesus' feet	John 11:1
Clopas's wife	John 19:25
Mother of John Mark	Acts 12:12
One of Paul's fellow workers	Rom. 16:6

Mary is the Greek form of the Hebrew version of Miriam.

Ireland, 1972

USA, 1976

Australia, 1993

USA, 1975

USSR, 1971

BIBLE LISTS

Stories Behind the Numbers

THREES OF THE BIBLE

References to the Number Three in the Bible	Reference
Noah had 3 sons: Shem, Ham, and Japheth.	Gen. 6:10; 7:13; 9:19
Abraham had 3 visitors who told him he would have a son and warned him about the destruction of Sodom and Gomorrah.	Gen. 18:1–2
Abraham served his visitors bread baked with 3 seahs of fine flour.	Gen. 18:6
There were 3 branches on the vine in the chief cupbearer's dream. These represented 3 days until Pharaoh would restore him.	Gen. 40:10–13
There were 3 baskets of bread in the chief baker's dream. These represented 3 days until Pharaoh would hang him.	Gen. 40:16–19
Joseph kept his brothers as prisoners for 3 days.	Gen. 42:14–17
Moses' mother hid him away for 3 months.	Exod. 2:1–3
Moses asked Pharaoh to allow the Israelites to take a 3-day journey into the wilderness to worship God.	Exod. 3:18; 5:3; 8:27
The Lord brought a plague of darkness to Egypt for 3 days.	Exod. 10:22–23
On the 3rd day, God appeared to the Israelites on Mount Sinai.	Exod. 19:10–16
The Israelites celebrated 3 annual festivals: The Festival of Unleavened Bread; the Festival of Weeks/Harvest; and the Festival of Tabernacles/Booths/Ingathering	Exod. 23:14–17; 34:23–24; Deut. 16:16
In the tabernacle, 3 branches were located on each side of the lampstand, and 3 cups were placed on each of the branches.	Exod. 25:32–33; 37:18–19
The altar in the tabernacle was 3 cubits high.	Exod. 27:1; 38:1
The curtains in the tabernacle had 3 posts and 3 bases.	Exod. 38:14–15
Sacrifices that remained on the 3rd day had to be burned.	Lev. 7:17–18; 19:6–7
Upon arriving in Canaan, the Israelites could not harvest from any fruit tree they planted for 3 years.	Lev. 19:23
The Israelites were given 3 blessings: "The Lord bless you and keep you." "The Lord make his face shine on you and be gracious to you." "The Lord turn his face toward you and give you peace."	Num. 6:24–26
The spies sent into Canaan brought back 3 types of fruit: grapes, figs, and pomegranates.	Num. 13:23
Anyone who touched a dead body had to be purified on the 3rd day.	Num. 19:12
Balaam beat his donkey 3 times.	Num. 22:28, 32–33
Balaam blessed Israel 3 times.	Num. 24:10
There were 3 cities of refuge located in Canaan and 3 across the Jordan.	Num. 35:13–14

References to the Number Three in the Bible	Reference
The Israelites were to store a tithe of the produce every 3 years.	*Deut. 14:28–29; 26:12*
A man could only be put to death on the testimony of 2 or 3 witnesses.	*Deut. 17:6; 19:15*
The Jordan River was divided 3 times.	*Josh. 3:16; 2 Kings 2:8, 14*
Caleb drove out the 3 Anakites from Hebron.	*Josh. 15:13–14*
From each tribe, 3 men were selected to survey the land.	*Josh. 18:4*
Samson lied to Delilah 3 times.	*Judg. 16:15*
Eli's sons used a 3-pronged fork to steal meat from the offering.	*1 Sam. 2:12–14*
God called to Samuel 3 times.	*1 Sam. 3:8*
King Saul was met by 3 men carrying 3 goats and 3 loaves of bread.	*1 Sam. 10:3*
Saul sent men to capture David at Naioth 3 times.	*1 Sam. 19:19–21*
Jonathan shot 3 arrows to warn David.	*1 Sam. 20:20–22*
An Egyptian slave went without food for 3 days and 3 nights.	*1 Sam. 30:11–12*
Saul's 3 sons all died on the same day.	*1 Sam. 31:2–8*
Zeruiah, David's step-sister, had 3 sons: Joab, Abishai, and Asahel.	*2 Sam. 2:18*
David's son Absalom fled to Geshur and stayed there 3 years.	*2 Sam. 13:38*
Absalom had 3 sons.	*2 Sam. 14:27*
Joab killed Absalom with 3 javelins.	*2 Sam. 18:14*
During David's reign, there was a famine for 3 years.	*2 Sam. 21:1*
David had 3 mighty men: Josheb-Basshebeth, Eleazar, and Shammah.	*2 Sam. 23:8–12, 16–17*
After David took the census, God gave him a choice of 3 consequences: 3 years of famine, 3 months of flight from his enemies, or 3 days of plague.	*2 Sam. 24:11–13*
King Abijah reigned for 3 years.	*1 Kings 15:1–2*
Elijah healed the Zarephath widow's son by stretching out on him 3 times.	*1 Kings 17:21*
During Elijah's time, there was no rain in the land for 3½ years.	*1 Kings 18:1; Luke 4:25*
Elijah ordered Baal's prophets to wet the wood and offering 3 times.	*1 Kings 18:34*
Men searched for Elijah for 3 days.	*2 Kings 2:17*
There were 3 miracle meals.	*2 Kings 4:42–43; Matt. 15:34, 38; Mark 6:38, 44*
Jehoash defeated Ben-Hadad 3 times.	*2 Kings 13:24–25*

180

References to the Number Three in the Bible	Reference
God healed Hezekiah on the 3rd day.	2 Kings 20:5–8
King Jehoahaz reigned for 3 months.	2 Kings 23:31
King Jehoiachin reigned for 3 months.	2 Kings 24:8
Benjamin had 3 sons: Bela, Beker, and Jediael.	1 Chron. 7:6
Obed-Edom kept the ark of the covenant for 3 months.	1 Chron. 13:14
Abraham is called God's friend 3 times.	2 Chron. 20:7; Isa. 41:8; James 2:23
The rebuilding of the temple was completed on the 3rd day of Adar.	Ezra 6:15
King Xerxes gave a banquet for his officials in the 3rd year of his reign.	Esther 1:3
Esther and the Israelites fasted for 3 days and 3 nights.	Esther 4:15–16
Job had 3 friends: Eliphaz, Bildad, and Zophar.	Job 2:11
After losing his first set of children, Job had 3 daughters: Jemimah, Keziah, and Keren-Happuch.	Job 42:13–15
"A cord of 3 strands is not quickly broken."	Eccles. 4:12
Seraphim cried "holy" 3 times.	Isa. 6:3
As a sign against Egypt, Isaiah went naked and barefoot for 3 years.	Isa. 20:1–3
The Trinity	Isa. 48:16
In Ezekiel's vision, there were 3 alcoves on each side of the east gate.	Ezek. 40:10, 21
In both Ezekiel's vision and John's revelation, there were 3 gates in each of the four corners of the city.	Ezek. 48:31; Rev. 21:13
Daniel and his friends trained for 3 years for the king's service.	Dan. 1:5
Daniel had 3 friends: Shadrach, Meshach, and Abednego.	Dan. 1:6–7
There were 3 warnings written on Nebuchadnezzar's wall.	Dan. 5:25–28
Daniel was one of 3 administrators over the satraps in the kingdom.	Dan. 6:1–2
Daniel prayed 3 times a day.	Dan. 6:10–13
A beast in Daniel's vision had 3 ribs in its mouth.	Dan. 7:5
Daniel had visions in the 3rd year of Belshazzar's and Cyrus's reigns.	Dan. 8:1; 10:1
Daniel mourned for 3 weeks over his vision.	Dan. 10:2–3
Jonah was inside the fish for 3 days and 3 nights.	Jon. 1:17; Matt. 12:40
It took 3 days to walk through Nineveh.	Jon. 3:3
God spoke to Jesus from heaven 3 times.	Matt. 3:17; 17:5; John 12:28

References to the Number Three in the Bible	Reference
The devil tempted Jesus 3 times, and Jesus rebuked him 3 times.	Matt. 4:1–11
Jesus raised 3 people from the dead: the synagogue leader's daughter, the widow's son, and Lazarus.	Matt. 9:23–26; Mark 5:39–42; Luke 7:12–15; 8:51–56; John 11:38–44
Jesus prayed 3 times in Gethsemane.	Matt. 26:44; Mark 14:41
Peter denied knowing Jesus 3 times.	Matt. 26:75
Jesus' death was followed by 3 hours of darkness.	Matt. 27:45
Jesus rose from the dead in 3 days.	Matt. 27:63; Mark 8:31
In the fig tree parable, the owner of the vineyard searched for fruit on the tree for 3 years.	Luke 13:6–7
Jesus questioned Peter 3 times in to restore him after his denial.	John 21:15–17
After the Damascus experience, Paul was blind for 3 days.	Acts 9:9
In Peter's vision, the sheet with unclean animals was let down from heaven 3 times.	Acts 10:16
There were 3 men who were sent to bring Peter to Cornelius.	Acts 11:11
Paul lists 3 gifts: faith, hope, and love.	1 Cor. 13:13
Paul was both shipwrecked and beaten 3 times.	2 Cor. 11:25
Paul was caught up into the 3rd heaven.	2 Cor. 12:2
Paul prayed for healing from the thorn in his flesh 3 times.	2 Cor. 12:8
People have 3 enemies: the world, the flesh, and the devil.	Gal. 5:17; Eph. 6:12; 1 John 2:15
People are made of 3 parts: spirit, soul, and body.	1 Thess. 5:23
There are 3 sources of temptation: the lust of the flesh, the lust of the eyes, and the pride of life.	1 John 2:16
These 3 testify that Jesus is the Christ: Spirit, water, and blood.	1 John 5:6–8
There are 3 forms of apostasy: the way of Cain, the error of Balaam, and the rebellion of Korah.	Jude 11
Jesus holds 3 offices: Prophet, Priest, and King.	Rev. 1:5
The creatures in John's Revelation cried "holy" 3 times.	Rev. 4:8
In John's Revelation, a 3rd of mankind was killed by 3 plagues: fire, smoke, and sulfur.	Rev. 9:18
In John's Revelation, 3 evil spirits that looked like frogs came out of the dragon's mouth.	Rev. 16:13
In John's Revelation, the great city split into 3 parts.	Rev. 16:19

FIVES OF THE BIBLE

References to the Number Five in the Bible	Reference
The Israelites were to present another corn offering to God 50 days after harvesting corn in the new land.	Lev. 23:15–16
Jubilee occurred every 50th year.	Lev. 25:10
Levites had to retire once they reached age 50.	Num. 8:23–26
The bride price was 50 shekels of silver.	Deut. 22:28–29
David chose 5 stones to use against Goliath.	1 Sam. 17:40
When he and his men were hungry, David asked for 5 loaves of bread	1 Sam. 21:1–3
David paid 50 shekels of silver for the threshing floor and oxen.	2 Sam. 24:24
During Josiah's Passover, the leaders of the Levites provided 5,000 Passover offerings and 500 head of cattle for the Levites.	2 Chron. 35:9
Job owned 500 yoke of oxen and 500 donkeys.	Job 1:3
Jesus fed 5,000 men with 5 loaves of bread. They sat in groups of 50.	Matt. 14:17–21; 16:9; Mark 6:38–44; 8:19; Luke 9:13–16; John 6:9–13
In Jesus' parable, there were 5 foolish virgins and 5 wise virgins.	Matt. 25:2
In the parables of the talents/minas, the man who had received 5 talents was considered wise.	Matt. 25:20–21; Luke 19:18–19
Elizabeth became pregnant and remained in seclusion for 5 months.	Luke 1:24
Jesus told a parable about forgiveness involving 500 denarii and 50 denarii.	Luke 7:41
In the parable of the rich man and Lazarus, the rich man wanted Abraham to send Lazarus to go and warn his 5 brothers.	Luke 16:28
The Samaritan woman had 5 husbands.	John 4:18
The Bethesda/Sheep Gate pool where Jesus healed a paralyzed man was surrounded by 5 covered colonnades.	John 5:1–2
Pentecost occurred 50 days after Jesus' resurrection.	Acts 2
After Peter and John preached, 5,000 men became believers.	Acts 4:1–4
After His resurrection, Jesus appeared to more than 500 people.	1 Cor. 15:6
Paul received 39 lashes 5 times.	2 Cor. 11:24

Sixes of the Bible

References to the Number Six in the Bible	Reference
Jacob and Leah had 6 sons together.	Gen. 30:20
Jacob worked for Laban for 6 years for his flocks.	Gen. 31:41
The Israelites were to work for only 6 days of the week.	Exod. 16:26; 20:9–11; Lev. 23:3
Hebrew servants were to serve only 6 years.	Exod. 21:2; Deut. 15:12
The glory of the Lord covered Mount Sinai for 6 days before God spoke to Moses.	Exod. 24:16
There were 6 branches that extended from the lampstand in the tabernacle.	Exod. 25:32–35; 37:18–21
The west end of the tabernacle had 6 frames.	Exod. 26:22; 36:27
Names of 6 of Jacob's sons were engraved onto the onyx stones for the ephod.	Exod. 28:9–12
Loaves of bread in the tent of meeting were to be set on the gold table in two rows of 6.	Lev. 24:6
Fields were to be worked for 6 years and then given rest.	Lev. 25:3–4
The leaders of the families of Israel brought 6 covered carts as an offering to the tabernacle.	Num. 7:3
There were 6 Levite towns that served as cities of refuge.	Num. 35:6–15
Israelites were instructed to eat unleavened bread for 6 days after the Passover.	Deut. 16:8
Joshua and his army were to march around Jericho once each day for 6 days.	Josh. 6:2–3, 14
Judah was allotted 6 cities in the desert.	Josh. 15:61–62
Judge Jephthah led Israel for 6 years.	Judg. 12:7
Boaz gave Ruth 6 measures of barley.	Ruth 3:15–17
After the ark of the covenant was carried 6 steps, David offered sacrifices and danced before the Lord.	2 Sam. 6:13–14
A giant at Gath had 6 toes on each foot and 6 fingers on each hand.	2 Sam. 21:20; 1 Chron. 20:6
The middle floor of the temple was 6 cubits wide.	1 Kings 6:6
Solomon's throne had 6 steps.	1 Kings 10:19–20; 2 Chron. 9:18–19

184

References to the Number Six in the Bible	Reference
Joab and his men stayed in Edom 6 months to defeat the Edomites.	*1 Kings 11:16*
King Omri ruled in Tirzah for 6 years.	*1 Kings 16:23*
Joash was hidden at the temple for 6 years.	*2 Kings 11:3;* *2 Chron. 22:11–12*
King Zechariah reigned for 6 months.	*2 Kings 15:8*
David had 6 sons in Hebron.	*1 Chron. 3:1–4*
Shekaniah, a member of the royal line after the exile, had 6 sons.	*1 Chron. 3:22*
Shimei, a descendant of Simeon, had 6 daughters.	*1 Chron. 4:27*
Azel, a descendant of Benjamin, had 6 sons.	*1 Chron. 8:38; 9:44*
Jeduthun had 6 sons who were assigned to minister through music.	*1 Chron. 25:3*
There were 6 Levites assigned as guards on the east gate.	*1 Chron. 26:17*
A total of 6 sheep were prepared each day for Nehemiah.	*Neh. 5:18*
Queen Esther was treated with oil of myrrh for 6 months, and perfumes and cosmetics for another 6 months.	*Esther 2:12*
Isaiah had a vision of seraphs with 6 wings.	*Isa. 6:2*
In Ezekiel's vision, a man held a measuring rod of 6 long cubits.	*Ezek. 40:5*
The alcoves at the east gate were 6 cubits square.	*Ezek. 40:12*
The width of the jambs in the outer sanctuary was 6 cubits on each side.	*Ezek. 41:1*
The entrance of the inner sanctuary was 6 cubits wide.	*Ezek. 41:3*
The wall of the temple was 6 cubits thick.	*Ezek. 41:5*
The foundation of the temple was 6 cubits long.	*Ezek. 41:8*
The gate of the inner court facing east was required to be shut for 6 working days.	*Ezek. 46:1*
On the Sabbath, 6 male lambs were to be offered as burnt offerings.	*Ezek. 46:4*
On the New Moon, 6 lambs were to be offered.	*Ezek. 46:6*
Jesus turned the water in 6 stone jars into wine.	*John 2:6*
Jesus arrived at Bethany 6 days before the Passover.	*John 12:1*
Peter was accompanied by 6 men to Caesarea.	*Acts 11:12*
Each living creature around the throne had 6 wings.	*Rev. 4:8*

SEVENS OF THE BIBLE

References to the Number Seven in the Bible	Reference
God rested from creation on the 7th day.	*Gen. 2:2; Heb. 4:4*
God blessed the 7th day and made it holy.	*Gen. 2:3*
God vowed that anyone who hurt Cain would be avenged 7 times over.	*Gen. 4:15*
Lamech claimed that if anyone harmed him, he should be avenged 77 times.	*Gen. 4:24*
God instructed Noah to take 7 pairs of every clean animal and bird into the ark.	*Gen. 7:1–3*
The ark came to rest on Mount Ararat in the 7th month.	*Gen. 8:4*
Abraham gave Abimelek 7 ewe lambs as a witness that he dug the well.	*Gen. 21:28–30*
Jacob worked 7 years for Leah and 7 years for Rachel.	*Gen. 29:18–20, 27–30*
After Jacob left, Laban pursued him for 7 days.	*Gen. 31:23*
Pharaoh dreamed that 7 gaunt cows ate 7 fat cows.	*Gen. 41:1–4, 17–21*
Pharaoh dreamed that 7 thin heads of grain ate 7 healthy heads of grain.	*Gen. 41:5–7, 22–24*
Pharaoh's dreams represented 7 years of famine.	*Gen. 41:25–54*
There were 70 members of the house of Jacob that resided in Egypt.	*Gen. 46:26–27; Exod. 1:5; Deut. 10:22*
The Egyptians mourned for Jacob 70 days.	*Gen. 50:1–3*
Joseph mourned for Jacob 7 days.	*Gen. 50:10*
The Israelites were to eat bread without yeast for 7 days in observance of Passover/Festival of Unleavened bread.	*Exod. 12:14–16; 23:15; Lev. 23:6; 2 Chron. 30:21*
The Israelites were to rest on the 7th day.	*Exod. 16:26–30; 20:10–11; Deut. 5:14*
Hebrew servants were to go free in the 7th year.	*Exod. 21:2; Jer. 34:14*
The land was to be allowed to rest in the 7th year.	*Exod. 23:10–11*
Moses appointed 70 elders who went up to Mount Sinai to worship God.	*Exod. 24:1, 9*
The tabernacle had 7 lamps.	*Exod. 25:37*
The ordination for Aaron and his sons lasted 7 days.	*Exod. 29:35; Lev. 8:33–35*
The blood from the sin offering had to be sprinkled 7 times in front of the curtain.	*Lev. 4:3–6*

186

SEVENS OF THE BIBLE (CONTINUED)

References to the Number Seven in the Bible	Reference
Those who were defiled would be unclean for 7 days.	*Lev. 12:1–2; 13:4; 15:13–28; Num. 19:11*
Young calves, lambs, or goats had to remain with their mothers for 7 days before being sacrificed.	*Lev. 22:27*
They were to offer 7 male lambs as burnt offerings.	*Lev. 23:18*
The Festival of Trumpets, the Day of Atonement, and the Festival of Tabernacles all took place in the 7th month.	*Lev. 23:23–34; Num. 29:1*
The Festival of Tabernacles lasted 7 days.	*Lev. 23:34–36*
The Year of Jubilee took place after 7 times 7 years.	*Lev. 25:8*
There were 7 enemy nations in the promised land.	*Deut. 7:1; Acts 13:19*
Debts had to be canceled after 7 years.	*Deut. 15:9*
On the 7th day, 7 priests marched around Jericho 7 times.	*Josh. 6:4–16; Heb. 11:30*
The land of Canaan was divided into 7 parts.	*Josh. 18:5–9*
Jerub-Baal had 70 sons, whom Abimelek murdered.	*Judg. 8:29–30; 9:2–5, 18, 24, 56*
Samson's wife cried for 7 days until he told her the riddle.	*Judg. 14:16–17*
Samson told Delilah that being tied with 7 fresh bowstrings and having his 7 braids weaved would take away his strength.	*Judg. 16:7–13*
There were 700 left-handed Benjamite soldiers from Gibeah.	*Judg. 20:15–16*
The ark of the covenant remained with the Philistines for 7 months.	*1 Sam. 6:1*
God killed 70 men from Beth Shemesh for looking into the ark of the covenant.	*1 Sam. 6:19*
Saul waited 7 days for Samuel but offered sacrifices before he arrived.	*1 Sam. 10:8; 13:8–10*
The people of Jabesh Gilead fasted for 7 days after the death of Saul.	*1 Sam. 31:11–13*
David reigned in Hebron 7 ½ years.	*2 Sam. 2:11; 5:5; 1 Kings 2:11; 1 Chron. 3:4*
David's son from Bathsheba died on the 7th day	*2 Sam. 12:17–18*
Seven of Saul's descendants that were handed over to the Gibeonites.	*2 Sam. 21:6–9*
After God sent a plague because of David's census, 70 thousand people died.	*2 Sam. 24:15; 1 Chron. 21:14*
It took Solomon 7 years to build the temple.	*1 Kings 6:38*
Solomon had 700 wives.	*1 Kings 11:3*

SEVENS OF THE BIBLE (CONTINUED)

References to the Number Seven in the Bible	Reference
Elijah sent his servant 7 times to check the sea for signs of rain.	*1 Kings 18:43–44*
God told Elijah that there were still 7,000 people who had not worshipped Baal.	*1 Kings 19:18; Rom. 11:4*
After the Shunammite's son woke from the dead, he sneezed 7 times.	*2 Kings 4:35*
Elisha instructed Naaman to go wash in the Jordan 7 times.	*2 Kings 5:10–14*
Joash was 7 years old when he became king.	*2 Kings 11:21*
During King Hezekiah's reign, 7 bulls, 7 rams, 7 male lambs, and 7 male goats were brought as a sin offering for the kingdom.	*2 Chron. 29:20–21*
In the 7th month, Ezra read the Book of the Law to the people.	*Neh. 8:1–2*
King Xerxes had 7 eunuchs.	*Esther 1:10*
King Xerxes asked his 7 nobles for advice regarding Queen Vashti.	*Esther 1:14–15*
Esther had 7 maids assigned to her.	*Esther 2:9*
Esther was brought to King Xerxes in the 7th year of his reign.	*Esther 2:16*
Job had 7 sons and 7,000 sheep.	*Job 1:2–3*
God promised to bring His people back to the land in 70 years.	*Jer. 29:10; Dan. 9:2*
Gabriel told Daniel, "Seventy 'sevens' are decreed for your people and your holy city to finish transgression, to put an end to sin, to atone for wickedness, to bring in everlasting righteousness, to seal up vision and prophecy and to anoint the Most Holy Place."	*Dan. 9:24–27*
Jesus fed the 4,000 with 7 loaves of bread, and there were 7 baskets of leftovers.	*Matt. 15:36–37; 16:10; Mark 8:5–8*
Jesus said we should forgive those who wrong us 7 times 70 times.	*Matt. 18:21–22; Luke 17:4*
Jesus drove out 7 demons from Mary Magdalene.	*Mark 16:9; Luke 8:2*
Jesus sent out 72 disciples.	*Luke 10:1, 17*
Emmaus was 7 miles from Jerusalem.	*Luke 24:13*
The disciples chose 7 men to oversee the distribution of food.	*Acts 6:1–3*
John wrote his revelation to 7 churches.	*Rev. 1:4*
The following can all be found in John's Revelation: 7 spirits, 7 golden candlesticks, 7 stars, 7 lamps, 7 seals, 7 horns, 7 eyes, 7 angels, 7 trumpets, 7 thunders, 7,000 slain in a great earthquake, 7 heads, 7 crowns, 7 last plagues, 7 bowls, 7 mountains, and 7 kings.	*Rev. 1–22*

TENS OF THE BIBLE

References to the Number Ten in the Bible	Reference
A 10th was set apart for God.	*Gen. 14:20; Deut. 14:22; 26:12; Matt. 23:23*
God gave the Israelites 10 commandments.	*Deut. 4:13; 10:4*
Haman's 10 sons were impaled on poles.	*Esther 9:10–14*
Daniel asked to be given only vegetables and water for 10 days.	*Dan. 1:12*
The beast in Daniel's and John's visions had 10 horns.	*Dan. 7:7–24; Rev. 13:1; 17:3, 7*
Jesus shared the parable of 10 virgins.	*Matt. 25:1*
In the parable of the bags of gold, the "good and faithful servant" had 10 bags of gold to give his master.	*Matt. 25:28*
In the parable of the lost coin, the woman had 10 coins.	*Luke 15:8*
Jesus healed 10 lepers.	*Luke 17:17*
In the parable of the minas, the nobleman gave 10 of his slaves 10 minas each.	*Luke 19:13*

189

Ten virgins

Ten Commandments

Ten lepers

TWELVES OF THE BIBLE

References to the Number Twelve in the Bible	Reference
There were 12 sons of Ishmael.	Gen. 25:13–16
There were 12 sons of Jacob.	Gen.35:23–36; 48:2–28; Acts 7:8
There were 12 springs at Elim, one of the Israelites' camp sites.	Exod. 15:27; Num. 33:9
There were 12 stone pillars set up at the foot of Mount Sinai, to represent the 12 tribes of Israel.	Exod. 24:4
There were 12 stones in the priest's breastpiece.	Exod. 28:15, 21; 39:14
Priests were to place 12 loaves of bread on a gold altar in the tent of meeting.	Lev. 24:5
The leaders of Israel were to bring 12 oxen before the Lord.	Num. 7:3
The leaders of Israel gave the following offering: 12 silver plates; 12 silver sprinkling bowls; 12 gold dishes; 12 bulls, 12 rams, and 12 male lambs for burnt offerings; 12 male goats for sin offerings.	Num. 7:84–87
The 12 staffs represented 12 tribes of Israel.	Num. 17:2, 6
Moses sent 12 spies into Canaan.	Deut. 1:23
There were 12 men, one from each tribe, who collected 12 stones from the Jordan River.	Josh. 4:2–9, 20
There were 12 cities of Benjamin.	Josh. 18:21–24
There were 12 cities of Zebulun.	Josh. 19:10–16
There were 12 cities for the descendants of the Levitical clan, Merari.	Josh. 21:7, 34–40; 1 Chron. 6:63
The Levite sent his concubine's body parts to each of the 12 tribes of Israel.	Judg. 19:29
Chosen for battle were 12 soldiers of David and 12 soldiers of Ish-Bosheth.	2 Sam. 2:14–15
Solomon had 12 district governors.	1 Kings 4:7–19
There were 12 bulls for temple furnishings.	1 Kings 7:25, 44; 2 Chron. 4:4, 15; Jer. 52:20
There were 12 lions for temple furnishings.	1 Kings 10:20; 2 Chron. 9:19
Ahijah the prophet tore his cloak into 12 pieces to represent 10 tribes given to Jeroboam and 2 given to David's family.	1 Kings 11:30

Twelves of the Bible (CONTINUED)

References to the Number Twelve in the Bible	Reference
King Omni reigned for 12 years.	*1 Kings 16:23*
Elijah used 12 stones to rebuild the altar on Mount Carmel.	*1 Kings 18:30–33*
Elisha had 12 yoke of oxen.	*1 Kings 19:19*
King Jehoshaphat reigned for 12 years.	*2 Kings 3:1*
Manasseh was 12 when he became king.	*2 Kings 21:1*
Nehemiah didn't eat the food allotted to the governor for 12 years.	*Neh. 5:14*
Esther underwent a 12-month beauty regimen.	*Esther 2:12*
A common measurement was 12 cubits.	*Ezek. 40:49; 43:16*
Jesus healed a woman who had been bleeding for 12 years.	*Matt. 9:20; Luke 8:43*
Jesus had 12 apostles.	*Matt. 10:2–4*
After Jesus fed 5,000 people, there were 12 baskets of leftovers.	*Matt. 14:20; Mark 6:43*
God would have sent Jesus 12 legions of angels.	*Matt. 26:53*
Jesus healed a 12-year-old girl.	*Mark 3:42; Luke 8:42*
Jesus was 12 when He was left in Jerusalem.	*Luke 2:42*
The apostles will sit on 12 thrones.	*Luke 22:30*
Paul laid hands on 12 men, who then spoke in tongues.	*Acts 19:7*
In his Revelation, John saw a woman wearing a crown with 12 stars on it.	*Rev. 12:1*
In his Revelation, John saw a heavenly Jerusalem with 12 pearl gates and 12 angels at the gates. On the gates were written the names of the 12 tribes of Israel. The wall of the city had 12 foundations. The city was 12,000 stadia long. The wall was 122 cubits thick.	*Rev. 21:12–21*
In his Revelation, John saw the tree of life bearing 12 crops of fruit.	*Rev. 22:2*

The Last Supper

FORTIES OF THE BIBLE

References to the Number Forty in the Bible	Reference
It rained for 40 days and 40 nights.	Gen. 7:4, 12, 17
Isaac was 40 years old when he married Rebekah.	Gen. 25:20
Esau was 40 years old when he married Judith.	Gen. 26:34
It took 40 days to embalm Jacob.	Gen. 50:2–3
Moses remained on Mount Sinai for 40 days and 40 nights.	Exod. 24:18; 28; 34 Deut. 9:9
There were 40 silver bases made for the south side of the tabernacle.	Exod. 26:18–19; 36:23–24
There were 40 silver bases made for the north side of the tabernacle.	Exod. 26:21, 25–26
The 12 spies explored Canaan for 40 days.	Num. 13:25
The Israelites wandered in the wilderness for 40 years.	Num. 14:33–34; Josh. 5:6; Ps. 95:10; Amos 2:10; Acts 7:36
Punishments were not to exceed 40 lashes.	Deut. 25:3
Caleb was 40 years old when he first explored Canaan.	Josh. 14:7
There were 40 years of peace during the time of the judges.	Judg. 3:11; 5:31; 8:28
The judge Abdon had 40 sons.	Judg. 12:13–14
Israel was ruled by the Philistines for 40 years.	Judg. 13:1
Eli judged Israel for 40 years.	1 Sam. 4:18
Goliath, the Philistine giant, mocked Israel for 40 days.	1 Sam. 17:16

Moses

The great flood

Isaac meets Rebekah

FORTIES OF THE BIBLE (CONTINUED)

References to the Number Forty in the Bible	Reference
Saul's son Ish-Bosheth was 40 years old when he became king.	2 Sam. 2:10
King David reigned for 40 years.	2 Sam. 5:4; 1 Kings 2:11; 1 Chron. 29:26–27
The main hall in Solomon's temple was 40 cubits long.	1 Kings 6:17
Each bronze basin in the temple held 40 baths.	1 Kings 7:38
King Solomon reigned for 40 years.	1 Kings 11:42; 2 Chron. 9:30
The prophet Elijah traveled 40 days and 40 nights to Mount Horeb.	1 Kings 19:8
The prophet Elisha received 40 camel-loads of gifts from Hazael.	2 Kings 8:9
King Joash reigned for 40 years.	2 Kings 12:1; 2 Chron. 24:1
Governors in Nehemiah's time took 40 shekels of silver from the people.	Neh. 5:15
The prophet Ezekiel lay on his side for 40 days, symbolically bearing Judah's sins.	Ezek. 4:6
God vowed to make Egypt desolate for 40 years.	Ezek. 29:11–13
The outer sanctuary in Ezekiel's vision was 40 cubits long.	Ezek. 41:2
The enclosed courts in Ezekiel's vision were 40 cubits long.	Ezek. 46:22
The prophet Jonah prophesied to the Ninevites that Nineveh would be destroyed in 40 days if they did not repent.	Jon. 3:4
Jesus fasted for 40 days and 40 nights.	Matt. 4:2; Mark 1:13; Luke 4:2
After His resurrection, Jesus appeared to the disciples for 40 days.	Acts 1:3
Moses was 40 years old when he fled to the Midian desert.	Acts 7:23–27
Moses spent 40 years in the Midian desert.	Acts 7:30
King Saul reigned for 40 years.	Acts 13:21
More than 40 men were involved in a plot to kill Paul.	Acts 23:12–13, 21

193

Jonah

Saul and David

David

Jesus

BIBLE LISTS

OFFICES, TITLES & POSITIONS

FALSE PROPHETS

False Prophet	Description	Reference
Ahab	Jeremiah predicted that he would be killed.	Jer. 29:21
Balaam	Rode a donkey and was confronted by an angel. God forced him to bless Israel.	*Num. 22–24*
Bar-Jesus (Elymas)	He tried to prevent the proconsul from believing Paul and Barnabas's message. He was struck blind.	*Acts 13:6–11*
Hananiah	Falsely prophesied that the Babylonian captivity would last two years	*Jer. 28:1–4*
Jezebel	Prophet at the church in Thyatira	*Rev. 2:20*
Noadiah	Prophet who tried to intimidate Nehemiah	*Neh. 6:14*
old prophet	Lied to another prophet and caused that prophet's death	*1 Kings 13:11–25*
Shemaiah	Sent untrue letters to the exiles. God vowed to eliminate his descendants.	*Jer. 29:24–32*
Zedekiah	Jeremiah predicted that he would be handed over to Babylon and killed.	*Jer. 29:21*

Zedekiah

Balaam

Elymas

JUDGES

Judge	Description	Reference
Abdon	Had forty sons and thirty grandsons	*Judg. 12:13–14*
Deborah	Assisted Barak in defeating the Canaanites	*Judg. 4:4–7*
Elon	Led Israel for ten years	*Judg. 12:11*
Gideon	Defeated the Midianites with three hundred men	*Judg. 7:4–7*
Ibzan	Had thirty sons and thirty daughters	*Judg. 12:8–9*
Jair	Had thirty sons who rode thirty donkeys	*Judg. 10:3–5*
Jephthah	Made a rash promise and lost his daughter as a result	*Judg. 11:30–40*
Othniel	First judge of Israel and Caleb's son-in-law	*Judg. 3:9*
Samson	Was given incredible physical strength and killed many Philistines	*Judg. 13–16*
Shamgar	Killed six hundred Philistines with an oxgoad	*Judg. 3:31*
Tola	Son of Dodo who led Israel for twenty-three years	*Judg. 10:1–2*

Jephthah and his daughter

Deborah

Samson

KINGS OF THE UNITED KINGDOM AND OF JUDAH

King of the United Kingdom	Additional Information	Reference
Saul	Israel's first king, who disqualified himself with repeated disobedience	*1 Sam. 11:14–15*
David	Israel's beloved king, a man after God's own heart despite his mistakes. His royal line would continue forever.	*2 Sam. 2:4; 5:3*
Solomon	Israel's wisest king, who had hundreds of wives and worshipped idols in his later years	*1 Kings 1:38–39*
THE KINGDOM DIVIDES : Judah (Southern Kingdom) & Israel (Northern Kingdom)		
King of Judah	**Additional Information**	**Reference**
Rehoboam	Solomon's son. Divided the kingdom with his harsh laws. Thus, he was the last king of the united kingdom and the first king of Judah.	*1 Kings 11:43*
Abijah	Led his army to a miraculous victory over northern Israel	*1 Kings 15:1*
Asa	Built fortified cities. Removed many idols. "Did what was right in the eyes of the LORD, as his father David had done." Lacked faith late in life.	*1 Kings 15:8–11*
Jehoshaphat	"Did what was right in the eyes of the LORD." Allied with the kings of Israel, which proved unwise. Saved his nation with prayer and fasting.	*1 Kings 15:24; 22:43*
Jehoram	Killed all his brothers and some of the rulers of Israel. Sanctioned Baal worship in Judah. Married Ahab's daughter.	*1 Kings 22:50*
Ahaziah	Reigned for one year. "Did evil in the eyes of the LORD." Allied with Israel.	*2 Kings 8:24, 27*
Joash	Hidden from his grandmother for six years. Became king at the age of seven. Restored Solomon's temple. Allowed idols back into Judah. Had Zechariah stoned.	*2 Kings 12:1*
Amaziah	"Did what was right in the eyes of the LORD," but not wholeheartedly. Was rebuked for idolatry.	*2 Kings 12:21; 14:3*
Uzziah/Azariah	"Did what was right in the eyes of the LORD." Was victorious over the Philistines and fortified Jerusalem. Famous and successful, his pride led to his downfall. The Lord afflicted him with leprosy.	*2 Kings 14:21; 15:3*

KINGS OF JUDAH (CONTINUED)

King of Judah	Additional Information	Reference
Jotham	Built the temple's upper gate and defeated the Ammonites. "Did what was right in the eyes of the LORD." Grew powerful because he walked steadfastly before the Lord.	*2 Kings 15:7, 34*
Ahaz	Worshipped idols. Sacrificed his children. Ignored the warnings of Isaiah, Hosea, and Micah.	*2 Kings 16:1*
Hezekiah	Restored the temple. Reinstituted Passover. Prayed for protection from Assyria. "He held fast to the LORD and did not stop following him."	*2 Kings 16:20; 18:6*
Manasseh	Worshipped idols. Sacrificed his children. Was captured by the Assyrians. He repented and was then brought back to Jerusalem, where he removed the idols and restored the altar of the Lord.	*2 Kings 21:1*
Amon	Worshipped idols. Was killed by his officials.	*2 Kings 21:18*
Josiah	Destroyed the idols. Repaired the temple. Once the Book of the Law was found, he renewed his nation's commitment to obedience.	*2 Kings 21:24*
Jehoahaz	"Did evil in the eyes of the LORD." Reigned for three months. Was captured by Egypt and died in captivity.	*2 Kings 23:31–32*
Jehoiakim	"Did evil in the eyes of the LORD." Was captured by Nebuchadnezzar and taken to Babylon.	*2 Kings 23:34–37*
Jehoiachin	"Did evil in the eyes of the LORD." Reigned for three months. Was captured by Nebuchadnezzar and taken to Babylon.	*2 Kings 24:6–9*
Zedekiah/Mattaniah	"Did evil in the eyes of the LORD." Was captured and taken to Babylon.	*2 Kings 24:17–19*

Rehoboam's insolence

KINGS OF ISRAEL

King of Israel	Additional Information	Reference
Jeroboam I	Created two golden calves for Israel to worship, a tradition that was followed by all the succeeding kings of Israel	*1 Kings 12:20*
Nadab	Was assassinated by Baasha	*1 Kings 14:20*
Baasha	Killed Nadab for the throne. Went to war with Asa of Judah.	*1 Kings 15:28*
Elah	Was killed by Zimri	*1 Kings 16:6*
Zimri	Killed Elah for his throne. He reigned for only seven days.	*1 Kings 16:15*
Tibni	Briefly ruled over half of Israel, but then Omri became king	*1 Kings 16:21*
Omri	Built the city of Samaria	*1 Kings 16:22*
Ahab	Married Jezebel and introduced Baal worship to Israel	*1 Kings 16:28*
Ahaziah	Worshipped Baal. Fell off a roof.	*1 Kings 22:40*
Joram/Jehoram	Discontinued worship of Baal. Allied with king of Judah. Consulted Elisha. Was killed by Jehu for his throne.	*2 Kings 1:17; 3:1–2*
Jehu	Used by God to destroy the house of Ahab. Also killed Jezebel and King Ahaziah of Judah.	*2 Kings 9:6*
Jehoahaz	Prayed for delivery from oppression, and God delivered Israel. Yet Israel continued to sin.	*2 Kings 10:35; 13:1–2*
Jehoash	Warred against Amaziah king of Judah. Wept at the death-bed of Elisha.	*2 Kings 13:9–11*
Jeroboam II	Restored Israel's boundaries. Recovered Damascus and Hamath.	*2 Kings 14:23–24*
Zechariah	Reigned for six months. Was killed by Shallum.	*2 Kings 15:8–9*
Shallum	Killed Zechariah for the throne. Reigned one month.	*2 Kings 15:10–13*
Menahem	Killed Shallum for the throne. Paid tribute (the price of protection) to Assyria.	*2 Kings 15:17–18*
Pekahiah	Menahem's son. "Did evil in the eyes of the LORD."	*2 Kings 15:22–24*
Pekah	Assassinated Pekahiah for the throne. During his reign, Assyria conquered Israel. Assassinated by Hoshea.	*2 Kings 15:27–28*
Hoshea	During his reign, Israelites were taken captive to Assyria.	*2 Kings 17:1–2*

"HE DID EVIL IN THE EYES OF THE LORD."

MAGICIANS AND THE DARK ARTS

Dark Art	Description	Reference
astrology	Study of heavenly bodies and their effects on the lives of humans	Forbidden as it is a type of divination (Lev. 19:26); practice mocked (Isa. 47:13; Jer. 10:2); astrologers advised King Nebuchadnezzar (Dan. 2:2–10); astrologers visited the newborn Christ (Matt. 2:1)
divination	The act of predicting the future through supernatural means	Forbidden (Lev. 19:26); Balaam's occupation (Josh. 13:22); Philistines asked diviners what to do with the ark (1 Sam. 6:2); part of the reason Israel was exiled (2 Kings 17:17); practiced by King Manasseh (2 Kings 21:6)
medium/spiritist	One who consults the dead	Forbidden (Lev. 19:31); consulted by King Saul (1 Sam. 28:7); consulted by King Manasseh (2 Kings 21:6)
sorcery/magic/witchcraft	The use of supernatural powers over others	Magicians typically served kings (Gen. 41:24; Dan. 1:20); sorcerers served in Pharaoh's court (Exod. 7:11); forbidden (Lev. 19:26; Rev. 21:8); part of the reason Israel was exiled (2 Kings 17:17); sorcerers served in King Nebuchadnezzar's court (Dan. 2:2); sorcerer named Simon tried to buy the ability to give the Holy Spirit (Acts 8:9–19); Bar-Jesus tried to discredit Paul's message (Acts 13:6–8); sorcerers repented (Acts 19:19)

Saul and the witch of Endor

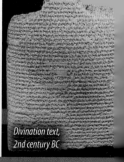

Divination text, 2nd century BC

NEW TESTAMENT LEADERS

Leader	Description	Reference
Andrew	One of the Twelve; Peter's brother	Matt. 10:1–4
Apollos	A preacher taught by Priscilla and Aquila	Acts 18:24
Aquila	Accompanied Paul to Ephesus	Acts 18:2
Barnabas	Accompanied Paul on his first missionary journey	Acts 4:36
Bartholomew (Nathanael)	One of the Twelve	Matt. 10:1–4
James	One of the Twelve. Brother of the apostle John. Member of Jesus' inner circle.	Matt. 4:21
James brother of Jesus	Jesus' brother. Leader of the church. Wrote the letter bearing his name.	Acts 15:13
James son of Alphaeus	One of the Twelve	Matt. 10:1–4
Jesus	Son of God	Matt. 1:1; 20:28
John the apostle	Apostle in Jesus' inner circle. Was charged with the care of Jesus' mother.	Matt. 4:21
Matthew (Levi)	One of the Twelve	Matt. 10:1–4
Paul/Saul	Apostle to the Gentiles. Wrote much of the New Testament.	Acts 13:9
Philip	One of the Twelve	Matt. 10:1–4
Philip	A prominent evangelist in the Christian community	Acts 6:5
Phoebe	A servant in the church in Cenchreae who assisted Paul and delivered his letter to the Romans.	Rom. 16:1–2
Priscilla	Aquila's wife. Risked her life for Paul and the church.	Acts 18:2–4
Silas	Joined Paul in his journeys	Acts 15:40
Simon Peter	Jesus' chief apostle	Matt. 4:18
Simon the Zealot	One of the Twelve	Matt. 10:1–4
Stephen	Was martyred for the cause of Christ	Acts 6:8–15
Thaddaeus (Judas)	One of the Twelve	Matt. 10:1–4
Thomas	One of the Twelve	Matt. 10:1–4
Timothy	Paul's protégé	Acts 16:1
Titus	Paul's protégé	2 Cor. 2:13

OCCUPATIONS

Vocation	Reference	Vocation	Reference
administrator	Dan. 2:49	magician	Dan. 2:2
apostle	Matt. 10:2	merchant	Matt. 13:45
archer	Gen. 21:20	metalworker	2 Tim. 4:14
armor-bearer	1 Sam. 14:12	midwife	Gen. 35:17
astrologer	Dan. 2:4	money changer	Matt. 21:12
baker	Gen. 40:1	musician	1 Chron. 15:16
barber	Ezek. 5:1	overseer/bishop	1 Tim. 3:1
butler	Gen. 40:1	pastor	Eph. 4:11
carpenter	Mark 6:3	perfumer	Neh. 3:8
centurion	Acts 10:1	physician	Col. 4:14
chariot driver	1 Kings 22:34	priest	Lev. 1:7
cook	1 Sam. 8:13	proconsul	Acts 13:7
craftsman	Exod. 31:1–5	prophet	Num. 12:6
cupbearer	Neh. 1:11	prostitute	Gen. 38:15
deacon	Phil. 1:1	queen	Esther 2:17
diviner	1 Sam. 6:2	reaper	Ps. 129:7
doorkeeper	1 Chron. 15:23	scribe	Jer. 36:32
elder	Exod. 3:16	seaman	Ezek. 27:27
embroiderer	Exod. 38:23	secretary	Ezra 4:8
farmer	Mark 4:3	servant	Gen. 16:8
fisherman	Matt. 4:18	shepherd	1 Sam. 16:11–13
gardener	John 20:15	silversmith	Acts 19:24
gatekeeper	2 Kings 7:10	slave master	Exod. 1:11
governor	Gen. 42:6	soldier	Num. 31:21
guard	Gen. 40:4	sorcerer	Acts 13:8
hunter	Gen. 25:27	tanner	Acts 9:43
inventor	Gen. 4:22	tax collector	Matt. 10:3
judge	2 Sam. 15:4	teacher	Ezra 7:6
king	1 Sam. 8:22	tentmaker	Acts 18:1–3
lawyer	Titus 3:13	treasurer	Ezra 1:8

PRIESTS

Priest	Description	Reference
Aaron	First high priest of Israel	*Deut. 10:6*
Abiathar	The only priest who escaped Saul	*1 Sam. 22:20–21*
Abihu	One of Aaron's sons. Was killed for unauthorized fire.	*Lev. 10:1–2*
Ahimelek	Priest who helped David and was killed by Saul.	*1 Sam. 21:1–6*
Ahimelek	Abiathar's son. Ahimelek's grandson.	*2 Sam. 8:17*
Amariah	A high priest during the reign of Jehoshaphat	*2 Chron. 19:11*
Amaziah	A priest of Bethel confronted by the prophet Amos	*Amos 7:10–17*
Ananias	High priest who brought accusations against Paul	*Acts 24:1*
Annas	High priest Caiaphas's father-in-law	*John 18:13*
Caiaphas	High priest who plotted Jesus' death	*John 11:47–53*
Eleazar	Israel's second high priest	*Num. 20:26–28*
Eli	Samuel's flawed mentor	*1 Sam. 1:3*
Eliashib	High priest during Nehemiah's time. Rebuilt the Sheep Gate.	*Neh. 3:1*
Elishama	A priest who taught during the reign of King Jehoshaphat	*2 Chron. 17:7–9*
Ezra	Returnee to Jerusalem who served as priest, scribe, and teacher	*Ezra 7:6*
Hilkiah	Found the Book of the Law during Josiah's reign	*2 Kings 22:8*
Hophni	One of Eli's corrupt sons. Was struck down by God.	*1 Sam. 2:34*
Ithamar	Aaron's youngest son	*Lev. 10:6*
Jahaziel	Zechariah's son	*2 Chron. 20:10–15*
Jehoiada	High priest whose wife hid young Joash from Athaliah	*2 Chron. 22:11*
Jehoram	A priest during the reign of King Jehoshaphat	*2 Chron. 17:7–9*
Joshua	First high priest after the Babylonian captivity	*Hag. 1:1*
Melchizedek	A priest who was not from Aaron's line. (Photo above)	*Gen. 14:17–20*
Nadab	One of Aaron's sons. Was killed for unauthorized fire.	*Lev. 10:1–2*
Pashhur	Had Jeremiah beaten and put in prison	*Jer. 20:1–2*
Phinehas	Israel's third high priest. Eleazar's son.	*Num. 25:7–13*
Phinehas	One of Eli's corrupt sons. Was struck down by God.	*1 Sam. 2:34*
Shelemiah	Priest whom Nehemiah put in charge of the storerooms	*Neh. 13:13*
Uriah	Built an altar for King Ahaz	*2 Kings 16:10–16*
Zadok	Priest during David's and Solomon's reigns	*1 Kings 1:34*
Zechariah	John the Baptist's father	*Luke 1:5*

PROPHETS

Prophet	Description	Reference
Aaron	God made him Moses' prophet.	*Exod. 7:1*
Agabus	Predicted a famine during the time of Paul	*Acts 11:28*
Ahijah	Prophesied to Jeroboam that he would become king	*1 Kings 11:29*
Amos	Wrote the book of Amos. A minor prophet. Prophesied in the time of King Uzziah.	*Amos 7:15*
Anna	Prophesied about Jesus	*Luke 2:36*
Azariah	Prophesied encouragement to King Asa	*2 Chron. 15:1–2*
Daniel	Wrote the book of Daniel. Interpreted dreams. Survived a lions' den.	*Dan. 1:3–7*
Deborah	Judge who led the Israelites in their victory over the Canaanites	*Judg. 5:7*
Elijah	Prophesied to King Ahab and King Ahaziah. Was on Mount Carmel for the face-off between Baal and Jehovah.	*1 Kings 17:1*
Elisha	Inherited a double portion of Elijah's spirit	*1 Kings 19:16*
Enoch	Called a prophet by Jude	*Jude 14*
Ezekiel	Wrote the book of Ezekiel. A priest who was among those taken captive to Babylon.	*Ezek. 1:3*
Gad	Joined David in his stronghold	*1 Chron. 29:29*
Habakkuk	Wrote the book of Habakkuk. A minor prophet. Contemporary of Jeremiah, Ezekiel, Daniel, and Zephaniah.	*Hab. 1:1*
Haggai	Wrote the book of Haggai. A minor prophet. Contemporary of Zechariah.	*Ezra 6:14*
Hanani	Made Asa angry when he rebuked him	*2 Chron. 16:7*
Hosea	Wrote the book of Hosea. A minor prophet. Prophesied during the reigns of Uzziah, Jotham, Ahaz, and Hezekiah.	*Hosea 1:1*
Huldah	Was consulted about the Book of the Law	*2 Kings 22:14*
Iddo	Prophesied regarding King Jeroboam	*2 Chron. 9:29*
Isaiah	Prophesied during the reigns of Uzziah, Jotham, Ahaz, and Hezekiah	*Isa. 1:1*
Jeduthun	Prophesied during David's reign	*2 Chron. 35:15*
Jehu	Prophesied against King Baasha	*1 Kings 16:7*
Jeremiah	Wrote the book of Jeremiah. A priest. Warned Judah of the exile. Prophesied from the reigns of King Josiah through King Jehoiachin.	*Jer. 1:1–2*

Prophet	Description	Reference
Joel	Wrote the book of Joel. A minor prophet. Probably prophesied during the reign of King Joash. Prophesied about God's Spirit being poured out.	Joel 2:28–32
Jonah	May have written the book of Jonah. A minor prophet. Reluctantly prophesied to Nineveh.	Jon. 1:1
Malachi	Wrote the book of Malachi. A minor prophet. Probably prophesied during Nehemiah's absence from Jerusalem.	Mal. 1:1
Micah	Wrote the book of Micah. A minor prophet. Prophesied about Samaria and Jerusalem during the reigns of Jotham, Ahaz, and Hezekiah.	Mic. 1:1
Micaiah	Prophesied against King Ahab, who threw him in prison	2 Chron. 18:7–25
Miriam	Assisted Moses in delivering Israel	Exod. 15:20
Moses	Called a prophet by God. Delivered the Israelites out of Egypt.	Deut. 18:18
Nahum	A minor prophet. Prophesied about Nineveh.	Nah. 1:1
Nathan	Prophesied during David's and Solomon's reigns	1 Kings 1:10
Obadiah	Wrote the book of Obadiah. A minor prophet. Prophesied about Edom. Probably a contemporary of Elijah and Elisha.	Obad. 1:1
Oded	Prophesied to the Aramean army. Prophesied in the time of King Ahaz and King Pekah.	2 Chron. 28:9–15
Philip's daughters	Philip had four unmarried daughters who prophesied.	Acts 21:9
Samuel	One of Israel's last judges. Prophesied to Eli and to King Saul.	1 Sam. 3:20
Shemaiah	Prophesied during the reign of King Rehoboam. Prophesied that Shishak would not destroy Israel.	2 Chron. 12:7
Zadok	High priest in the time of David and Solomon	2 Sam. 15:27
Zechariah	Wrote the book of Zechariah. A minor prophet. A priest. Prophesied about Jesus. A contemporary of Haggai. He prophesied during the reign of Persian King Darius.	Zech. 1:1
Zephaniah	Wrote the book of Zephaniah. A minor prophet. A descendant of King Hezekiah. Prophesied during King Josiah's reign.	Zeph. 1:1

Ezekiel

Jeremiah

Nathan

ZECHARIAH

ROLES OF PRIESTS

Role or Responsibility	Reference
Keep the lamps burning	Exod. 27:21
Keep the altar fire burning	Lev. 6:12–13
Diagnose leprosy	Lev. 13:2–59
Make atonement for the people	Lev. 15:30–31
Offer firstfruits	Lev. 23:10–11
Prepare the bread of the Presence	Lev. 24:5–9
Set values for vowed items	Lev. 27:8
Cover tabernacle items before moving them	Num. 4:5–15
Decide whether or not adultery had been committed	Num. 5:14–15
Bless the Israelites	Num. 6:23–27
Blow trumpets	Num. 10:8–10
Oversee the tabernacle	Num. 18:1–7
Act as judges	Deut. 17:8–13
Address armies before they went into battle	Deut. 20:2–4
Carry the ark	Josh. 3:6
Offer sacrifices	2 Chron. 29:34
Act as teachers	Mal. 2:7
Burn incense	Luke 1:9

Table of Showbread

Altar of Incense

Altar for offerings

TEACHERS AND MENTORS

Teacher or Mentor	Student	Reference
Barnabas	Paul	Acts 9:26–28
Barnabas	John Mark	Acts 15:39
Eli	Samuel	1 Sam. 3:1
Elijah	Elisha	1 Kings 19:19
Ezra	Exiles	Ezra 7:10
Gamaliel	Paul	Acts 5:34–39
Jesus	Apostles	Matt. 10:2
Moses	Israelites	Exod. 12:35
Moses	Joshua	Num. 11:28
Naomi	Ruth	Ruth 1:22
Paul	Silas	Acts 15:40
Paul	Timothy	Acts 16:1–3
Paul	Priscilla and Aquila	Acts 18:1–3
Paul	Titus	Gal. 2:1
Priscilla and Aquila	Apollos	Acts 18:24–26
Samuel	Saul	1 Sam. 9:17
Zechariah	King Uzziah	2 Chron. 26:5

schoolteacher lecturer faculty member adviser Barnabas
pedagogue Naomi supervisor trainer
preceptor Gamaliel assistant Samuel Zechariah educator
Ezra Jesus
Aquila professor
Paul
teach pundit Priscilla Moses scholar tutor guide Elijah instructor
disciplinarian coach mentor Eli

BIBLE LISTS

PROMISES,
CHURCH &
THE CHRISTIAN LIFE

25 GREAT PROMISES OF GOD

#	Great Promise	Reference
1	God will never again destroy the earth by flood.	*Gen. 9:11*
2	God will bless all peoples of the earth through Abraham.	*Gen. 12:3*
3	David's kingdom will never end.	*2 Sam. 7:16*
4	God promised to cleanse us from sin.	*Isa. 1:18*
5	The Prince of Peace will be born and will reign forever.	*Isa. 9:6–7*
6	God has a plan for us.	*Jer. 29:11*
7	God promised to bring the Israelites back from captivity.	*Jer. 29:13–14*
8	God will bless those who are faithful in giving.	*Mal. 3:10–12*
9	God will answer prayers.	*Matt. 7:7*
10	Jesus will come again.	*Matt. 24*
11	Whoever believes in Jesus will have eternal life.	*John 3:16*
12	God will give us the Holy Spirit.	*John 14:16–17*
13	The Holy Spirit will guide us.	*John 16:13*
14	In Jesus we will have peace.	*John 16:33*
15	All things work together for good to those who love God.	*Rom. 8:28*
16	Nothing can separate us from the love of God.	*Rom. 8:38–39*
17	If we declare Jesus aloud, we will be saved.	*Rom. 10:9*
18	The message of the cross is the power of God.	*1 Cor. 1:18*
19	God will help us withstand temptation.	*1 Cor. 10:13*
20	In Christ, we are new creations.	*2 Cor. 5:17*
21	We are not slaves to the desires of the flesh.	*Gal. 5:16*
22	God will meet all our needs.	*Phil. 4:19*
23	We will be rewarded for serving the Lord.	*Col. 3:23–24*
24	The dead will be resurrected.	*1 Thess. 4:16*
25	God will give us rest.	*Heb. 4:1, 9*

BAPTISMS

Person (or People) Baptized	Baptized by	Reference
The Israelites at Sinai	Moses	*Exod. 24:6–8; Heb. 9:19–20*
Those made clean after being defiled	The priest or someone who was clean	*Lev. 14:4–7, 49–53; Num. 19:18–19*
The Levites	Moses	*Num. 8:7*
People from Judea	John the Baptist	*Matt. 3:6*
Jesus (photo above)	John the Baptist	*Matt. 3:13*
Tax collectors	John the Baptist	*Luke 3:12*
3,000 people	Peter and most likely other disciples	*Acts 2:41*
Many people in Samaria	Philip	*Acts 8:12*
Simon the sorcerer	Philip	*Acts 8:13*
The Ethiopian eunuch	Philip	*Acts 8:38*
Paul/Saul	Ananias (or an unnamed person)	*Acts 9:17–18*
Gentiles at Caesarea	Peter	*Acts 10:48*
Lydia and her household	Paul	*Acts 16:14–15*
The jailer and his household	Paul/Silas	*Acts 16:33*
Crispus and his household	Paul	*Acts 18:8*
Disciples at Ephesus	Paul	*Acts 19:1, 5*
Gaius	Paul	*1 Cor. 1:14*
Stephanas's household	Paul	*1 Cor. 1:16*

Depictions of Jesus' baptism

LIFE

BENEFITS OF BEING IN CHRIST

Benefit	Reference
We are dead to sin but alive to God.	*Rom. 6:11*
We have eternal life.	*Rom. 6:23*
There is no condemnation.	*Rom. 8:1*
Nothing can separate us from God's love.	*Rom. 8:39*
We are made alive.	*1 Cor. 15:22*
We can stand firm.	*2 Cor. 1:21*
The old covenant has been taken away.	*2 Cor. 3:14*
We are new creations.	*2 Cor. 5:17*
God reconciled the world to Himself.	*2 Cor. 5:19*
Our sins are not counted against us.	*2 Cor. 5:19*
We are free.	*Gal. 2:4*
We are justified by faith.	*Gal. 2:16*
We are God's children.	*Gal. 3:26; Eph. 1:5*
We are blessed with spiritual blessings.	*Eph. 1:3*
We were chosen before the creation of the world.	*Eph. 1:4, 11*
Our sins are forgiven.	*Eph. 1:7*
We were sealed with the Holy Spirit.	*Eph. 1:13*
We are seated in heavenly realms.	*Eph. 2:6*
We are blessed with the riches of His grace.	*Eph. 2:7*
We have been brought near to Christ.	*Eph. 2:13*
We have been given fullness in Christ.	*Col. 2:10*

GOD'S CONCERN FOR THE POOR

God's Concern for the Poor	Reference
He wants the poor to be defended.	*Exod. 23:6; Prov. 31:9*
He wants provisions made for the poor.	*Exod. 23:11; Lev. 19:10; Deut. 15:7*
He wants families to financially look after other poor family members.	*Lev. 25:25*
He wants the poor to maintain dignity.	*Lev. 25:39*
He does not want people to take advantage of the poor.	*Deut. 24:14*
He wants the wages of the poor to be paid each day before sunset.	*Deut. 24:15*
He provides refuge for the poor.	*Ps. 14:6; 34:6; Isa. 25:4*
He wants to maintain justice for the poor.	*Ps. 140:12; Prov. 22:22; 29:13–15*
He wants the poor to be befriended.	*Prov. 19:4; Jer. 39:9–11; Luke 14:13*
He wants the poor to be treated with kindness.	*Prov. 19:7; 29:7; Zech. 7:10*
He does not want the poor to be ignored or forgotten.	*Prov. 21:13; Acts 9:35–37; 2 Cor. 9:9*
He wants the gospel preached to the poor.	*Matt. 11:5; Luke 4:16–21; 7:22*

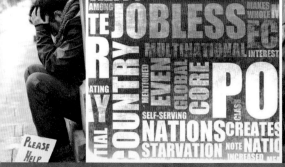

GOD'S MESSAGES TO EMPLOYERS

God's Message to Employers	Reference
Pay wages that are due.	Lev. 19:13; Deut. 24:15; Matt. 10:10; Luke 10:7; Rom. 4:4; 1 Tim. 5:18
Do not be ruthless in your position.	Lev. 25:43
Do not take advantage of employees.	Deut. 24:14
Treat employees with respect.	Eph. 6:9
Treat employees fairly.	Col. 4:1
If you cheat your employees, God will judge you.	James 5:4

Do not cheat them
Treat employees with respect Accountable to God Do not be ruthless
Do not take advantage
Pay wages that are due *Treat fairly*

GOD'S MESSAGES TO EMPLOYEES

God's Message to Employees	Reference
God created work.	Gen. 2:15
Do not demand more pay than you agreed to.	Matt. 20:9–12
Respect and obey your employer just as you would God.	Eph. 6:5–8; 1 Tim. 6:1–2
Work with all your heart, as if working for God not for people.	Col. 3:22–24
Work to provide for your needs.	2 Thess. 3:10
Submit to employers, even those who are harsh.	1 Pet. 2:18–19

Work as if working for God

Respect and your employer

Work with all your heart

Obey authority

God created work

Submit to employers

Work to provide for yourself

Stick to your agreements

GOD'S PROMISES DURING TEMPTATION

God's Promise during Temptation	Reference
We will not be overcome with any temptation that others haven't had to go through.	*1 Cor. 10:13; 1 Pet. 4:12*
We will not be tempted beyond what we can handle.	*1 Cor. 10:13*
When we are tempted, God will give us a way to escape that temptation.	*1 Cor. 10:13*
We can stand firm against temptation if we put on the armor of God.	*Eph. 6:11–17*
Jesus can help us in our temptations because He Himself was tempted, but He did not sin.	*Heb. 2:18; 4:15*
Temptation can produce perseverance and maturity.	*James 1:1–4*
We will be rewarded if we overcome temptation.	*James 1:12; 1 Pet. 1:7*
God does not tempt anyone.	*James 1:13*
Temptation leads to sin, which then leads to death.	*James 1:15*
If we resist the devil, he will flee.	*James 4:7*

215

Adam and Eve

Temptation of Christ

Joseph and Potiphar's wife

David and Bathsheba

GOD'S PROMISES FOR PROTECTION

God's Promise for Protection	Reference
"When you go to war against your enemies. . .the LORD your God, . . .will be with you."	*Deut. 20:1–4*
"Be strong and courageous. Do not be afraid or terrified because of them, for the LORD your God goes with you; he will never leave you nor forsake you."	*Deut. 31:6*
"He will guard the feet of his faithful servants. . . ."	*1 Sam. 2:9*
". . .you alone, LORD, make me dwell in safety."	*Ps. 4:8*
"The Lord is a refuge for the oppressed. . . ."	*Ps. 9:9*
"The LORD is my rock, my fortress and my deliverer. . . ."	*Ps. 18:2–3*
"God is our refuge and strength. . . ."	*Ps. 46:1–3*
"He will cover you with his feathers, and under his wings you will find refuge. . . ."	*Ps. 91:3–7*
"He will not let your foot slip—he who watches over you will not slumber. . . ."	*Ps. 121:3–8*
"No one will be able to stand against you all the days of your life. As I was with Moses, so I will be with you; I will never leave you nor forsake you."	*Josh. 1:5*
"Unless the LORD builds the house, the builders labor in vain. Unless the LORD watches over the city, the guards stand watch in vain."	*Ps. 127:1*
"The Lord watches over all who love him, but all the wicked he will destroy."	*Ps. 145:20*
"Whoever listens to me will live in safety and be at ease, without fear of harm."	*Prov. 1:33*
"For the LORD will be at your side and will keep your foot from being snared."	*Prov. 3:26*
"The name of the LORD is a fortified tower. . . ."	*Prov. 18:10*
"It will be a shelter and shade from the heat of the day, and a refuge and hiding place from the storm and rain."	*Isa. 4:6*
"Like birds hovering overhead, the LORD Almighty will shield Jerusalem."	*Isa. 31:5*
"So do not fear, for I am with you; do not be dismayed, for I am your God. I will strengthen you and help you; I will uphold you with my righteous right hand."	*Isa. 41:10*
"From the west, people will fear the name of the LORD, and from the rising of the sun, they will revere his glory. For he will come like a pent-up flood that the breath of the LORD drives along."	*Isa. 59:19*
"I give them eternal life, and they shall never perish; no one will snatch them out of my hand."	*John 10:28–29*
"The Lord is faithful, and he will strengthen and protect you from the evil one."	*2 Thess. 3:3*

GOD'S PROMISES TO ANSWER PRAYER

God's Promise to Answer Prayer	Reference
God listens to a sinless heart.	Isa. 59:1–2; Ps. 66:18
When we pray in secret, God will reward us.	Matt. 6:6
If two of us agree about what we ask for, it will be done.	Matt. 18:19
God will grant whatever is asked in faith.	Matt. 21:22; Mark 11:24
Our prayers will be heard if we forgive others.	Mark 11:25
God answers persistent prayers.	Luke 11:5–13; 18:1–7
God will give the Holy Spirit to those who ask Him.	Luke 11:13
Prayers asked in Jesus' name will be answered.	John 14:13–14; 15:16; 16:23–26
Our prayers will be answered if we abide in Christ.	John 15:7
The Holy Spirit will pray on our behalf when we do not know what to pray for.	Rom. 8:26–27
When we pray, we don't have to be anxious.	Phil. 4:6
God will help those who approach Him with confidence in Him.	Heb. 4:16
God will grant the prayers of those who ask without doubting.	James 1:5–7
God will answer prayers that are made with the right motives.	James 4:3
A prayer offered in faith will heal the sick.	James 5:15
The prayer of a righteous person is effective.	James 5:16–18; 1 Pet. 3:12
Husbands can prevent the hindering of their prayers by being considerate and respectful to their wives.	1 Pet. 3:7
God will answer our prayers if we are obedient.	1 John 3:22
God will answer prayers made according to His will.	1 John 5:14
If we see a Christian commit a sin that does not lead to death, God will give them life if we pray.	1 John 5:16

Prayer at wailing wall in Jerusalem

GOD'S PROMISES OF GUIDANCE

God's Promise of Guidance	Reference
God promises to guide his people into peace.	*Ps. 23:2*
God promises to guide his people.	*Ps. 25:9*
God promises to guide his people through the end of their lives.	*Ps. 48:14*
God promises wisdom in making decisions.	*Ps 73:24*
God promises to be present when we feel uncertain.	*Isa. 42:16*
God promises to lead his people into truth.	*John 16:13*

LIGHT AND DARKNESS

Important Scriptures on Light and Darkness	Reference
"And God said, 'Let there be light,' and there was light. . . ."	*Gen. 1:3–18*
"You, LORD, are my lamp; the LORD turns my darkness into light."	*2 Sam. 22:29*
"May the day of my birth perish, and the night that said, 'A boy is conceived!' That day—may it turn to darkness; . . ."	*Job 3:3–5*
"Turn night into day; in the face of the darkness light is near."	*Job 17:12*
"The light in his tent becomes dark; the lamp beside him goes out."	*Job 18:6*
"He is driven from light into the realm of darkness and is banished from the world."	*Job 18:18*
"In the dark, thieves break into houses, but by day they shut themselves in; they want nothing to do with the light."	*Job 24:16*
"He marks out the horizon on the face of the waters for a boundary between light and darkness."	*Job 26:10*
"How I long for the months gone by, for the days when God watched over me, when his lamp shone on my head and by his light I walked through darkness!"	*Job 29:2–3*
"Yet when I hoped for good, evil came; when I looked for light, then came darkness."	*Job 30:26*
"What is the way to the abode of light? And where does darkness reside?"	*Job 38:19*
"You, LORD, keep my lamp burning; my God turns my darkness into light."	*Ps. 18:28*
"Even in darkness light dawns for the upright, for those who are gracious and compassionate and righteous."	*Ps. 112:4*
"If I say, 'Surely the darkness will hide me and the light become night around me,' even the darkness will not be dark to you; the night will shine like the day, for darkness is as light to you."	*Ps. 139:11–12*
"I saw that wisdom is better than folly, just as light is better than darkness."	*Eccles. 2:13*
"Woe to those who call evil good and good evil, who put darkness for light and light for darkness, who put bitter for sweet and sweet for bitter."	*Isa. 5:20*
"The people walking in darkness have seen a great light; on those living in the land of deep darkness a light has dawned."	*Isa. 9:2*
"I form the light and create darkness, I bring prosperity and create disaster; I, the LORD, do all these things."	*Isa. 45:7*
"Give glory to the LORD your God before he brings the darkness, before your feet stumble on the darkening hills. You hope for light, but he will turn it to utter darkness and change it to deep gloom."	*Jer. 13:16*

Description	Reference
"He reveals deep and hidden things; he knows what lies in darkness, and light dwells with him."	*Dan. 2:22*
"The people living in darkness have seen a great light; on those living in the land of the shadow of death a light has dawned."	*Matt. 4:16*
"The eye is the lamp of the body. If your eyes are healthy, your whole body will be full of light. But if your eyes are unhealthy, your whole body will be full of darkness. If then the light within you is darkness, how great is that darkness!"	*Matt. 6:22–23*
"The light shines in the darkness, and the darkness has not overcome it."	*John 1:5*
"This is the verdict: Light has come into the world, but people loved darkness instead of light because their deeds were evil. Everyone who does evil hates the light, and will not come into the light for fear that their deeds will be exposed. . . ."	*John 3:19–21*
"Jesus spoke again to the people, he said, 'I am the light of the world. Whoever follows me will never walk in darkness, but will have the light of life.'"	*John 8:12*
"I have come into the world as a light, so that no one who believes in me should stay in darkness."	*John 12:46*
"Therefore judge nothing before the appointed time; wait until the Lord comes. He will bring to light what is hidden in darkness and will expose the motives of the heart. At that time each will receive their praise from God."	*1 Cor. 4:5*
"For you were once darkness, but now you are light in the Lord. . . ."	*Eph. 5:8–14*
"You are all children of the light and children of the day. We do not belong to the night or to the darkness. . . ."	*1 Thess. 5:5–8*
"But you are a chosen people, a royal priesthood, a holy nation, God's special possession, that you may declare the praises of him who called you out of darkness into his wonderful light."	*1 Pet. 2:9*
"This is the message we have heard from him and declare to you: God is light; in him there is no darkness at all. If we claim to have fellowship with him and yet walk in the darkness, we lie and do not live out the truth. But if we walk in the light, as he is in the light, we have fellowship with one another, and the blood of Jesus, his Son, purifies us from all sin."	*1 John 1:5–7*

220

SEE ALSO: *Exod. 14:19–20; Job 10:20–22; Job 12:22–25; Isa. 5:30; Isa. 42:16; Isa. 59:9; Lam. 3:1–2; Ezek. 32:7–8; Luke 11:34–36; John 12:35–36; Acts 26:15–18; Rom. 2:17–21; Rom. 13:11–12; 2 Cor. 6:14; 2 Pet. 1:19; 1 John 2:8–11.*

MANAGING MONEY

What the Bible Says about Money	Reference
Jews were not to charge interest to other Jews.	*Lev. 25:35–37; Ps. 15:5*
A percentage of our earnings belongs to God.	*Lev. 27:30; 1 Cor. 16:2*
God owns everything, including our money.	*Deut. 10:14*
Being debt-free is a blessing.	*Deut. 28:1–2, 12*
Being in debt is a curse.	*Deut. 28:15, 43–44*
No one should accept money as a bribe.	*Ps. 15:5*
Money acquired dishonestly will not last long.	*Prov. 13:11*
Working for money increases a person's wealth.	*Prov. 13:11*
Wise people save for the future.	*Prov. 21:20*
Foolish people spend all that they earn.	*Prov. 21:20*
Those who borrow money become slaves to their lenders.	*Prov. 22:7*
It is wrong to promise to pay and then not follow through.	*Eccles. 5:5*
Those who love money never have enough.	*Eccles. 5:10*
Those who are responsible with the money given to them will receive more.	*Matt. 25:14–29; Luke 19:12–26*
Sacrificial giving is more important than giving large amounts.	*Mark 12:41–44*
We should be satisfied with the money we earn and not try to get more by stealing or lying.	*Luke 3:14*
We should not be greedy.	*Luke 12:15; 1 Pet. 5:2*
Our lives cannot be measured by the things that we own.	*Luke 12:15*
If we are unable to handle money, we can't be trusted with heavenly riches.	*Luke 16:10–11*
We cannot serve both God and money; they compete with each other and only one can win.	*Luke 16:13*
Give whatever you decide to give to God, but don't lie about its amount or source. If you do so, you are only lying to God.	*Acts 5:2–10*
The love of money is the cause of various kinds of evil, leading many to depart from the faith.	*1 Tim. 3:3; 6:10; 2 Tim. 3:2; Heb. 13:5*
Those who want to be rich often find themselves tempted and trapped by their desires.	*1 Tim. 6:9*

"One Another's" of the Faith

Christian Actions toward "One Another"	Reference
Do not deceive one another.	*Lev. 19:11*
Wash one another's feet.	*John 13:14*
Love one another.	*John 13:34; Rom. 12:10; 1 Pet. 4:8; 1 John 4:7*
Honor one another above yourselves.	*Rom. 12:10*
Live in harmony with one another.	*Rom. 12:16; 1 Thess. 5:13*
Accept one another.	*Rom. 15:7*
Instruct one another.	*Rom. 15:14*
Agree with one another.	*1 Cor. 1:10*
Serve one another in love.	*Gal. 5:13*
Be completely humble, gentle, and patient with one another in love.	*Eph. 4:2*
Be kind and compassionate to one another.	*Eph. 4:32*
Forgive one another.	*Eph. 4:32*
Speak to one another with psalms, hymns, and songs from the Spirit.	*Eph. 5:19*
Teach and admonish one another.	*Col. 3:16*
Encourage one another.	*1 Thess. 4:18; 5:11*
Spur one another on toward love and good deeds.	*Heb. 10:24*
Offer hospitality to one another.	*1 Pet. 4:9*

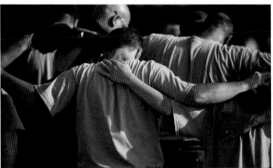

PASSAGES ABOUT FORGIVING

Important Scriptures on Forgiveness	Reference
"The Lᴏʀᴅ, the Lᴏʀᴅ, the compassionate and gracious God, slow to anger, . . . and forgiving wickedness, rebellion and sin. . . ."	Exod. 34:6–7
"Hear from heaven, your dwelling place, and when you hear, forgive."	1 Kings 8:30
"Blessed is the one whose transgressions are forgiven. . . ."	Ps. 32:1–2
"Praise the Lᴏʀᴅ, . . .who forgives all your sins and heals all your diseases."	Ps. 103:2–3
"For I will forgive their wickedness and will remember their sins no more."	Jer. 31:34
"Lord, listen! Lord, forgive! Lord, hear and act! . . ."	Dan. 9:19
"And forgive us our debts, as we also have forgiven our debtors."	Matt. 6:12, 14–15
". . . 'Take heart, son; your sins are forgiven. . . .'"	Matt. 9:2–6
"How many times shall I forgive my brother or sister? . . ."	Matt. 18:21–22
The Parable of the Unmerciful Servant	Matt. 18:23–35
"This is my blood of the covenant, which is poured out for many for the forgiveness of sins."	Matt. 26:28
"If you hold anything against anyone, forgive them. . . ."	Mark 11:25
". . .Whoever has been forgiven little loves little. . . ."	Luke 7:47–49
"If your brother or sister sins against you, rebuke them; and if they repent, forgive them. . . ."	Luke 17:3–4
"Jesus said, 'Father, forgive them, for they do not know what they are doing.'"	Luke 23:34
"If you forgive anyone's sins, their sins are forgiven. . . ."	John 20:23
"Anyone you forgive, I also forgive. . . ."	2 Cor. 2:10
"In him we have redemption through his blood, the forgiveness of sins . . ."	Eph. 1:7
"Be kind. . .forgiving each other, just as in Christ God forgave you."	Eph. 4:32
"God made you alive with Christ. He forgave us all our sins, having canceled the charge of our legal indebtedness, which stood against us and condemned us; he has taken it away, nailing it to the cross."	Col. 2:13–14
"Bear with each other and forgive one another if any of you has a grievance against someone. Forgive as the Lord forgave you."	Col. 3:13
"For I will forgive their wickedness and will remember their sins no more."	Heb. 8:12
"Without the shedding of blood there is no forgiveness."	Heb. 9:22
"If we confess our sins, he is faithful and just and will forgive us our sins and purify us from all unrighteousness."	1 John 1:9

THE ROLE OF THE CHURCH

Role of the Church	Reference
To care for widows	*Exod. 22:22; 1 Tim. 5:4; James 1:27*
To care for orphans	*Exod. 22:22; James 1:27*
To gently restore members	*Matt 18:12–14; Gal. 6:1*
To discipline members	*Matt. 18:15–20*
To spread the gospel	*Matt. 28:19; Acts 16:10; 1 Thess. 3:2*
To rebuke sin	*Luke 17:3; 1 Tim. 5:20*
To be a witness	*Acts 1:8; 22:15; 26:16*
To give to the needy	*Acts 2:44–45; 4:32–35*
To shepherd the church	*Acts 20:28; 1 Pet. 5:2*
To serve others	*Rom. 12:7; Eph. 5:21; 6:7*
To love others	*Rom. 12:10; 13:8; Heb. 13:1*
To stand against false doctrines	*Gal. 1:6–9; Eph. 4:14–16; Titus 1:9*
To preach and teach	*1 Tim. 4:11–13; 2 Tim. 2:2; 4:2*

THEMES IN PROVERBS

Theme	Reference
Abominations	6:16–18; 11:1, 20
Alcohol	20:1; 23:29–35
Anger	12:16; 21:14
Attributes of God	5:21; 18:10
Discipline	13:24; 19:18
Enemies	25:21–22
Fear of the Lord	9:10; 22:4
Fool	11:29; 15:5, 14
Glad Heart	12:20; 21:15
Gossip & Speech	11:13; 13:3; 15:1, 28; 20:19
Hatred	10:12; 15:17
Honesty	23:10–11; 28:8, 21
Humility	22:4, 19; 30:32
Immoral Women	9:13–18; 22:14
Kings and Rulers	19:6, 10, 12
Laziness	15:19; 20:4, 13
Marriage	21:9, 19; 24:3–4
Money	19:4, 6, 17; 23:4–8
Neighbors	21:10; 29:5
Parenting	23:13–14, 24
Poor People	13:23; 14:31; 19:1
Receiving Instruction	9:7–9; 17:10
Reward and Penalty	11:18–21, 23; 19:5, 9, 29
Right and Wrong	28:11
Righteous People	22:5
Trust in God	20:22, 24; 21:30
Wicked People	13:17; 15:8–9
Wisdom	9:1–18
Young People	13:1; 17:2, 25
Your Friends	13:20; 14:7

TREATMENT OF ALIENS

Treatment of Foreigners and Aliens	Reference
They were not to eat the Passover unless they were circumcised.	Exod. 12:43–48
They were not to be mistreated or oppressed.	Exod. 22:21
They were to be treated as family.	Lev. 19:34
Animals for sacrifice were not to be accepted from them.	Lev. 22:25
Food was to be left behind for them.	Lev. 23:22
They were to be loved.	Deut. 10:19
They could be expected to repay loans made to them.	Deut. 15:1–3
They were not allowed to be rulers over Israel.	Deut. 17:15
They could be charged interest.	Deut. 23:20
They were to be given justice.	Deut. 24:17
They would be given preference if Israel was disobedient.	Deut. 28:43–45
Israel was not allowed to intermarry with them.	Ezra 10:2
If Israel was disobedient, they would be handed over to them.	Ezek. 28:7

Artist depictions of Ruth and Boaz

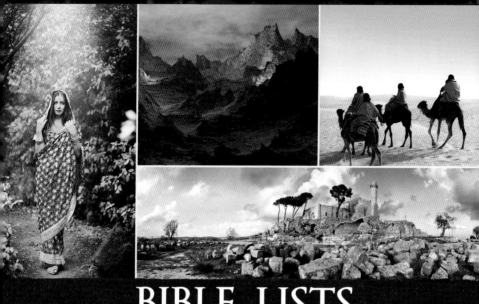

BIBLE LISTS

PSALMS,
PRAYER &
WORSHIP

PRAY

25 PSALMS WORTH PRAYING

Psalm	Description
Ps. 3	God is our shield.
Ps. 13	Trust in God's love.
Ps. 16	God will protect his people.
Ps. 17	God will listen to and protect his people.
Ps. 23	"The Lord is My Shepherd".
Ps. 25	God is gracious and forgiving.
Ps. 27	God offers salvation.
Ps. 28	God is a rock.
Ps. 30	God turns mourning into dancing.
Ps. 38	God forgives sins.
Ps. 51	God restores his people after they sin.
Ps. 56	God is gracious.
Ps. 61	God is worthy of praise.
Ps. 63	God is worth thirsting after.
Ps. 71	God is a refuge.
Ps. 84	A day in God's courts is better than 10,000 elsewhere.
Ps. 86	God will grant his favor.
Ps. 101	God is worthy of following.
Ps. 103	Blessed is God.
Ps. 123	Praise the Lord.
Ps. 138	God provides forgiveness and is to be feared.
Ps. 141	God turns his heart to his people.
Ps.142	God looks out for his people.
Ps. 143	God will hear prayers.
Ps. 145	God is to be exalted.

ALTARS BUILT

Altar Builder	Purpose/Occasion	Reference
Abraham	To worship, and to sacrifice Isaac	*Gen. 12:7–8; 13:4, 18; 22:9*
Ahab	Built for the god Baal	*1 Kings 16:30–32*
Asa	Repaired the altar	*2 Chron. 15:8*
Baal's prophets	To call on Baal	*1 Kings 18:26*
David	To stop the plague	*2 Sam. 24:18–25*
Elijah	To call on God to show Himself more powerful than Baal	*1 Kings 18:30–32*
Gideon	After seeing the angel of the Lord	*Judg. 6:22–24*
Isaac	After God promised him numerous descendants	*Gen. 26:23–25*
Jacob	To worship	*Gen. 33:18–20; 35:1–7*
Jeroboam	Built as an alternative place to worship	*1 Kings 12:33*
Joshua	In obedience to Moses' instructions	*Josh. 8:30–31*
Manasseh	Built for the god Baal, for the temple in Jerusalem, and for the heavenly hosts	*2 Kings 21:3–5*
Moses	As thanks for defeating the Amalekites; as preparation for the making of the covenant	*Exod. 17:15–16; 24:4*
Noah	After exiting the ark, to sacrifice	*Gen. 8:20*
Reuben, Gad, and the half-tribe of Manasseh	To remind everyone they were a part of Israel	*Josh. 22:10–34*
Samuel	For worship	*1 Sam. 7:15–17*
Saul	For worship	*1 Sam. 14:34–35*
Solomon	For worship	*1 Kings 9:25*
Uriah the priest	Built as instructed by King Ahaz	*2 Kings 16:11*
Zerubbabel and other priests	For worship	*Ezra 3:2–3*

Sacrifice of Isaac

Abraham

Noah's sacrifice

CELEBRATORY SONGS

Singer(s)	Context	Reference
David	Deliverance from Saul	Ps. 18
David	Dedication of the temple	Ps. 30
Deborah and Barak	Defeat of Sisera and Jabin	Judg. 5:1–31
Israel	The gift of water	Num. 21:17–18
Mary	Thanks for the Son promised to her	Luke 1:46–55
Moses and Miriam	The defeat of the Egyptians (photo above)	Exod. 15:1–21
Simeon	Thanks for allowing him to see the Messiah	Luke 2:26–32
Zechariah	Thanks for the son God had given him	Luke 1:67–79

Song of Miriam

King David dances

An angel with
a lute

MORNING PRAYERS AND WORSHIP

Morning Prayer Offered	Reference
"On the morning of the third day there was thunder and lightning, with a thick cloud over the mountain, and a very loud trumpet blast. Everyone in the camp trembled. Then Moses led the people out of the camp to meet with God, and they stood at the foot of the mountain."	*Exod. 19:16–17*
"He got up early the next morning and built an altar at the foot of the mountain and set up twelve stone pillars representing the twelve tribes of Israel. Then he sent young Israelite men, and they offered burnt offerings and sacrificed young bulls as fellowship offerings to the Lord."	*Exod. 24:4–5*
"So Moses chiseled out two stone tablets like the first ones and went up Mount Sinai early in the morning, as the Lord had commanded him; and he carried the two stone tablets in his hands. Then the Lord came down in the cloud and stood there with him and proclaimed his name, the Lord."	*Exod. 34:4–5*
"Early the next morning they arose and worshiped before the Lord."	*1 Sam. 1:19*
"They were also to stand every morning to thank and praise the Lord."	*1 Chron. 23:30*
"Every morning and evening they present burnt offerings and fragrant incense to the Lord."	*2 Chron. 13:11*
"Early in the morning he would sacrifice a burnt offering for each of them, thinking, 'Perhaps my children have sinned and cursed God in their hearts.' This was Job's regular custom."	*Job 1:5*
"In the morning, Lord, you hear my voice; in the morning I lay my requests before you and wait expectantly."	*Ps. 5:3*
"But I will sing of your strength, in the morning I will sing of your love; for you are my fortress, my refuge in times of trouble."	*Ps. 59:16*
"In the morning the word of the Lord came to me."	*Ezek. 12:8*
"Very early in the morning, while it was still dark, Jesus got up, left the house and went off to a solitary place, where he prayed."	*Mark 1:35*

MUSIC AND MUSICAL INSTRUMENTS

Musical Instrument	Reference
cymbal	1 Chron. 16:5; Ps. 150:5; 1 Cor. 13:1
flute	Dan. 3:5, 7, 10, 15
harp	Ps. 137:2; Ezek. 26:13; Dan. 3:5
horn	2 Chron. 15:14; Dan. 3:5
lyre	1 Sam. 10:5; Neh. 12:27; Dan. 3:5
pipes	Gen. 4:21; Dan. 3:5, 10, 15; Luke 7:32
sistrum	2 Sam. 6:5
strings	Ps. 45:8; 150:4
timbrel/tambourine	Exod. 15:20; Job 21:12; Ps. 150:4
trumpet	Exod. 19:16; 2 Kings 11:14; 2 Chron. 29:27
zither	Dan. 3:5, 7, 10, 15

Trumpet

Harp

Pipes

OFFERINGS

Offering	Description	Reference
burnt	A male without defect; consumed by fire	*Lev. 1:3*
drink	Wine or drink; usually poured around the altar; offered with meat offerings	*Gen. 35:14; Exod. 29:40; Num. 15:5*
fellowship	Celebrated peace with God	*Lev. 3:1; 7:11*
firstfruits	First of the harvest and firstborn of people and animals	*Exod. 22:29; Deut. 18:4*
freewill	A voluntary sacrifice or gift; not required	*Lev. 23:38; Deut. 16:10*
grain	The finest flour	*Lev. 2:1; Num. 15:4*
guilt	To make restitution for causing loss to another	*Lev. 5:15–16; 6:6; 7:1*
incense	Offered along with meat offerings; was offered daily in the holy place; a symbol of prayer	*Exod. 30:8; Mal. 1:11; Luke 1:9*
jealousy	The offering the husband was to bring when charging his wife with adultery	*Num. 5:15*
sin	Made for sins committed	*Lev. 4:3; 6:25; 10:17*
thank	Made as an expression of thankfulness	*Lev. 7:12; 22:29; Ps. 50:14*
tithe	One-tenth of everything from the land	*Lev. 27:30; Num. 18:21; Deut. 14:22*
wave	Parts of offerings sometimes waved by priests	*Exod. 29:26; 35:22; Lev. 7:30*

Grain

Noah's altar

Firstfruits

OLD TESTAMENT TEMPLES

Category	First Temple	Second Temple
Location	Mount Moriah on the threshing floor (2 Chron. 3:1)	Mount Moriah on the threshing floor (Ezra 6:2–12)
Person responsible	Built by David's decree (2 Sam. 7:2)	Built by Cyrus's decree (Ezra 1:1–2)
Builders	Solomon and his men (1 Chron. 17:12)	Ezra, Nehemiah, and exiles (Ezra/Neh.)
Materials	Provided by Hiram (1 Kings 5:6)	Provided by Tyre and Sidon (Ezra 3:7)
Improvements		Improved by Herod, which took forty-six years (John 2:20)
Time spent	Seven years (1 Kings 6:38)	Approximately 20 years (Ezra 4:24; 6:15)
Dimensions	Sixty cubits long, twenty cubits wide, thirty cubits high. The portico at the front of the temple extended a width of twenty cubits and projected ten cubits from the front of the temple. (1 Kings 6:2–10)	Not mentioned. We might assume it was in accordance with the instructions for the first temple since they had it in writing and probably wouldn't make changes.
Missing items		Ark of the covenant, tables of stone, pot of manna, Aaron's rod. Some of the original temple items were brought back from Babylon, where King Nebuchadnezzar had taken them. (Ezra 1:7–11)

The Islamic Dome of the Rock and Jewish Wailing Wall in modern-day Jerusalem

PSALMS OF PRAISE

Title	Psalm	Title	Psalm
The Lord's Glory and Man's Dignity	Ps. 8	The Lord Exalts the Humble	Ps. 113
The Works and the Word of God	Ps. 19	God's Deliverance of Israel from Egypt	Ps. 114
Praise for Deliverance	Ps. 21	The One True God	Ps. 115
A Cry of Anguish and a Song of Praise	Ps. 22	A Song of Praise	Ps. 117
The Voice of the Lord in the Storm	Ps. 29	Meditations and Prayers relating to God's Law	Ps. 119
Praise to the Creator and Preserver	Ps. 33	Prayer for the Peace of Jerusalem	Ps. 122
Wickedness of Men and Loving-Kindness of God	Ps. 36	Prayer for the Lord's Blessing upon the Sanctuary	Ps. 132
God's Abundant Favor to Earth and Man	Ps. 65	A Call to Praise God	Ps. 134
God Humbles the Proud but Exalts the Righteous	Ps. 75	Praise the Lord's Wonderful Works and the Vanity of Idols	Ps. 135
Longing for the Temple Worship	Ps. 84	Thanks for the Lord's Goodness to Israel	Ps. 136
Praise for the Lord's Goodness	Ps. 92	Praise for the Lord's Goodness	Ps. 145
All Men Exhorted to Praise God	Ps. 100	The Lord an Abundant Helper	Ps. 146
Praise for the Creator	Ps. 104	Praise for Jerusalem's Restoration and Prosperity	Ps. 147
The Lord's Wonderful Works in Behalf of Israel	Ps. 105	A Call for the Universe to Praise God	Ps. 148
Israel's Rebellion and the Lord's Deliverance	Ps. 106	Israel Invoked to Praise the Lord	Ps. 149
The Lord's Deliverance from Troubles	Ps. 107	A Psalm of Praise	Ps. 150
The Lord Praised for His Goodness	Ps. 111		

PSALMS OF CONFESSION

PSALMS OF THANKSGIVING

Title	Psalm
Thanksgiving for God's Justice	Ps. 9
David's Song of Victory	Ps. 18
Thanksgiving for Deliverance from Death	Ps. 30
Thanksgiving for Confession and Forgiveness	Ps. 32
The Lord, a Provider and Deliverer	Ps. 34
God Sustains His Servant	Ps. 40
God's Abundant Favor to Earth and Man	Ps. 65
Praise for God's Mighty Deeds and for His Answer to Prayer	Ps. 66
The Nations Exhorted to Praise God	Ps. 67
Praise for the Lord's Mercies	Ps. 103
The Lord's Deliverance from Troubles	Ps. 107
Thanksgiving for Deliverance from Death	Ps. 116
Thanksgiving for the Lord's Saving Goodness	Ps. 118
Prayer for the Peace of Jerusalem	Ps. 122
Praise for Rescue from Enemies	Ps. 124
Thanksgiving for Return from Captivity	Ps. 126
Thanksgiving for the Lord's Favor	Ps. 138

PSALMS OF SUPPLICATION

Psalms of Supplication (continued)

Title	Psalm
Prayer of an Old Man for Deliverance	*Ps. 71*
A Prayer for National Deliverance	*Ps. 74*
Comfort in Times of Distress	*Ps. 77*
A Prayer for the Nation's Deliverance	*Ps. 79*
A Prayer for the Nation's Restoration	*Ps. 80*
A Prayer for the Defeat of Israel's Enemies	*Ps. 83*
Prayer for God's Mercy on the Nation	*Ps. 85*
A Psalm of Supplication and Trust	*Ps. 86*
A Petition to Be Saved from Death	*Ps. 88*
A Hymn in Time of National Trouble	*Ps. 89*
God's Eternity and Man's Temporary Nature	*Ps. 90*
The Lord Implored to Avenge His People	*Ps. 94*
Prayer of an Afflicted Man for Mercy on Himself and on Zion	*Ps. 102*
Prayer for Deliverance from the Treacherous	*Ps. 120*
Prayer for Mercy	*Ps. 123*
A Prayer for the Destruction of Israel's Enemies	*Ps. 129*
A Lament of the Israelites in Exile	*Ps. 137*
Prayer for Protection against the Wicked	*Ps. 140*
An Evening Prayer for Sanctification and Protection	*Ps. 141*
Prayer for Help in Trouble	*Ps. 142*

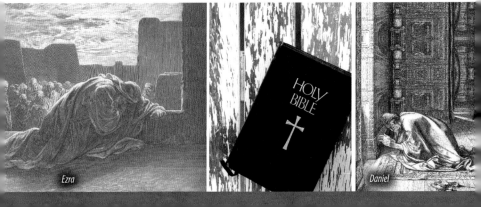

Ezra

Daniel

TABERNACLE/TEMPLE ARTICLES

Article or Item	Reference
altar (bronze)	2 Chron. 4:1
altar (gold)	2 Chron. 4:19
ark of the covenant	Exod. 26:33; 1 Kings 6:19
basins	2 Chron. 4:6
bowls	2 Chron. 4:8
bull figures	2 Chron. 4:3
capitals	2 Chron. 3:15
censers	2 Chron. 4:22
cherubim	2 Chron. 3:11
curtain	Exod. 26:1; 2 Chron. 3:14
dishes	2 Chron. 4:22
firepans	Exod. 27:3
floral work (gold)	2 Chron. 4:21
lamps	2 Chron. 4:20
lampstands (gold)	2 Chron. 4:7
meat forks	Exod. 27:3; 2 Chron. 4:16
oil	Exod. 27:20
pillars	2 Chron. 3:15
poles	Exod. 27:6
pomegranates (chained)	2 Chron. 3:16
pots	Exod. 27:3; 2 Chron. 4:11
rings	Exod. 27:4
sea of cast metal	2 Chron. 4:2
shovels	Exod. 27:3; 2 Chron. 4:11
sprinkling bowls	Exod. 27:3; 2 Chron. 4:22
stands	2 Chron. 4:14
tables	2 Chron. 4:8
tongs (gold)	2 Chron. 4:21
wick trimmer (gold)	2 Chron. 4:22

BIBLE LISTS

VITAL VERSES &
READING PLANS

ENCOURAGING PASSAGES

Important Scriptures on Encouragement	Reference
"Moses answered the people, 'Do not be afraid. Stand firm and you will see the deliverance the LORD will bring you today. . . .'"	*Exod. 14:13–14*
"The LORD himself goes before you and will be with you; he will never leave you nor forsake you. Do not be afraid; do not be discouraged."	*Deut. 31:8*
"Shadrach, Meshach and Abednego replied to him, 'King Nebuchadnezzar, we do not need to defend ourselves before you in this matter. If we are thrown into the blazing furnace, the God we serve is able to deliver us from it, and he will deliver us from Your Majesty's hand. But even if he does not, we want you to know, Your Majesty, that we will not serve your gods or worship the image of gold you have set up.'"	*Dan. 3:16–18*
"The LORD is my shepherd. . . ."	*Ps. 23*
"Whoever dwells in the shelter of the Most High will rest in the shadow of the Almighty. . . ."	*Ps. 91:1–4*
"Blessed are the poor in spirit, for theirs is the kingdom of heaven. . . ."	*Matt. 5:3–12*
"Do not be afraid of those who kill the body but cannot kill the soul. . . ."	*Matt. 10:28–31*
". . .But seek his kingdom, and these things will be given to you as well"	*Luke 12:22–31*
"For God so loved the world that he gave his one and only Son, that whoever believes in him shall not perish but have eternal life. For God did not send his Son into the world to condemn the world, but to save the world through him."	*John 3:16–17*
"Do not let your hearts be troubled. You believe in God; believe also in me. . . ."	*John 14:1–4*
". . . And hope does not put us to shame, because God's love has been poured out into our hearts through the Holy Spirit, who has been given to us."	*Rom. 5:1–5*
"But God demonstrates his own love for us in this: While we were still sinners, Christ died for us."	*Rom. 5:8*
"No, in all these things we are more than conquerors through him who loved us. For I am convinced that neither death nor life, neither angels nor demons, neither the present nor the future, nor any powers, neither height nor depth, nor anything else in all creation, will be able to separate us from the love of God that is in Christ Jesus our Lord."	*Rom. 8:37–39*
"Do you not know that in a race all the runners run, but only one gets the prize? Run in such a way as to get the prize. Everyone who competes in the games goes into strict training. They do it to get a crown that will not last; but we do it to get a crown that will last forever."	*1 Cor. 9:24–25*
"Therefore, if anyone is in Christ, the new creation has come: The old has gone, the new is here! All this is from God, who reconciled us to himself. . . ."	*2 Cor. 5:17–19*

Important Scriptures on Encouragement	Reference
"Therefore, if you have any encouragement from being united with Christ, if any comfort from his love, if any common sharing in the Spirit, if any tenderness and compassion, then make my joy complete by being like-minded, having the same love, being one in spirit and of one mind."	*Phil. 2:1–2*
"I am not saying this because I am in need, for I have learned to be content whatever the circumstances. I know what it is to be in need, and I know what it is to have plenty. I have learned the secret of being content in any and every situation, whether well fed or hungry, whether living in plenty or in want. I can do all this through him who gives me strength."	*Phil. 4:11–13*
"You were dead in your sins and in the uncircumcision of your flesh, God made you alive with Christ. He forgave us all our sins, having canceled the charge of our legal indebtedness, which stood against us and condemned us. . . ."	*Col. 2:13–15*
". . .We will be with the Lord forever. Therefore encourage one another with these words."	*1 Thess. 4:13–18*
"But you, man of God, flee from all this, and pursue righteousness, godliness, faith, love, endurance and gentleness. Fight the good fight of the faith. Take hold of the eternal life to which you were called when you made your good confession in the presence of many witnesses. . . ."	*1 Tim. 6:11–16*
". . .Let us then approach God's throne of grace with confidence, so that we may receive mercy and find grace to help us in our time of need."	*Heb. 4:14–16*
"Now faith is confidence in what we hope for and assurance about what we do not see."	*Heb. 11:1*
"Therefore, since we are surrounded by such a great cloud of witnesses, let us throw off everything that hinders and the sin that so easily entangles. And let us run with perseverance the race marked out for us, fixing our eyes on Jesus, the pioneer and perfecter of faith. For the joy set before him he endured the cross, scorning its shame, and sat down at the right hand of the throne of God. Consider him who endured such opposition from sinners, so that you will not grow weary and lose heart."	*Heb. 12:1–3*
"My dear children, I write this to you so that you will not sin. But if anybody does sin, we have an advocate with the Father—Jesus Christ, the Righteous One. He is the atoning sacrifice for our sins, and not only for ours but also for the sins of the whole world."	*1 John 2:1–2*
"See what great love the Father has lavished on us, that we should be called children of God! And that is what we are! The reason the world does not know us is that it did not know him. Dear friends, now we are children of God, and what we will be has not yet been made known. But we know that when Christ appears, we shall be like him, for we shall see him as he is. All who have this hope in him purify themselves, just as he is pure."	*1 John 3:1–3*

GREAT BIBLE PRAYERS

Prayer of the Bible	Author	Reference
"...I am unworthy of all the kindness and faithfulness you have shown your servant. I had only my staff when I crossed this Jordan, but now I have become two camps...."	Jacob	*Gen. 32:9–12*
"Lord Almighty, if you will only look on your servant's misery and remember me, and not forget your servant but give her a son, then I will give him to the Lord for all the days of his life, and no razor will ever be used on his head."	Hannah	*1 Sam. 1:11*
"Who am I, Sovereign Lord, and what is my family, that you have brought me this far?..."	David	*2 Sam. 7:18–29*
"...'Lord my God, let this boy's life return to him!'"	Elijah	*1 Kings 17:20–21*
"...Answer me, Lord, answer me, so these people will know that you, Lord, are God, and that you are turning their hearts back again."	Elijah	*1 Kings 18:36–37*
"I have been very zealous for the Lord God Almighty. The Israelites have rejected your covenant, torn down your altars, and put your prophets to death with the sword. I am the only one left, and now they are trying to kill me too."	Elijah	*1 Kings 19:10*
"Lord, the God of Israel, ... you alone are God over all the kingdoms of the earth. You have made heaven and earth...."	King Hezekiah	*2 Kings 19:15–19*
"I am too ashamed and disgraced, my God, to lift up my face to you, because our sins are higher than our heads and our guilt has reached to the heavens...."	Ezra	*Ezra 9:6–15*
"Lord, the God of heaven, the great and awesome God, who keeps his covenant of love with those who love him and keep his commandments, let your ear be attentive and your eyes open to hear the prayer your servant is praying before you...."	Nehemiah	*Neh. 1:5–11*
"You are always righteous, Lord, when I bring a case before you...."	Jeremiah	*Jer. 12:1–4*
"Lord, the great and awesome God, who keeps his covenant of love with those who love him and keep his commandments, we have sinned and done wrong. We have been wicked and have rebelled; we have turned away from your commands and laws. We have not listened to your servants the prophets, who spoke in your name to our kings, our princes and our ancestors, and to all the people of the land...."	Daniel	*Dan. 9:4–19*

Prayer of the Bible	Author	Reference
"Our Father in heaven, hallowed be your name, your kingdom come, your will be done, on earth as it is in heaven. Give us today our daily bread. And forgive us our debts, as we also have forgiven our debtors. And lead us not into temptation, but deliver us from the evil one."	Jesus	*Matt. 6:9–13*
"My Father, if it is possible, may this cup be taken from me. Yet not as I will, but as you will. . . . My Father, if it is not possible for this cup to be taken away unless I drink it, may your will be done."	Jesus	*Matt. 26:39, 42*
"My God, my God, why have you forsaken me?"	Jesus	*Matt. 27:46*
"Father, forgive them, for they do not know what they are doing."	Jesus	*Luke 23:34*
"Father, into your hands I commit my spirit."	Jesus	*Luke 23:46*
"Father, the hour has come. Glorify your Son, that your Son may glorify you. For you granted him authority over all people that he might give eternal life to all those you have given him. Now this is eternal life: that they know you, the only true God, and Jesus Christ, whom you have sent. . . ."	Jesus	*John 17*
"Receive my spirit. . . . Lord, do not hold this sin against them."	Stephen	*Acts 7:59–60*
"I keep asking that the God of our Lord Jesus Christ, the glorious Father, may give you the Spirit of wisdom and revelation, so that you may know him better. I pray that the eyes of your heart may be enlightened in order that you may know the hope to which he has called you, the riches of his glorious inheritance in his holy people. . . ."	Paul	*Eph. 1:17–21*
"I pray that out of his glorious riches he may strengthen you with power through his Spirit in your inner being, so that Christ may dwell in your hearts through faith. And I pray that you, being rooted and established in love, may have power, together with all the Lord's holy people, to grasp how wide and long and high and deep is the love of Christ, and to know this love that surpasses knowledge—that you may be filled to the measure of all the fullness of God."	Paul	*Eph. 3:16–19*

GOD AS CREATOR

God the Creator	Reference
"God made two great lights—the greater light to govern the day and the lesser light to govern the night. He also made the stars."	*Gen. 1:16*
"For in six days the LORD made the heavens and the earth, the sea, and all that is in them, but he rested on the seventh day. . . ."	*Exod. 20:11*
"I will send you rain in its season, and the ground will yield its crops. . . ."	*Lev. 26:4*
"Ask now about the former days, long before your time, from the day God created human beings on the earth; ask from one end of the heavens to the other. Has anything so great as this ever happened, or has anything like it ever been heard of?"	*Deut. 4:32*
"To the LORD your God belong the heavens. . . ."	*Deut. 10:14, 22*
"You alone are the LORD. You made the heavens. . . ."	*Neh. 9:6*
"He provides rain for the earth; he sends waters on the countryside."	*Job 5:10*
"You have set your glory in the heavens. . . . When I consider your heavens, the work of your fingers, the moon and the stars, which you have set in place, what is mankind that you are mindful of them, human beings that you care for them?"	*Ps. 8:1, 3–4*
"The heavens declare the glory of God; the skies proclaim the work of his hands."	*Ps. 19:1*
"For since the creation of the world God's invisible qualities—his eternal power and divine nature—have been clearly seen, being understood from what has been made, so that people are without excuse. . . ."	*Rom. 1:20, 25*
"For everything God created is good, and nothing is to be rejected if it is received with thanksgiving."	*1 Tim. 4:4*
"He also says, 'In the beginning, Lord, you laid the foundations of the earth, and the heavens are the work of your hands.'"	*Heb. 1:10*
"By faith we understand that the universe was formed at God's command, so that what is seen was not made out of what was visible. . . . And so from this one man, and he as good as dead, came descendants as numerous as the stars in the sky and as countless as the sand on the seashore."	*Heb. 11:3, 12*
"He said in a loud voice, 'Fear God and give him glory, because the hour of his judgment has come. Worship him who made the heavens, the earth, the sea and the springs of water.'"	*Rev. 14:7*

READING PLAN: BIBLE OVERVIEW

#	Title	Reference
Day 1	Creation and the Entrance of Sin	*Gen. 1–3*
Day 2	The Flood	*Gen. 6:9–8:22*
Day 3	Abraham and Isaac	*Gen. 22:1–19*
Day 4	The Life of the Patriarch Joseph	*Gen. 37–50*
Day 5	The Call of Moses	*Exod. 3*
Day 6	The Ten Commandments	*Exod. 20:3–17*
Day 7	Moses Pleads for God's Presence	*Exod. 33*
Day 8	God's Instructions to Joshua	*Josh. 1*
Day 9	The Defeat of Jericho	*Josh. 6:15–21*
Day 10	Joshua's Farewell Address	*Josh. 23–24*
Day 11	The Story of Samson	*Judg. 13–16*
Day 12	David's Battle with Goliath	*1 Sam. 17:12–54*
Day 13	David's Sin with Bathsheba	*2 Sam. 11:1–12*
Day 14	The Temple Built	*1 Kings 6*
Day 15	Solomon's Prayer	*2 Chron. 6:12–42*
Day 16	A Blessed Man	*Ps. 1*
Day 17	The Shepherdhood of God	*Ps. 23*
Day 18	Isaiah's Call	*Isa. 6:1–8*
Day 19	Three Godly Men and a Fiery Furnace	*Dan. 3:8–30*
Day 20	Daniel in the Lions' Den	*Dan. 6*
Day 21	The Story of the Prophet Jonah	*Jon. 1–4*
Day 22	Christ's Birth	*Luke 2:1–20*

Reading Plan: Bible Overview (continued)

#	Title	Reference
Day 23	Jesus' Baptism and Temptation	*Matt. 3:13–4:11*
Day 24	Christ's Sermon on the Mount	*Matt. 5–7*
Day 25	Christ's Transfiguration	*Matt. 17:1–8*
Day 26	Two Great Commandments	*Matt. 22:34–40*
Day 27	Christ's Death and Resurrection	*Matt. 27:27–28:10*
Day 28	A Model Prayer	*Luke 11:2–4*
Day 29	The New Birth in Christ	*John 3:1–21*
Day 30	The Samaritan Woman at the Well	*John 4:1–42*
Day 31	Jesus and Lazarus	*John 11*
Day 32	Jesus' Pre-Crucifixion Address to the Disciples	*John 13–16*
Day 33	Jesus' "High Priestly" Prayer	*John 17*
Day 34	Believers Receive the Holy Spirit and the Church Built	*Acts 2*
Day 35	Saul's Conversion	*Acts 9:1–9*
Day 36	Jesus before Pontius Pilate	*Matt. 27:1–26*
Day 37	The Love Chapter	*1 Cor. 13*
Day 38	The Promise of Eternal Life	*1 Cor. 15:12–27*
Day 39	The "Faith Hall of Fame"	*Heb. 11*
Day 40	A New Heaven and Earth	*Rev. 21*

Conversion of Paul

READING PLAN: CHRISTMAS

#	Title	Reference
Day 1	Jesus, the Word, Becomes Flesh	*John 1:1–18*
Day 2	Jesus' Genealogy; The Angels Appear to Joseph	*Matt. 1:1–25*
Day 3	Prophecies Concerning Jesus' Birth, Life, and Death	*Gen. 49:10; 2 Sam. 7:12–16; Isa. 7:14; Jer. 23:1–8; 33:14–16; Mic. 5:2; Zech. 12:10; 13:1*
Day 4	John the Baptist's Birth Foretold	*Luke 1:5–25*
Day 5	The Angel Appears to Mary	*Luke 1:26–38*
Day 6	Mary Visits Elizabeth	*Luke 1:39–45*
Day 7	The Magnificat (Mary's Song)	*Luke 1:46–56*
Day 8	Zechariah's Song of Praise	*Luke 1:67–80*
Day 9	The Birth of Jesus	*Luke 2:1–7*
Day 10	The Angels Deliver Good News	*Luke 2:8–14*
Day 11	The Shepherds Visit Jesus	*Luke 2:15–20*
Day 12	Simeon and Anna	*Luke 2:21–40*
Day 13	Promise of a Child Who Brings New Hope and Peace	*Isa. 9:2–7; 11:1–13; 12:1–6*
Day 14	The Visit of the Magi	*Matt. 2:1–12*
Day 15	Jesus' Family Flees to Egypt	*Matt. 2:13–23*
Day 16	Jesus at the Temple as a Boy	*Luke 2:41–52*
Day 17	The Public Introduction	*Luke 3:1–20; John 1:19–28*
Day 18	The Baptism of Jesus	*Mark 1:9–13*
Day 19	Jesus, the Lamb of God	*Isa. 53:6–10; John 1:29–34; 1 Pet. 1:18–21*
Day 20	The New Life Jesus Came to Bring	*Isa. 62:10–12; Mal. 4:2; John 3:16; Rom. 12:1–2; 2 Cor. 5:17–21; Heb. 12:1–3; 1 John 3:1–3; 4:9*
Day 21	Jesus: The Ultimate Prophet	*Deut. 18:14–22; Acts 3:17–23*
Day 22	Jesus: The Ultimate Priest	*Heb. 7:11–17; 7:23–8:2; 8:7–13; 10:11–14*
Day 23	Jesus: The Ultimate King	*Num. 24:15–19; Ps. 72:1–19; 132:11–18; Phil. 2:5–11*
Day 24	The Hope of Christmas: Promise of New Life	*Jer. 31:1–14, 23–34; Ezek. 36:24–29*
Day 25	Attributes of Christ	*Matt. 28:20; John 8:12; 10:11–16; 14:6; Col. 1:15–16; 1 Tim. 1:16–17; Heb. 13:8; Rev. 22:13*

READING PLAN: EASTER

#	Title	Reference
Day 1	The Fall (The Need for Easter)	*Gen. 3:1–24*
Day 2	Jesus is an Exalted Priest	*Ps. 110:1–7*
Day 3	God Restores His People	*Isa. 40:1–31*
Day 4	God Will Look Upon His People with Favor	*Isa. 61:1–11*
Day 5	John the Baptist Introduces Jesus	*Matt. 3:1–17*
Day 6	God Will Judge Sin	*Isa. 63:1–19*
Day 7	Jesus is God's Servant	*Isa. 49:1–7*
Day 8	Can this Be the Christ?	*John 7:14–8:11*
Day 9	God Will Protect His People	*Ps. 69:1–36*
Day 10	The Resurrection Is Real	*Mark 12:1–12*
Day 11	Events Leading Up to the Crucifixion	*Matt. 26:1–35; 27:1–10*
Day 12	Betrayal and Arrest of Jesus	*Matt. 26:36–56*
Day 13	God Hears Our Earnest Cries	*Ps. 55:1–23*
Day 14	Peter Denies Christ	*Matt. 26:57–75*
Day 15	The Crucifixion of Christ	*Matt. 27:11–44*
Day 16	Jesus Prayer on the Cross	*Ps. 22:1–31*
Day 17	The Death and Burial of Jesus	*Matt. 27:45–66*
Day 18	The Suffering Servant	*Isa. 52:13–53:12*
Day 19	The Coming Restoration	*Isa. 49:8–26*
Day 20	God Will Protect and Restore His people	*Ps. 16:1–11*
Day 21	The Resurrection of Christ	*Mark 16:1–20*
Day 22	Jesus Reveals God	*Heb. 1:1–13*
Day 23	Jesus the Great High Priest	*Heb. 4:14–5:10*
Day 24	The New Heaven and Earth	*Rev. 21:1–27*
Day 25	Jesus Will Return	*Rev. 22:1–21*

250

The resurrection

Jesus appears to Mary

Shroud of Turin

JESUS

READING PLAN: FINDING COMFORT

#	Title	Reference
Day 1	The God Who Sees	*Gen. 16:1–16; 21:8–21*
Day 2	The Gift of a Redeemer	*Ruth 1; 4:13–17*
Day 3	Back from the Dead	*1 Kings 17:8–24*
Day 4	Refuge for the Oppressed	*Ps. 9*
Day 5	You Are Never Forsaken	*Ps. 22*
Day 6	The Lord Is My Shepherd	*Ps. 23*
Day 7	In His Favour Is Life	*Ps. 30*
Day 8	Cast Your Burden on Him	*Ps. 55*
Day 9	Comfort in Affliction	*Ps. 119:49–76*
Day 10	Not unto Thine Own Understanding	*Prov. 3:1–20*
Day 11	A Season for Everything	*Eccles. 3:1–15*
Day 12	This Is Our God	*Isa. 25*
Day 13	In Perfect Peace	*Isa. 26*
Day 14	God's Word Stands Forever	*Isa. 40*
Day 15	Awake, Awake, Put On Strength	*Isa. 51*
Day 16	I Will Rejoice in Jerusalem	*Isa. 65:17–66:24*
Day 17	With an Everlasting Love	*Jer. 31:1–26*
Day 18	His Compassions Fail Not	*Lam. 3:1–33*
Day 19	I Will Turn Back Your Captivity	*Zeph. 3:9–20*
Day 20	Blessed Are They That Mourn	*Matt. 5:1–16*
Day 21	A Resurrection and a Commission	*Matt. 28*
Day 22	The Bread of Life	*John 6*
Day 23	I Lay Down My Life	*John 10*
Day 24	Way, Truth, Life	*John 14*
Day 25	I Have Overcome the World	*John 16:16–33*
Day 26	Gospel Mystery	*1 Cor. 15:42–58*
Day 27	The God of All Comfort	*2 Cor. 1:1–11*
Day 28	Consolation in Christ	*Phil. 2:1–11*
Day 29	New Heaven and New Earth	*Rev. 21*
Day 30	When Jesus Comes	*Rev. 22*

READING PLAN: FORGIVENESS

#	Title	Reference
Day 1	A Brother Forgives	*Gen. 32:1–21; 33:1–11*
Day 2	The Trespass of Thy Brethren	*Gen. 50:1–21*
Day 3	God, Merciful and Gracious	*Exod. 34*
Day 4	No God Like Thee	*1 Kings 8:22–53*
Day 5	The Good Lord Pardons	*2 Chron. 30:1–20*
Day 6	Remember, O Lord, Thy Mercies	*Ps. 25*
Day 7	Blessed Are the Forgiven	*Ps. 32*
Day 8	Show Us Mercy	*Ps. 85*
Day 9	God Abundantly Pardons	*Isa. 55*
Day 10	He Delights in Mercy	*Mic. 7*
Day 11	Forgive Us Our Debts	*Matt. 6:5–15*
Day 12	Parable of the Unforgiving Servant	*Matt. 18:15–35*
Day 13	Blood Shed for Remission of Sins	*Matt. 26:17–29*
Day 14	Authority to Forgive	*Mark 2:1–17*
Day 15	Forgive, and Be Forgiven	*Luke 6:27–42*
Day 16	A Sinful Woman Forgiven	*Luke 7:36–50*
Day 17	If He Repents, Forgive Him	*Luke 16:19–17:4*
Day 18	Father Forgive Them	*Luke 23:26–43*
Day 19	Neither Do I Condemn Thee	*John 7:53–8:11*
Day 20	That They May Receive Forgiveness	*Acts 26:1–23*
Day 21	Peace with God, Eternal Life	*Rom. 5*
Day 22	Forgive and Comfort	*2 Cor. 2:1–11*
Day 23	Dead in Sin, Alive in Christ	*Eph. 1:3–2:10*
Day 24	Forgiving One Another	*Eph. 4:17–32*
Day 25	Reconciled by His Death	*Col. 1:3–23*
Day 26	As Christ Forgave You	*Col. 3:1–17*
Day 27	Mediator of a New Testament	*Heb. 9:11–10:10*
Day 28	Our Great High Priest	*Heb. 10:11–39*
Day 29	Patience and Prayer	*James 5:7–20*
Day 30	Confess Your Sins	*1 John 1:5–2:6*

READING PLAN: FRIENDSHIP

#	Title	Reference
Day 1	Envy Destroys Relationships	*Gen. 37; Acts 7:9*
Day 2	Father-in-Law/Son-in-Law	*Exod. 4:18; 18*
Day 3	The Friend of God	*Exod. 33:8–23; James 2:23*
Day 4	No Partiality	*Lev. 19:14–15; James 2:1–13*
Day 5	Loving Thy Neighbor	*Lev. 19:16–18; Matt. 22:34–40*
Day 6	Respecting the Elderly	*Lev. 19:32–37; 1 Tim. 5:1–2*
Day 7	Beware the Influence of Friends	*Deut. 13:1–8*
Day 8	Mother-in-Law/Daughter-in-Law	*Ruth 1–2*
Day 9	Respecting Widows	*1 Kings 17; Jer. 7:5–7*
Day 10	Grieving Together	*Job 2:11–13*
Day 11	Deceit Destroys Relationships	*Ps. 109*
Day 12	Debt Destroys Relationships	*Prov. 6:1–5; 17:18*
Day 13	Listening to Wise Advice	*Prov. 12*
Day 14	Anger Destroys Relationships	*Prov. 15:17–18; 22:24–25*
Day 15	Gossip Destroys Relationships	*Prov. 16:27–28*
Day 16	Being a Friend	*Prov. 18:24*
Day 17	Speaking the Truth in Love	*Prov. 27:5–11; Eph. 4:14–29*
Day 18	Strength in Numbers	*Eccles. 4:9–12; Dan. 1*
Day 19	Husbands and Wives	*Song of Sol. 5:16; Eph. 5*
Day 20	Sharing What the Lord Has Done	*Mark 5:1–20*
Day 21	Jesus, Friend of Sinners	*Luke 7*
Day 22	Rejoicing Together	*Luke 15*
Day 23	Laying Down Your Life	*John 15*
Day 24	Working toward Peace	*Rom. 14:13–23*
Day 25	Edifying Others	*Eph. 4:1–13*
Day 26	Humbly Esteeming Others	*Phil. 2:1–8*
Day 27	Forgive, as Christ Forgave You	*Col. 3:1–17*
Day 28	Brotherly Love	*Heb. 13:1–3; 1 John 2:1–14*
Day 29	Friendship with the World	*James 4:4–17*
Day 30	A Friend in Need	*1 Pet. 4:8–11*

READING PLAN: KNOWING GOD

#	Title	Reference
Day 1	God the Creator	*Gen. 1:1–2:3*
Day 2	God the Sustainer	*Gen. 2:4–24*
Day 3	God of Promises	*Gen. 15*
Day 4	God of Holiness	*Exod. 3*
Day 5	God the Victor	*Exod. 15:1–21*
Day 6	God of Purity	*Exod. 20*
Day 7	God of Glory	*Exod. 33:7–23*
Day 8	God of Blessing	*Deut. 28*
Day 9	God of Judgment	*Judg. 10:6–16*
Day 10	God the Unrivaled	1 Kings 18:16–46
Day 11	God of Majesty	*Ps. 8*
Day 12	God of Life	*Ps. 16*
Day 13	God of Supremacy	*Ps. 19*
Day 14	God the Shepherd	*Ps. 23*
Day 15	God of Peace	*Ps. 29*
Day 16	God of Greatness	*Ps. 48*
Day 17	God the Protector	*Ps. 91*
Day 18	God of Refuge	*Ps. 94*
Day 19	God of Deliverance	*Ps. 118*
Day 20	God of Purpose	*Isa. 42:1–9*
Day 21	God of Forgiveness	*Isa. 43:22–44:5*
Day 22	God the Servant	*John 13:1–17*
Day 23	God of the Trinity	*John 14*
Day 24	God the Life Giver	*John 15:1–16:16*
Day 25	God the Savior	*John 19:1–37*
Day 26	God of the Resurrection	*Mark 16*
Day 27	God Our Friend	*1 John 1:1–2:14*
Day 28	God the Praiseworthy	*Rev. 4:1–5:14*
Day 29	God of Salvation	*Rev. 19*
Day 30	God the Approachable	*Rev. 22*

READING PLAN: LIFE OF CHRIST

#	Title	Reference
Day 1	The Birth of Jesus Foretold	*Luke 1:26–38*
Day 2	The Birth of Jesus	*Matt. 1:18–25*
Day 3	The Birth of Jesus	*Luke 2:1–20*
Day 4	The Magi	*Matt. 2:1–12*
Day 5	The Word Became Flesh	*John 1:1–28*
Day 6	The Baptism of Jesus	*Mark 1:2–13*
Day 7	A Light Has Risen	*Matt. 4:12–17*
Day 8	Ministry in Galilee	*Luke 4:14–37*
Day 9	Jesus Chooses the First Disciples	*John 1:35–51*
Day 10	Jesus Appoints the Twelve	*Mark 3:13–35*
Day 11	Jesus Cleanses the Temple; Nicodemus Visits Jesus	*John 2:12–3:21*
Day 12	Parables	*Mark 4:1–34*
Day 13	The Heart	*Mark 7:1–23*
Day 14	Jesus and John the Baptist	*Luke 7:18–35*
Day 15	The Authority of the Son	*John 5:1–47*
Day 16	The Sermon on the Mount	*Matt. 5:1–48*
Day 17	The Sermon on the Mount Continues	*Matt. 6:1–34*
Day 18	Keep Asking, Searching, Knocking	*Matt. 7:1–29*
Day 19	Jesus' Power over Nature	*Luke 8:22–56*
Day 20	Healings	*Matt. 8:1–17*
Day 21	Jesus Heals an Official's Son	*John 4:46–54*
Day 22	The Man with Leprosy; The Paralytic	*Luke 5:12–26*
Day 23	The Twelve Disciples; Instructions for Service	*Matt. 10:1–42*
Day 24	The Cost of Discipleship	*Mark 8:34–9:1*
Day 25	The Transfiguration	*Mark 9:2–13*
Day 26	Who Is the Greatest?	*Luke 9:46–62*
Day 27	Greatness in the Kingdom	*Matt. 18:1–35*
Day 28	Blessing the Children	*Mark 10:13–16*
Day 29	Jesus Heals a Disabled Woman on the Sabbath	*Luke 13:10–17*
Day 30	Lord of the Sabbath	*Matt. 12:1–21*

READING PLAN: LIFE OF CHRIST (CONTINUED)

#	Title	Reference
Day 31	Jesus and Beelzebub	*Matt. 12:22–45*
Day 32	Jesus Teaches at the Festival	*John 7:1–8:11*
Day 33	Peter's Declaration about Jesus	*Matt. 16:13–28*
Day 34	The Plot to Kill Jesus	*John 11:45–12:11*
Day 35	Jesus Enters Jerusalem	*Matt. 21:1–17*
Day 36	A Story about a Vineyard	*Mark 12:1–12*
Day 37	Jesus Is Anointed	*Mark 14:1–11*
Day 38	Jesus Judges the Pharisees and the Teachers of the Law	*Matt. 23:1–39*
Day 39	Signs of the End of the Age	*Matt. 24:1–25:13*
Day 40	The Institution of the Lord's Supper	*Mark 14:12–31*
Day 41	The World's Hatred	*John 15:18–16:33*
Day 42	Betrayal and Arrest of Jesus	*Luke 22:39–23:25*
Day 43	Jesus Dies	*John 19:28–42*
Day 44	The Empty Tomb	*John 20:1–18*
Day 45	"I am Coming Soon"	*Rev. 22:1–21*

READING PLAN: THANKSGIVING

#	Title	Reference
Day 1	Give Thanks: God Is Our Defender	Ps. 7:1–17
Day 2	Give Thanks: God Reigns	Ps. 9:1–20
Day 3	Give Thanks: God Is Merciful	Ps. 28:1–9
Day 4	Give Thanks: God Is Faithful	1 Chron. 16:7- 36
Day 5	Give Thanks: God Is Accessible	Ps. 42:1–4
Day 6	Give Thanks: God Is Good	Ezra 3:7–13
Day 7	Give Thanks: God Provides for Us	Ps. 67:1–7
Day 8	Give Thanks: God Is Praiseworthy	Ps. 69:30–36
Day 9	Give Thanks: God Saves Us	Isa. 12:1–6
Day 10	Give Thanks: God Works on Our Behalf	Ps. 75:1–10
Day 11	Give Thanks: God Restores Us	Jer. 30:18–22
Day 12	Give Thanks: God Is Our Creator	Ps. 95:1–7
Day 13	Give Thanks: God Mends the Broken	Jer. 33:1–11
Day 14	Give Thanks: God Cares for Us	Ps. 100:1–5
Day 15	Give Thanks: God Sees the Big Picture	2 Cor. 4:7–18
Day 16	Give Thanks: God Gives More Than Deserved	2 Cor. 9:6–15
Day 17	Give Thanks: God Preserves Our History	Ps. 106:9–48
Day 18	Give Thanks: God Blesses Us	Eph. 1:3–14
Day 19	Give Thanks: God Raised Jesus	Eph. 1:15–23
Day 20	Give Thanks: God Helps Us	Ps. 118:1–12
Day 21	Give Thanks: God Fights for Us	Ps. 118:13–24
Day 22	Give Thanks: God's Love Endures Forever	Ps. 136:1–26
Day 23	Give Thanks: God Makes Us Righteous	2 Thess. 1:3–12
Day 24	Give Thanks: God Heals the Broken Heart	Ps. 147:1–20
Day 25	Give Thanks: God Conquers All	Rev. 7:9–17

Verses about Marriage

Important Scriptures on Marriage	Reference
"If a man has recently married, he must not be sent to war or have any other duty laid on him. For one year he is to be free to stay at home and bring happiness to the wife he has married."	*Deut. 24:5*
"It has been said, 'Anyone who divorces his wife must give her a certificate of divorce.' But I tell you that anyone who divorces his wife, except for sexual immorality, makes her the victim of adultery, and anyone who marries a divorced woman commits adultery."	*Matt. 5:31–32*
"Jesus replied, 'Not everyone can accept this word, but only those to whom it has been given. For there are eunuchs who were born that way, and there are eunuchs who have been made eunuchs by others—and there are those who choose to live like eunuchs for the sake of the kingdom of heaven. The one who can accept this should accept it.'"	*Matt. 19:11–12*
"At the resurrection people will neither marry nor be given in marriage; they will be like the angels in heaven."	*Matt. 22:30*
"For example, by law a married woman is bound to her husband as long as he is alive, but if her husband dies, she is released from the law that binds her to him. So then, if she has sexual relations with another man while her husband is still alive, she is called an adulteress. But if her husband dies, she is released from that law and is not an adulteress if she marries another man."	*Rom. 7:2–3*
"But since sexual immorality is occurring, each man should have sexual relations with his own wife, and each woman with her own husband. The husband should fulfill his marital duty to his wife, and likewise the wife to her husband. The wife does not have authority over her own body but yields it to her husband. In the same way, the husband does not have authority over his own body but yields it to his wife. Do not deprive each other except perhaps by mutual consent and for a time, so that you may devote yourselves to prayer. Then come together again so that Satan will not tempt you because of your lack of self-control."	*1 Cor. 7:2–5*
"Now to the unmarried and the widows I say: It is good for them to stay unmarried, as I do. But if they cannot control themselves, they should marry, for it is better to marry than to burn with passion."	*1 Cor. 7:8–9*
"To the married I give this command (not I, but the Lord): A wife must not separate from her husband. But if she does, she must remain unmarried or else be reconciled to her husband. And a husband must not divorce his wife."	*1 Cor. 7:10–11*

Important Scriptures on Marriage	Reference
"To the rest I say this (I, not the Lord): If any brother has a wife who is not a believer and she is willing to live with him, he must not divorce her. And if a woman has a husband who is not a believer and he is willing to live with her, she must not divorce him. For the unbelieving husband has been sanctified through his wife, and the unbelieving wife has been sanctified through her believing husband. Otherwise your children would be unclean, but as it is, they are holy. But if the unbeliever leaves, let it be so. The brother or the sister is not bound in such circumstances; God has called us to live in peace. How do you know, wife, whether you will save your husband? Or, how do you know, husband, whether you will save your wife?"	*1 Cor. 7:12–16*
"Now about virgins: I have no command from the Lord, but I give a judgment as one who by the Lord's mercy is trustworthy. Because of the present crisis, I think that it is good for a man to remain as he is. Are you pledged to a woman? Do not seek to be released. Are you free from such a commitment? Do not look for a wife. But if you do marry, you have not sinned; and if a virgin marries, she has not sinned. But those who marry will face many troubles in this life, and I want to spare you this."	*1 Cor. 7:25–28*
"I would like you to be free from concern. An unmarried man is concerned about the Lord's affairs—how he can please the Lord. But a married man is concerned about the affairs of this world—how he can please his wife—and his interests are divided. An unmarried woman or virgin is concerned about the Lord's affairs: Her aim is to be devoted to the Lord in both body and spirit. But a married woman is concerned about the affairs of this world—how she can please her husband. . . ."	*1 Cor. 7:32–35*
"If anyone is worried that he might not be acting honorably toward the virgin he is engaged to, and if his passions are too strong and he feels he ought to marry, he should do as he wants. He is not sinning. They should get married. But the man who has settled the matter in his own mind, who is under no compulsion but has control over his own will, and who has made up his mind not to marry the virgin—this man also does the right thing. So then, he who marries the virgin does right, but he who does not marry her does better."	*1 Cor. 7:36–38*
"A woman is bound to her husband as long as he lives. But if her husband dies, she is free to marry anyone she wishes, but he must belong to the Lord. In my judgment, she is happier if she stays as she is—and I think that I too have the Spirit of God."	*1 Cor. 7:39–40*
"Marriage should be honored by all, and the marriage bed kept pure, for God will judge the adulterer and all the sexually immoral."	*Heb. 13:4*

Verses on Strength

Important Scriptures on Strength	Reference
"The Lord is my strength and my defense; he has become my salvation. . . ."	*Exod. 15:2*
"Love the Lord your God with all your heart and with all your soul and with all your strength."	*Deut. 6:5*
"Be strong and courageous. Do not be afraid or terrified because of them, for the Lord your God goes with you; he will never leave you nor forsake you."	*Deut. 31:6*
"Be strong and courageous, because you will lead these people to inherit the land I swore to their ancestors to give them. Be strong and very courageous. Be careful to obey all the law my servant Moses gave you; do not turn from it to the right or to the left, that you may be successful wherever you go."	*Josh. 1:6–7*
"After putting him to sleep on her lap, she called for someone to shave off the seven braids of his hair, and so began to subdue him. And his strength left him."	*Judg. 16:19*
"Be strong and courageous. Do not be afraid or discouraged because of the king of Assyria and the vast army with him, for there is a greater power with us than with him."	*2 Chron. 32:7*
"They are your servants and your people, whom you redeemed by your great strength and your mighty hand."	*Neh. 1:10*
"Nehemiah said, 'Go and enjoy choice food and sweet drinks, and send some to those who have nothing prepared. This day is holy to our Lord. Do not grieve, for the joy of the Lord is your strength.'"	*Neh. 8:10*
"The Lord is my strength and my shield; my heart trusts in him, and he helps me. My heart leaps for joy, and with my song I praise him."	*Ps. 28:7*
"Ants are creatures of little strength, yet they store up their food in the summer."	*Prov. 30:25*
"But those who hope in the Lord will renew their strength. They will soar on wings like eagles; they will run and not grow weary, they will walk and not be faint."	*Isa. 40:31*
"The Sovereign Lord is my strength; he makes my feet like the feet of a deer, he enables me to tread on the heights."	*Hab. 3:19*
"We who are strong ought to bear with the failings of the weak and not to please ourselves."	*Rom. 15:1*
"He will also keep you firm to the end, so that you will be blameless on the day of our Lord Jesus Christ."	*1 Cor. 1:8*
"For the foolishness of God is wiser than human wisdom, and the weakness of God is stronger than human strength."	*1 Cor. 1:25*

Verses on Strength (CONTINUED)

Important Scriptures on Strength	Reference
"But God chose the foolish things of the world to shame the wise; God chose the weak things of the world to shame the strong."	*1 Cor. 1:27*
"I pray that the eyes of your heart may be enlightened in order that you may know the hope to which he has called you, the riches of his glorious inheritance in his holy people, and his incomparably great power for us who believe. That power is the same as the mighty strength he exerted when he raised Christ from the dead and seated him at his right hand in the heavenly realms."	*Eph. 1:18–20*
"I can do all this through him who gives me strength."	*Phil. 4:13*
"You then, my son, be strong in the grace that is in Christ Jesus."	*2 Tim. 2:1*
"And what more shall I say? I do not have time to tell about Gideon, Barak, Samson and Jephthah, about David and Samuel and the prophets, who through faith conquered kingdoms, administered justice, and gained what was promised; who shut the mouths of lions, quenched the fury of the flames, and escaped the edge of the sword; whose weakness was turned to strength; and who became powerful in battle and routed foreign armies."	*Heb. 11:32–34*
"If anyone speaks, they should do so as one who speaks the very words of God. If anyone serves, they should do so with the strength God provides, so that in all things God may be praised through Jesus Christ. To him be the glory and the power for ever and ever. Amen."	*1 Pet. 4:11*
"And the God of all grace, who called you to his eternal glory in Christ, after you have suffered a little while, will himself restore you and make you strong, firm and steadfast."	*1 Pet. 5:10*
"I write to you, fathers, because you know him who is from the beginning. I write to you, young men, because you are strong, and the word of God lives in you, and you have overcome the evil one."	*1 John 2:14*
"I know your deeds. See, I have placed before you an open door that no one can shut. I know that you have little strength, yet you have kept my word and have not denied my name."	*Rev. 3:8*

261

ZINGERS FROM MOSES

Zinger from Moses	Reference
" 'Just as you say,' Moses replied, 'I will never appear before you again.' "	*Exod. 10:29*
" 'There will be loud wailing throughout Egypt—worse than there has ever been or ever will be again. But among the Israelites not a dog will bark at any person or animal.' Then you will know that the LORD makes a distinction between Egypt and Israel."	*Exod. 11:6–7*
"Do not be afraid. Stand firm and you will see the deliverance the LORD will bring you today. The Egyptians you see today you will never see again. The LORD will fight for you; you need only to be still."	*Exod. 14:13–14*
"Why should your anger burn against your people, whom you brought out of Egypt with great power and a mighty hand? Why should the Egyptians say, 'It was with evil intent that he brought them out, to kill them in the mountains and to wipe them off the face of the earth'? Turn from your fierce anger; relent and do not bring disaster on your people."	*Exod. 32:11–12*
"Did I conceive all these people? Did I give them birth? Why do you tell me to carry them in my arms, as a nurse carries an infant, to the land you promised on oath to their ancestors?"	*Num. 11:12*
"Here I am among six hundred thousand men on foot, and you say, 'I will give them meat to eat for a whole month!' Would they have enough if flocks and herds were slaughtered for them? Would they have enough if all the fish in the sea were caught for them?"	*Num. 11:21–22*
" 'If you put all these people to death, leaving none alive, the nations who have heard this report about you will say, 'The LORD was not able to bring these people into the land he promised them on oath, so he slaughtered them in the wilderness.' "	*Num. 14:15–16*
"O God, the God who gives breath to all living things, will you be angry with the entire assembly when only one man sins?"	*Num. 16:22*
"Listen, you rebels, must we bring you water out of this rock?"	*Num. 20:10*
"And here you are, a brood of sinners, standing in the place of your fathers and making the LORD even more angry with Israel. If you turn away from following him, he will again leave all this people in the wilderness, and you will be the cause of their destruction."	*Num. 32:14–15*
"Has any other people heard the voice of God speaking out of fire, as you have, and lived? Has any god ever tried to take for himself one nation out of another nation, by testings, by signs and wonders, by war, by a mighty hand and an outstretched arm, or by great and awesome deeds, like all the things the LORD your God did for you in Egypt before your very eyes?"	*Deut. 4:33–34*

Zinger from Moses	Reference
"These commandments that I give you today are to be on your hearts. Impress them on your children. Talk about them when you sit at home and when you walk along the road, when you lie down and when you get up. Tie them as symbols on your hands and bind them on your foreheads. Write them on the doorframes of your houses and on your gates."	*Deut. 6:6–9*
"When the LORD your God brings you into the land he swore to your fathers, to Abraham, Isaac and Jacob, to give you—a land with large, flourishing cities you did not build, houses filled with all kinds of good things you did not provide, wells you did not dig, and vineyards and olive groves you did not plant—then when you eat and are satisfied, be careful that you do not forget the LORD, who brought you out of Egypt, out of the land of slavery."	*Deut. 6:10–12*
"In the future, when your son asks you, 'What is the meaning of the stipulations, decrees and laws the LORD our God has commanded you?' tell him: 'We were slaves of Pharaoh in Egypt, but the LORD brought us out of Egypt with a mighty hand. Before our eyes the LORD sent signs and wonders—great and terrible—on Egypt and Pharaoh and his whole household.'"	*Deut. 6:20–22*
"The LORD did not set his affection on you and choose you because you were more numerous than other peoples, for you were the fewest of all peoples. But it was because the LORD loved you and kept the oath he swore to your ancestors that he brought you out with a mighty hand and redeemed you from the land of slavery, from the power of Pharaoh king of Egypt."	*Deut. 7:7–8*
"Remember how the LORD your God led you all the way in the wilderness these forty years, to humble and test you in order to know what was in your heart, whether or not you would keep his commands. He humbled you, causing you to hunger and then feeding you with manna, which neither you nor your ancestors had known, to teach you that man does not live on bread alone but on every word that comes from the mouth of the LORD. Your clothes did not wear out and your feet did not swell during these forty years."	*Deut. 8:2–4*
"See, I am setting before you today a blessing and a curse—the blessing if you obey the commands of the LORD your God that I am giving you today; the curse if you disobey the commands of the LORD your God and turn from the way that I command you today by following other gods, which you have not known."	*Deut. 11:26–28*
"The LORD will make you the head, not the tail. If you pay attention to the commands of the LORD your God that I give you this day and carefully follow them, you will always be at the top, never at the bottom."	*Deut. 28:13*
"You who were as numerous as the stars in the sky will be left but few in number, because you did not obey the LORD your God."	*Deut. 28:62*

ZINGERS FROM SOLOMON

Zinger from Solomon	Reference
"[Lord,] give your servant a discerning heart to govern your people and to distinguish between right and wrong. For who is able to govern this great people of yours?"	*1 Kings 3:9*
"Cut the living child in two and give half to one and half to the other."	*1 Kings 3:25*
"Like a gold ring in a pig's snout is a beautiful woman who shows no discretion."	*Prov. 11:22*
"Whoever loves discipline loves knowledge, but whoever hates correction is stupid."	*Prov. 12:1*
"Whoever spares the rod hates their children, but the one who loves their children is careful to discipline them."	*Prov. 13:24*
"The Lord works out everything to its proper end—even the wicked for a day of disaster."	*Prov. 16:4*
"In their hearts humans plan their course, but the Lord establishes their steps."	*Prov. 16:9*
"Pride goes before destruction, a haughty spirit before a fall."	*Prov. 16:18*
"There is a way that appears to be right, but in the end it leads to death."	*Prov. 16:25*
"The lot is cast into the lap, but its every decision is from the Lord."	*Prov. 16:33*
"Better to live on a corner of the roof than share a house with a quarrelsome wife."	*Prov. 21:9*
"The rich rule over the poor, and the borrower is slave to the lender."	*Prov. 22:7*
"Do not answer a fool according to his folly, or you yourself will be just like him."	*Prov. 26:4*
"A quarrelsome wife is like the dripping of a leaky roof in a rainstorm; restraining her is like restraining the wind or grasping oil with the hand."	*Prov. 27:15–16*
"As iron sharpens iron, so one person sharpens another."	*Prov. 27:17*
" 'Meaningless! Meaningless!' says the Teacher. 'Utterly meaningless! Everything is meaningless.' "	*Eccles. 1:2*
"Yet when I surveyed all that my hands had done and what I had toiled to achieve, everything was meaningless, a chasing after the wind; nothing was gained under the sun."	*Eccles. 2:11*

Zinger from Solomon	Reference
"There is a time for everything, and a season for every activity under the heavens: a time to be born and a time to die, a time to plant and a time to uproot, a time to kill and a time to heal, a time to tear down and a time to build, a time to weep and a time to laugh, a time to mourn and a time to dance, a time to scatter stones and a time to gather them, a time to embrace and a time to refrain from embracing, a time to search and a time to give up, a time to keep and a time to throw away, a time to tear and a time to mend, a time to be silent and a time to speak, a time to love and a time to hate, a time for war and a time for peace."	*Eccles. 3:1–8*
"Whoever loves money never has enough; whoever loves wealth is never satisfied with their income. This too is meaningless."	*Eccles. 5:10*
"This is the evil in everything that happens under the sun: The same destiny overtakes all. The hearts of people, moreover, are full of evil and there is madness in their hearts while they live, and afterward they join the dead. Anyone who is among the living has hope—even a live dog is better off than a dead lion!"	*Eccles. 9:3–4*
"Whatever your hand finds to do, do it with all your might, for in the realm of the dead, where you are going, there is neither working nor planning nor knowledge nor wisdom."	*Eccles. 9:10*
"I have seen something else under the sun: The race is not to the swift or the battle to the strong, nor does food come to the wise or wealth to the brilliant or favor to the learned; but time and chance happen to them all."	*Eccles. 9:11*
"As dead flies give perfume a bad smell, so a little folly outweighs wisdom and honor."	*Eccles. 10:1*
"Remember him—before the silver cord is severed, and the golden bowl is broken; before the pitcher is shattered at the spring, and the wheel broken at the well, and the dust returns to the ground it came from, and the spirit returns to God who gave it."	*Eccles. 12:6–7*

Zingers from Jesus

Zinger from Jesus	Reference
"If your right eye causes you to stumble, gouge it out and throw it away. It is better for you to lose one part of your body than for your whole body to be thrown into hell."	*Matt. 5:29*
"Why do you look at the speck of sawdust in your brother's eye and pay no attention to the plank in your own eye? How can you say to your brother, 'Let me take the speck out of your eye,' when all the time there is a plank in your own eye? You hypocrite, first take the plank out of your own eye, and then you will see clearly to remove the speck from your brother's eye."	*Matt. 7:3–5*
"Enter through the narrow gate. For wide is the gate and broad is the road that leads to destruction, and many enter through it. But small is the gate and narrow the road that leads to life, and only a few find it."	*Matt. 7:13–14*
"Many will say to me on that day, 'Lord, Lord, did we not prophesy in your name and in your name drive out demons and in your name perform many miracles?' Then I will tell them plainly, 'I never knew you. Away from me, you evildoers!'"	*Matt. 7:22–23*
"Foxes have dens and birds have nests, but the Son of Man has no place to lay his head."	*Matt. 8:20*
"Do not be afraid of those who kill the body but cannot kill the soul. Rather, be afraid of the One who can destroy both soul and body in hell."	*Matt. 10:28*
"Are not two sparrows sold for a penny? Yet not one of them will fall to the ground outside your Father's care. And even the very hairs of your head are all numbered."	*Matt. 10:29–30*
"Whoever acknowledges me before others, I will also acknowledge before my Father in heaven. But whoever disowns me before others, I will disown before my Father in heaven."	*Matt. 10:32–33*
"A wicked and adulterous generation asks for a sign! But none will be given it except the sign of the prophet Jonah. For as Jonah was three days and three nights in the belly of a huge fish, so the Son of Man will be three days and three nights in the heart of the earth."	*Matt. 12:39–40*
"Whoever has will be given more, and they will have an abundance. Whoever does not have, even what they have will be taken from them."	*Matt. 13:12*
"It is not right to take the children's bread and toss it to the dogs."	*Matt. 15:26*
"The Son of Man will go just as it is written about him. But woe to that man who betrays the Son of Man! It would be better for him if he had not been born."	*Matt. 26:24*

Zingers from Jesus (continued)

Zinger from Jesus	Reference
"Am I leading a rebellion, that you have come out with swords and clubs to capture me?"	*Matt. 26:55*
"Indeed, it is easier for a camel to go through the eye of a needle than for someone who is rich to enter the kingdom of God."	*Luke 18:25*
"If they keep quiet, the stones will cry out."	*Luke 19:40*
"Judas, are you betraying the Son of Man with a kiss?"	*Luke 22:48*
"Have I not chosen you, the Twelve? Yet one of you is a devil!"	*John 6:70*
"Has not Moses given you the law? Yet not one of you keeps the law. Why are you trying to kill me?"	*John 7:19*
"'You do not know me or my Father,' Jesus replied. 'If you knew me, you would know my Father also.'"	*John 8:19*
"You belong to your father, the devil, and you want to carry out your father's desires. He was a murderer from the beginning, not holding to the truth, for there is no truth in him. When he lies, he speaks his native language, for he is a liar and the father of lies."	*John 8:44*
"Before Abraham was born, I am!"	*John 8:58*
"No one takes it from me, but I lay it down of my own accord. I have authority to lay it down and authority to take it up again."	*John 10:18*
"I am the way and the truth and the life. No one comes to the Father except through me."	*John 14:6*
"Anyone who has seen me has seen the Father."	*John 14:9*
"I always taught in synagogues or at the temple, where all the Jews come together. I said nothing in secret. Why question me? Ask those who heard me. Surely they know what I said."	*John 18:20–21*

APPENDIX

BIBLE &
WORLD
TIMELINES

TIME LINE
CREATION – 2200 BC

????—Creation of the world; Adam and Eve. Date unknown. Many conservative Christians date the creation of the world between 5000 BC and 4000 BC.

???

????—Cain and Abel

????—Noah and the Flood (early date)

????—Tower of Babel (early date)

3200

????—Invention of the wheel
????—Invention of pottery

????—Development of sailing ships

????—Development of the Sumerian alphabet (if Flood is at early date)

????—Early Egyptian dynasties founded (if Flood is at early date)

269

2700

2300—Noah and the Flood (late date)

????—Tower of Babel (late date)

2200

2166—Birth of Abraham

????—Life of Job

2300—Archaeological evidence points to the practice of cannibalism
2215—The death of Sargon

????—Silk creation begins in China
2200—First editions of the *Epic of Gilgamesh*
2200—Egyptians begin worshipping Ra, the sun god

All dates are uncertain.

TIME LINE
2200 BC – 1500 BC

BIBLE EVENT | WORLD EVENT

2200

2166—Birth of Abraham

2100—Ziggurat built in Ur

2080—Birth of Ishmael
2066—Birth of Isaac
2005—Birth of Jacob

2000

270

1950—Amorites conquer Mesopotamia
1940—City of Ur falls

1914—Birth of Joseph
1884—Joseph's rise in Egypt
1876—Joseph's family moves to Egypt

1800

1766—Shang dynasty begins in China
1750—Code of Hammurabi created

?????—Israelites enslaved in Egypt

1600

1600—Hittites defeat Babylon; rise of Hittites

1526—Birth of Moses

All dates are approximate.

TIME LINE
1500 BC – 1000 BC

BIBLE EVENT   WORLD EVENT

1500

1500—The Aryans invade India
1500—The Lydians occupy Mycenae

1446—The Exodus; crossing of the Red Sea
1446–1406—Hebrews wander in the
wilderness; God gives the Ten Commandments; building of the tabernacle

1406—Death of Moses; Joshua leads the Hebrews
in their conquest of Canaan

1400

1400—The creation of the cuneiform tablets in
the royal library and temple of Ugarit

1372—Reign of Pharaoh Amenhotep (aka Ikhnaton)
1360—King Tut begins reign in Egypt

1350—The first judges; the Hebrew people
begin their struggle with the Philistines

271

1300

1304—Rameses II begins reign in Egypt
1300—Reign of Shalmaneser in Assyria

Judges lead the Hebrews:
Othniel	Jair
Ehud	Jephthah
Shamgar	Ibzan
Deborah	Elon
Gideon	Abdon
Tola	Samson

1200

1200—The fall of the Hittite Empire and
the beginning of the Iron Age
1190—The Trojan War

1100

1100—Greece enters her Dark Ages
1100—Tiglath-Pileser I begins reign in Assyria

1100—Eli becomes a priest and judge

1060–1020—The ministry of Samuel
1051—Saul becomes king

1050—Zhou dynasty begins in China
1050—Development of the Phoenician alphabet

1011—David becomes king

1000

1000—The Mayan Empire is founded in Central
America

All dates are approximate.

Time Line
1000 BC – 750 BC

BIBLE EVENT   WORLD EVENT

1000

978—Hiram begins reign in Tyre

971—Solomon begins reign

931—The kingdom divides

NORTHERN KINGDOM
Dates when they begin reign
931—Jeroboam

SOUTHERN KINGDOM
Dates when they begin reign
931—Rehoboam
913—Abijah
911—Asa

945—Shishak I begins reign in Egypt; Egypt briefly unified again

910—Nadab
909—Baasha

900

886—Elah
885—Zimri and Tibni
885—Omri
874—Ahab
873—Ahaziah

873—Jehoshaphat
853—Joram
842—Ahaziah
841—Athaliah
835—Joash

858—Shalmaneser III begins reign in Assyria
850—Assyria pushes back the Aramaeans
841—Israel begins paying tribute to Assyria

852—Joram
841—Jehu

814—Jehoahaz

800

800—Greek city-states begin to organize

798—Jehoash
793—Jeroboam II

796—Amaziah
792—Uzziah

783—Shalmaneser IV reigns in Assyria
776—First Olympic Games

753—Zechariah
752—Shallum
752—Menahem

753—Rome is founded; Romulus is king
750—Homer writes the *Iliad* in Greece

740—Jotham

700

Prophets
870—Elijah begins ministry
845—Elisha begins ministry
770—Jonah goes to Nineveh
760—Isaiah begins ministry
758—Hosea begins ministry
755—Amos begins ministry

272

All dates are approximate.

TIME LINE
750 BC – 500 BC

BIBLE EVENT   WORLD EVENT

NORTHERN KINGDOM
Dates when they begin reign

SOUTHERN KINGDOM
Dates when they begin reign

750

742—Pekahiah
740—Pekah
732—Hoshea   **732**—Ahaz
722—Fall of Israel
                    716—Hezekiah
PROPHETS
738—Micah begins ministry

750—Greece settles Sicily
744—Tiglath-Pileser III reigns in Assyria
726—Shalmaneser V reigns in Assyria
722—Sargon II reigns in Assyria and conquers the northern kingdom

700

                    697—Manasseh

704—Sennacherib reigns in Assyria

650

658—Nahum begins ministry
650—Jeremiah begins ministry
                    643—Amon
640—Zephaniah begins ministry **640**—Josiah

660—Japanese culture begins to emerge   273

600

620—Birth of Daniel
620—Ezekiel begins ministry
                    609—Jehoahaz
                    609—Jehoiakim
608—Habakkuk begins ministry
                    598—Jehoiachin
                    597—Zedekiah
590—Obadiah begins ministry **586**—Fall of Judah

612—Nineveh falls to the Babylonians
609—Pharaoh Neco battles in Carchemesh but is hindered en route by Josiah
605—Nebuchadnezzar II reigns in Babylon
586—Nebuchadnezzar attacks Judah
570—Confucius teaches in China

550

539—Cyrus the Great begins reign in Persia
539—Persia conquers Babylon; Darius the Mede reigns in Babylon
538—Cyrus allows the Jews to return to Israel
536—The Jews begin rebuilding the temple
521—Darius reigns in Persia
509—Establishment of the Roman Republic

500

522—Zechariah begins ministry
520—Haggai begins ministry

All dates are approximate.

TIME LINE
500 BC – 400 BC

516—Jewish temple is completed

500

492–479—Greco-Persian Wars
485—Xerxes I begins reign in Persia

478—Esther becomes queen

274   **465**—Malachi begins ministry

469—Birth of Socrates
464—Artaxerxes reigns in Persia
461—Peloponnesian War

457—Ezra sent to Judah

450—Joel begins ministry

450

444—Nehemiah sent to Judah

441—Euripides writes his first play

431—Peloponnesian War renewed

404—Artaxerxes II reigns in Persia

400

All dates are approximate.

TIME LINE
400 BC – 1 BC

| BIBLE | EVENT | WORLD | EVENT |

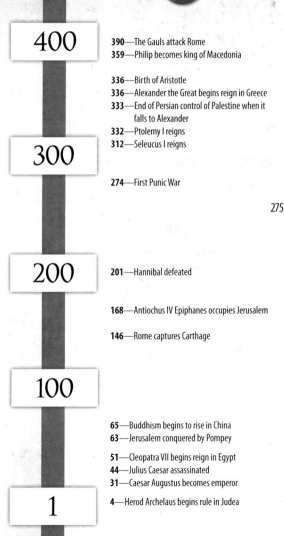

400

390—The Gauls attack Rome
359—Philip becomes king of Macedonia

336—Birth of Aristotle
336—Alexander the Great begins reign in Greece
333—End of Persian control of Palestine when it
falls to Alexander
332—Ptolemy I reigns
312—Seleucus I reigns

300

274—First Punic War

275

The "400 Silent Years"

200

201—Hannibal defeated

168—Antiochus IV Epiphanes occupies Jerusalem

146—Rome captures Carthage

100

65—Buddhism begins to rise in China
63—Jerusalem conquered by Pompey

51—Cleopatra VII begins reign in Egypt
44—Julius Caesar assassinated
31—Caesar Augustus becomes emperor

1

4—Herod Archelaus begins rule in Judea

5—Birth of John the Baptist
4—Birth of Jesus Christ
2—Visit of the Magi; Herod orders the death of
innocent children Jesus' family flees to
Egypt

All dates are approximate.

TIME LINE
AD 1 — AD 100

AD 1

8—Jesus amazes the religious leaders when He visits the temple as a child

                    14—Tiberius becomes emperor of Rome

26—John baptizes Jesus
30—Jesus crucified and raised from the dead

25

32—Stephen, the deacon, is martyred
37—Paul is converted   **26**—Pontius Pilate becomes governor of Judea
44—James is martyred
45—James written   **37**—Caligula becomes emperor of Rome; birth
47—Paul begins first missionary journey   of Josephus
49—Council of Jerusalem; Paul begins second   **43**—Claudius conquers portions of Britain
       missionary journey; Galatians written
51—1 & 2 Thessalonians written
52—Paul begins third missionary journey

50

55—1 & 2 Corinthians written
57—Romans written
60—Ephesians, Philippians, Colossians, Philemon   **54**—Nero becomes emperor of Rome
       written
63—Titus written
65—1 Peter, 1 Timothy written   **64**—Rome burns; Nero blames the Christians
67—2 Timothy, Hebrews, 2 Peter written   **66**—The Jews rebel against Rome
68—Peter and Paul both martyred   **70**—Titus sacks Israel; temple destroyed
70—Jude written?

75

85—John exiled to Patmos; 1, 2, 3 John written
90—Revelation written   **79**—Pompeii destroyed by Mt. Vesuvius
                    81—Domitian becomes emperor of Rome

All four Gospels were written in the first century. Their exact dates are difficult to determine.

                    90—Domitian persecutes the Christians

100

CREDITS

page 2 • BANNER: *Crosses in Wood* (Source: Thinkstock.)

page 7 • BANNER: *Cross on Wall* (Source: Thinkstock.) BOTTOM: *Person with Bible; Father and Son; Man on Dock; Pointing to a Verse* (Source: Thinkstock.)

page 8 • Full page, *Genesis with Necklace* (Source: Thinkstock.)

page 10 • BANNER: *Hippopotamus* (Source: Thinkstock.) BOTTOM: *Mouse* (Source: Thinkstock.)

page 11 • BANNER: *Dove* (Source: Thinkstock.) BOTTOM: *Spotted Eagle Owl; Turkish Stork; Falcon* (Source: Thinkstock.)

page 12 • BANNER: *Camels* (Source: Thinkstock.) BOTTOM: *Weasel; Chameleon; Sheep* (Source: Thinkstock.)

page 13 • BANNER: *Hoopoe* (Source: Thinkstock.) BOTTOM: *Ostrich* (Source: Thinkstock.)

page 14 • BANNER: *Crocodile* (Source: Thinkstock.) BOTTOM: *Edible Frog (Rana esculenta)* (Source: Thinkstock.)

page 15 • BANNER: *Honeycomb* (Source: Thinkstock.) BOTTOM: *Scorpion; Honey Bees; Ants* (Source: Thinkstock.)

page 16 • BANNER: *Acacia Tree* (Source: Thinkstock.)

page 18 • BOTTOM: *Pomegranate* (Source: Thinkstock.)

page 20 • BANNER: *Bible Held in Hands* (Source: Thinkstock.)

page 21 • BOTTOM: *Cross Against Blue Sky* (Source: Thinkstock.)

page 22 • BOTTOM: *Cross* (Source: Thinkstock.)

page 23 • BANNER: *Scribe Writing in Hebrew* (Source: Thinkstock.) BOTTOM: *The Great Isaiah Scroll* (Source: Wikimedia Commons.)

page 24 • BOTTOM: *King Solomon and the Queen of Sheba*, Konrad Witz (ca. 1400–1447), (Source: Wikimedia Commons.) BOTTOM: *Hosea*, Statue by Antônio Francisco Lisboa (1738–1814). Photo by Eric Gaba. This image is licensed under the

BOTTOM: *The Prophet Amos*, Gustave Doré (1832–1883). (Source: Wikimedia Commons.)

page 25 • BANNER: *Number Collage* (Source: Thinkstock.)

page 26 • BANNER: *KJV Woodcut*, Title page from the Holy Bible, King James Version printed in 1611 by the Church of England. Source: (Source: Wikimedia Commons.) BOTTOM: *Notebook* (Source: Thinkstock.)

page 27 • BANNER: *Bible and Chinese Calculator* (Source: Thinkstock.) BOTTOM: *Top Ten Most Used Words in the Bible*, From the library of TheBiblePeople.com. Used by permission.

page 28 • BANNER: *Library* (Source: Thinkstock.) BOTTOM: *King Solomon in Old Age*, Gustave Doré (1832–1883). (Source: Wikimedia Commons.) BOTTOM: *Collage of Books Used in the Bible*, From the library of TheBiblePeople.com. Used by permission.

page 29 • BANNER: *Scroll and Hanukkah* (Source: Thinkstock.) BOTTOM: *The Martyrdom of the Seven Brothers*, original artist unknown, ca. 1450s–1470s. (Source: Wikimedia Commons.) BOTTOM: *Shadrach, Meshach, Abednego* (Source: Thinkstock.)

page 30 • BANNER: *Rainbow Landscape* (Source: Thinkstock.) BOTTOM: *Bible and the Sacrament* (Source: Thinkstock.)

page 31 • BANNER: *Russian Dolls* (Source: Thinkstock.)

page 32 • BANNER: *Person in Prayer* (Source: Thinkstock.) BOTTOM: *Norwich Cathedral (Norwich, England); Dove; Christ the King (Lisbon, Portugal); Man with Bible* (Source: Thinkstock.)

page 33 • BANNER: *Greek Inscription* (Source: Thinkstock.) BOTTOM:

Codex Arabicus, The underlying text (ca. 500) is in Syriac. The overlying text (ca. 900) is in Arabic. (Source: Wikimedia Commons.)

page 34 • BANNER: *Jewish Rabbi* (Source: Thinkstock.) BOTTOM: *Marriage of the Virgin*, Alexandre-François Caminade (1783–1862). (Source: Wikimedia Commons.) BOTTOM: *High Priest Offering Incense on the Altar and High Priest Offering a Sacrifice of a Goat*, Illustration from *Treasures of the Bible* by Henry Davenport Northrop, 1894. (Source: Wikimedia Commons.) BOTTOM: *Furniture of the Biblical Tabernacle*, Illustration from The *Holy Bible* published by Holman in 1890. (Source: Wikimedia Commons.)

page 35 • BANNER: *Stone Tablets* (Source: Thinkstock.) BOTTOM: *Ten Commandments Word Art*, From the library of TheBiblePeople. com. Used by permission.

page 36 • BANNER: *Scales* (Source: Thinkstock.) BOTTOM: *Ruler* (Source: Thinkstock.)

page 37 • BANNER: *Open Bible* (Source: Thinkstock.) BOTTOM: *Jewish Man Holding Torah* (Source: Thinkstock.)

page 39 • BANNER: *Woman with Scissors* (Source: Thinkstock.) BOTTOM: *Samson and Delilah*, Josef Worlicek (1824–1897). (Source: Wikimedia Commons.) BOTTOM: *Samson and Delilah*, Cover from *Samson and Delilah: Spectacular Feature #11*. Comic book published by Fox Feature Syndicate in 1950. (Source: Wikimedia Commons.) BOTTOM: *Samson and Delilah*, Michelangelo Merisi da Caravaggio (1571–1610). (Source: Wikimedia Commons.)

page 40 • BANNER: *Genesis Page* (Source: Thinkstock.) BOTTOM: *God Took Enoch*, Gerard Hoet (1648–1733). (Source: Wikimedia Commons.) BOTTOM: *Adam and Eve* (Source: Thinkstock.) BOTTOM: *Hagar and Ishmael Banished by Abraham*, Pieter Jozef Verhaghen (1728–1811). (Source: Wikimedia

Commons.) Bottom: *Moses and the Daughters of Jethro,* Ciro Ferri (1634–1689). (Source: Wikimedia Commons.)

page 41 • Bottom: *Israel in Egypt,* Edward Poynter (1836–1919). (Source: Wikimedia Commons.)

page 42 • Banner: *Ezra Page* (Source: Thinkstock.) Bottom: *Tomb of Cyrus,* photo by Alireza Shakernia. This photo is licensed under the Creative Commons Attribution-ShareAlike 3.0 Unported license. (Source: Wikimedia Commons.) Bottom: *Absalom,* Albert Weisgerber (1878–1915). (Source: Wikimedia Commons.) Bottom: *King Asa,* Seventeenth-century painting by unknown artist. (Source: Wikimedia Commons.)

page 43 • Bottom: *Five Smooth Stones* (Source: Thinkstock.)

page 44 • Bottom: *Solomon's Sin,* Published as a Bible card by the Providence Lithograph Company in 1901. (Source: Wikimedia Commons.) Bottom: *Saul Attacking David,* Giovanni Francesco Barbieri (best known as Guercino, 1591–1666). (Source: Wikimedia Commons.)

page 45 • Banner: *Gospel of John Opening* (Source: Thinkstock.) Bottom: *Madonna and Child* (Source: Thinkstock.) Bottom: *Pontius Pilate,* Statue in Bom Jesus, Braga, Portugal. Photo by Jose Goncalves. This image is licensed under the Creative Commons Attribution-ShareAlike 3.0 Unported license. (Source: Wikimedia Commons.) Bottom: *Gabriel* (Source: Thinkstock.) Bottom: *Simon the Zealot,* photo by Tony Bowden. Statue of Simon the Zealot by Hermann Schievelbein at the roof of the Helsinki Cathedral, 1849. (Source: Wikimedia Commons.)

page 46 • Bottom: *Cross* (Source: Thinkstock.)

page 47 • Banner: *Romans Book Opener* (Source: Thinkstock.)

page 48 • Bottom: *Roman Slaves,* original artist and date unknown (2nd century). (Source: Wikimedia Commons.)

page 49 • Banner: *Friends Walking* (Source: Thinkstock.) Bottom: *Two Friends Sitting on Grass* (Source: Thinkstock.) Bottom: *Shadrach, Meshach, and Abednego Preserved from the Burning Fiery Furnace,* Simeon Solomon (1840–1905). (Source: Wikimedia Commons.) Bottom: *Rock Climbers* (Source: Thinkstock.)

page 50 • Banner: *King David Playing the Harp,* original artist unknown, ca. 1770. (Source: Wikimedia Commons.) Bottom: *King David Stained Glass* (Source: Thinkstock.)

page 51 • Banner: *Walking on the Water* (Source: Thinkstock.) Bottom: *Fall of Jericho,* Published as a Bible card by the Providence Lithograph Company in 1901. (Source: Wikimedia Commons.) Bottom: *Gideon's Victory,* Published as a Bible card by the Providence Lithograph Company in 1901. (Source: Wikimedia Commons.) Bottom: *Naomi and Ruth,* Published as a Bible card by the Providence Lithograph Company in 1901. (Source: Wikimedia Commons.)

page 52 • Bottom: *Healing of the Blind Man,* Duccio di Buoninsegna (ca. 1260–1318). (Source: Wikimedia Commons.) Bottom: *Christ Healing the Paralytic at Capernaum,* Engraving, ca. 1790, by Bernhard Rode (1725–1797). (Source: Wikimedia Commons.) Bottom: *Woman with the Alabaster Jar* (Source: Thinkstock.)

page 53 • Banner: *Noah's Ark* (Source: Thinkstock.) Bottom: *Rainbow Mosaic* (Source: Thinkstock.)

page 54 • Banner: *Satellite View of Northern Africa,* Courtesy of NASA. (Source: Wikimedia Commons.) Bottom: *Pyramid* (Source: Thinkstock.)

page 55 • Banner: *Kids* (Source: Thinkstock.) Bottom: *Lazarus, Mary, and Martha,* original artist unknown, ca. 1475. (Source: Wikimedia Commons.) Bottom: *Abraham, Sarah and Hagar, Bible Pictures with Brief Descriptions* by Charles Foster, published in 1897. (Source: Wikimedia Commons.) Bottom: *Miriam and Moses,* Paul Delaroche (1797–1856). (Source: Wikimedia Commons.)

page 56 • Banner: *Woman behind Veil* (Source: Thinkstock.)

page 57 • Banner: *Thumbs Up and Down* (Source: Thinkstock.) Bottom: *The First Mourning,* William-Adolphe Bouguereau (1825–1905). (Source: Wikimedia Commons.) Bottom: *Abraham and Isaac* (Source: Thinkstock.) Bottom: *Salome Receives the Head of John the Baptist,* Carlo Sellitto (1581–1614). (Source: Wikimedia Commons.)

page 58 • Banner: *The Creation of Adam,* Michelangelo Buonarroti (1475–1564). (Source: Wikimedia Commons.) Bottom: *King David* (Source: Thinkstock.)

page 59 • Bottom: *Moses* (Source: Thinkstock.) Bottom: *Elijah and the Woman's Son* (Source: Thinkstock.) Bottom: *Daniel in the Lions' Den* (Source: Thinkstock.)

page 60 • Banner: *Mary and Joseph* (Source: Thinkstock.) Bottom: *Rings* (Source: Thinkstock.)

page 61 • Background: *Biological Signs* (Source: Thinkstock.) Bottom: *Scarves,* photo by Joe Mabel. This image is licensed under the Creative Commons Attribution-ShareAlike 3.0 Unported license. (Source: Wikimedia Commons.)

page 62 • Banner: *Candle; Wine; Cheese* (Source: Thinkstock.) Bottom: *Eliezer Meets Rebekah at the Well,* Julius Schnorr von Carolsfeld (1794–1872). (Source: Wikimedia Commons.) Bottom: *Abraham and the Three Angels,* Giovanni Battista Tiepolo (1696–1770). (Source: Wikimedia

Commons.) Bottom: *The Harlot of Jericho and the Two Spies,* James Tissot (1836–1902). (Source: Wikimedia Commons.) Bottom: *Zacchaeus in the Sycamore Awaiting the Passage of Jesus,* James Tissot (1836–1902). (Source: Wikimedia Commons.)

page 63 • Banner: *Conversion of St. Paul,* Nicolas-Bernard Lépicié (1735–1784). (Source: Wikimedia Commons.)

page 64 • Banner: *Crib* (Source: Thinkstock.)

page 65 • Banner: *Empty Plate* (Source: Thinkstock.) Bottom: *Temptation of Christ,* Sandro Botticelli (1445–1510). (Source: Wikimedia Commons.)

page 66 • Banner: *Fire* (Source: Thinkstock.) Bottom: *Cain and Abel,* Ivory panel from the Cathedral of Salerno. Original artist unknown, ca. 1084. (Source: Wikimedia Commons.)

page 67 • Banner: *St. Paul,* Statue in the Vatican. Photo by M. Trischler. This image is licensed under the Creative Commons Attribution-ShareAlike 2.5 Generic license. (Source: Wikimedia Commons.) Bottom: *Title Page from 1 Corinthians* (Source: Thinkstock.) Bottom: *Collage of Names,* From the library of TheBiblePeople.com. Used by permission.

page 68 • Banner: *Mosaic of Daniel in the Lions' Den* (Source: Thinkstock.) Bottom: *Samson in the Treadmill,* Carl Heinrich Bloch (1834–1890). (Source: Wikimedia Commons.) Bottom: *Sacrifice of Isaac,* Andrea del Sarto (1486–1530). (Source: Wikimedia Commons.) Bottom: *Moses Floating on the Water, Bible Pictures with Brief Descriptions* by Charles Foster, published in 1897. (Source: Wikimedia Commons.) Bottom: *David and Goliath* (Source: Thinkstock.)

page 69 • Bottom: *Fiery Furnace,* Gustave Doré (1832–1883). (Source: Wikimedia Commons.)

page 71 • Banner: *Olive Tree Bark,* Jerusalem, Israel. Photo by

Juandev. This image is licensed under the Creative Commons Attribution-ShareAlike 3.0 Unported licence. (Source: Wikimedia Commons.) Bottom: *Acacia Wood,* photo by B. Navez. This image is licensed under the Creative Commons Attribution-ShareAlike 3.0 Unported licence. (Source: Wikimedia Commons.) Bottom: *Juniper Tree* (Source: Thinkstock.) Bottom: *Gold* (Source: Thinkstock.) Bottom: *Olive Tree,* photo by Juandev. This image is licensed under the Creative Commons Attribution-ShareAlike 3.0 Unported licence. (Source: Wikimedia Commons.)

page 72 • Banner: *Replica of the Garden Tomb* (Source: Thinkstock.)

page 73 • Bottom: *Rachel's Tomb,* This image is licensed under the Creative Commons Attribution-ShareAlike 2.5 Generic license. (Source: Wikimedia Commons.) Bottom: *Hebron,* photo by A. E. Breen (1913). (Source: Wikimedia Commons.) Bottom: *Traditional and Probable Grave of Joseph,* photo published in *Sacred Books and Literature of the East,* 1917. (Source: Wikimedia Commons.)

page 74 • Banner: *Looking behind Doors* (Source: Thinkstock.) Bottom: *Question Marks* (Source: Thinkstock.) Bottom: *The Soldiers Casting Lots for Christ's Garments,* William Blake (1757–1827). (Source: Wikimedia Commons.) Bottom: *Yes, No, Dice* (Source: Thinkstock.)

page 75 • Banner: *Torah* (Source: Thinkstock.) Bottom: *Circumcision of Ishmael,* Gerard Hoet (1648–1733). (Source: Wikimedia Commons.) Bottom: *Circumcision of Jesus,* Andrea Mantegna (1431–1506). (Source: Wikimedia Commons.)

page 76 • Banner: *Clothing* (Source: Thinkstock.) Bottom: *Fig Leaf* (Source: Thinkstock.) Bottom: *Ancient Sandal,* photo by the U.S. National Park Service. (Source:

Wikimedia Commons.)

page 77 • Banner: *Grasshopper* (Source: Thinkstock.) Bottom: *Lentils; Honey; Almonds* (Source: Thinkstock.)

page 78 • Banner: *Coins* (Source: Thinkstock.)

page 79 • Banner: *Temple of Baal,* photo by Jerzy Strzelecki. This image is licensed under the Creative Commons Attribution-ShareAlike 3.0 Unported license. (Source: Wikimedia Commons.)

page 80 • Banner: *Calendar* (Source: Thinkstock.) Bottom: *Jewish Months and their Modern Equivalent, Quickview Bible* © 2012 Zondervan Publishers (www.zondervan.com). Used by permission.

page 81 • Banner: *Menorah* (Source: Thinkstock.) Bottom: *Shofar* (Source: Thinkstock.) Bottom: *City of Booths in Jerusalem,* This image is licensed under the Creative Commons Attribution-ShareAlike 2.5 Generic license. (Source: Wikimedia Commons.) Bottom: *Unleavened Bread* (Source: Thinkstock.)

page 82 • Banner: *Camels* (Source: Thinkstock.)

page 83 • Banner: *Postage Meters* (Source: Thinkstock.)

page 84 • Banner: *Gold Bars* (Source: Thinkstock.) Bottom: *Coins* (Source: Thinkstock.)

page 85 • Banner: *Wailing Wall in Jerusalem* (Source: Thinkstock.) Bottom: *Theater at Ephesus,* photo by Norman Herr. (Source: Wikimedia Commons.) Bottom: *Tower of Babel* (Source: Thinkstock.) Bottom: *Model of the Tabernacle,* This image is licensed under the Creative Commons Attribution-ShareAlike 3.0 Unported license. (Source: Wikimedia Commons.)

page 86 • Banner: *Bronze Swords,* Late Bronze Age (ca. 1000–900 BC). Photo by Laténium. This image is licensed under the Creative Commons Attribution-ShareAlike 3.0 Unported

page 104 • Banner: *Greetings on Bulletin Board* (Source: Thinkstock.) Bottom: *Aloha* (Source: Thinkstock.)

page 105 • Banner: *Laughing Donkey* (Source: Thinkstock.) Bottom: *Paper Faces; Smiling Girl; Laughing Couple* (Source: Thinkstock.)

page 106 • Banner: *Jesus with Lamb* (Source: Thinkstock.) Bottom: *Jesus' Parables,* Sweet Publishing released these images, which are taken from now-out-of-print *Read'n Grow Picture Bible Illustrations* (Biblical illustrations by Jim Padgett, courtesy of Sweet Publishing, Ft. Worth, TX, and Gospel Light, Ventura, CA. Copyright 1984), under new license, CC-BY-SA 3.0. (Source: Wikimedia Commons.)

page 107 • Banner: *Paper Bag Faces* (Source: Thinkstock.)

page 108 • Bottom: *Job and His Friends,* Ilya Yefimovich Repin (1844–1930). (Source: Wikimedia Commons.) Bottom: *Jesus Mocked by the Soldiers,* Édouard Manet (1832–1883). (Source: Wikimedia Commons.) Bottom: *David and Goliath,* Gebhard Fugel (1863–1939). (Source: Wikimedia Commons.)

page 109 • Banner: *Golden Calf* (Source: Thinkstock.) Bottom: *The Denying of Peter,* Jan Miense Molenaer (1610–1668). (Source: Wikimedia Commons.) Bottom: *Joseph Receives His Father,* Salomon de Bray (1597–1664). (Source: Wikimedia Commons.) Bottom: *Samson's Final Victory,* unknown artist, ca. 1650. (Source: Wikimedia Commons.)

page 110 • Banner: *Water* (Source: Thinkstock.) Bottom: *Noah's Ark* (Source: Thinkstock.) Bottom: *Moses Strikes the Rock,* James Tissot (1836–1902). (Source: Wikimedia Commons.) Bottom: *Person in Water* (Source: Thinkstock.)

page 111 • Banner: *John's Vision of Heaven,* Matthias Gerung (1500–1570). (Source: Wikimedia Commons.) Bottom:

Leviathan, Gustave Doré (1832–1883). (Source: Wikimedia Commons.) Bottom: *Worship before God's Throne,* unknown artist and date. (Source: Wikimedia Commons.) Bottom: *Ezekiel's Vision,* Hans Holbein the Younger (1497–1543). (Source: Wikimedia Commons.)

page 113 • Banner: *Desert in Judah* (Source: Thinkstock.) Bottom: *Desert in Judah* (Source: Thinkstock.)

page 114 • Banner: *Rameses II Statues in Abu Simbel, Egypt.* Photo by Brian Snelson. This image is licensed under the Creative Commons Attribution 2.0. Generic license. Bottom: *Egyptian Pyramids* (Source: Thinkstock.) Bottom: *King Tut's Mask,* photo by Steve Evans. This image is licensed under the Creative Commons Attribution 2.0. Generic license. (Source: Wikimedia Commons.) Bottom: *Carved Owl* (Source: Thinkstock.)

page 115 • Banner: *Hittite Sculpture* (Source: Thinkstock.) Bottom: *Samson Defeats the Philistines* (Source: Thinkstock.) Bottom: *Enemies of Israel,* From the library of TheBiblePeople.com. Used by permission. Bottom: *King Saul Falls in Battle* (Source: Thinkstock.)

page 116 • Banner: *Island of Patmos* (Source: Thinkstock.) Bottom: *Island of Cyprus* (Source: Thinkstock.) Bottom: *Island of Crete* (Source: Thinkstock.) Bottom: *Island of Malta* (Source: Thinkstock.)

page 117 • Banner: *Sea of Galilee* (Source: Thinkstock.) Bottom: *Images of the Dead Sea* (Source: Thinkstock.)

page 118 • Banner: *Mountains of Ebal and Gerizim,* photo by Asad. This image is licensed under the Creative Commons Attribution-ShareAlike 3.0 Unported license. (Source: Wikimedia Commons.) Bottom: *Ararat* (Source: Thinkstock.) Bottom: *Mt. Carmel,* photo by Hana. This image is licensed under the Creative Commons Attribution-

ShareAlike 3.0 Unported license. (Source: Wikimedia Commons.) Bottom: *Mt. Sinai* (Source: Thinkstock.)

page 119 • Banner: *Model of Jerusalem* (Source: Thinkstock.) Bottom: *Tower of David* (Source: Thinkstock.) Bottom: *Children in Jerusalem* (Source: Thinkstock.) Bottom: *Dome of the Rock and the Wailing Wall in Jerusalem* (Source: Thinkstock.)

page 120 • Banner: *Sculpture* (Source: Thinkstock.)

page 121 • Banner: *Inscription from Xerxes,* photo by Bjørn Christian Tørrissen. This image is licensed under the Creative Commons Attribution-ShareAlike 3.0 Unported license. (Source: Wikimedia Commons.) Bottom: *Map of the Persian Empire,* Map created by Department of History, United States Military Academy, West Point. Bottom: *Cyrus the Great* (Source: Wikimedia Commons.) Bottom: *Xerxes,* photo by Jona Lendering. This image is licensed under the Creative Commons Attribution-ShareAlike 3.0 Unported license. (Source: Wikimedia Commons.)

page 122 • Banner: *Map of Israel* (Source: Thinkstock.) Bottom: *Moses Seeing the Promised Land,* Christian Rohlfs (1849–1938). (Source: Wikimedia Commons.) Bottom: *Moses Views the Promised Land,* Frederic Leighton (1830–1896). (Source: Wikimedia Commons.) Bottom: *Moses,* Illustration from The Holy Bible published by Holman in 1890. (Source: Wikimedia Commons.) Bottom: *Moses,* James Tissot (1836–1902). (Source: Wikimedia Commons.)

page 123 • Banner: *Unknown River* (Source: Thinkstock.) Bottom: *Nile River* (Source: Thinkstock.) Bottom: *Tigris River,* This image is licensed under the Creative Commons Attribution-ShareAlike 3.0 Unported license. (Source: Wikimedia Commons.)

page 124 • Banner: *Aqueduct in Caesarea* (Source:

Thinkstock.) Bottom: *Roman Theater in Caesarea* (Source: Thinkstock.)

page 125 • Banner: *Judean Valley* (Source: Thinkstock.)

page 127 • Banner: *Crown of Thorns and Bible* (Source: Thinkstock.) Bottom: *Woman at the Well*, Carl Heinrich Bloch (1834–1890). (Source: Wikimedia Commons.) Bottom: *Suffer the Children*, Carl Heinrich Bloch (1834–1890). (Source: Wikimedia Commons.) Bottom: *Jesus Tempted*, Carl Heinrich Bloch (1834–1890). (Source: Wikimedia Commons.) Bottom: *The Transfiguration*, Carl Heinrich Bloch (1834–1890). (Source: Wikimedia Commons.)

page 128 • Banner: *Sketch of Jesus with Halo* (Source: Thinkstock.) Bottom: *Jesus Breaking Bread* (Source: Thinkstock.) Bottom: *Cross in Sky* (Source: Thinkstock.) Bottom: *Sheep* (Source: Thinkstock.) Bottom: *One Way* (Source: Thinkstock.)

page 129 • Banner: *Sheep* (Source: Thinkstock.) Bottom: *Sheep* (Source: Thinkstock.)

page 130 • Banner: *Hand Nailed to Cross* (Source: Thinkstock.) Bottom: *The Crucifixion*, Giotto di Bondone (1266–1337). (Source: Wikimedia Commons.)

page 131 • Banner: *The Touch of Christ* (Source: Thinkstock.) Bottom: *Catch of Fish* (Source: Thinkstock.) Bottom: *Loaves and Fishes* (Source: Thinkstock.) Bottom: *Walking on the Water* (Source: Thinkstock.)

page 132 • Bottom: *Widow's Son* (Source: Thinkstock.) Bottom: *Jairus's Daughter* (Source: Thinkstock.) Bottom: *Resurrection of Lazarus*, Duccio di Buoninsegna (ca. 1260–1318). (Source: Wikimedia Commons.)

page 133 • Banner: *Jesus Inscription* (Source: Thinkstock.)

page 134 • Bottom: *Brick Building* (Source: Thinkstock.) Bottom:

Bread and Grain (Source: Thinkstock.) Bottom: *Wedding Invitation* (Source: Thinkstock.) Bottom: *Stethoscope* (Source: Thinkstock.)

page 135 • Banner: *Jesus' Name in Wood* (Source: Thinkstock.) Bottom: *Candle* (Source: Thinkstock.) Bottom: *Sunrise from Space* (Source: Thinkstock.) Bottom: *Alpha and Omega*, This image is licensed under the Creative Commons Attribution-ShareAlike 3.0 Unported license. (Source: Wikimedia Commons.) Bottom: *Jesus and Bread* (Source: Thinkstock.) Bottom: *Rock* (Source: Thinkstock.)

page 136 • Banner: *Names of God* (Source: Thinkstock.) Bottom: *Fortress* (Source: Thinkstock.) Bottom: *Shepherd Staff* (Source: Thinkstock.) Bottom: *New Growth* (Source: Thinkstock.) Bottom: *Judge* (Source: Thinkstock.) Bottom: *Light* (Source: Thinkstock.)

page 137 • Banner: *Man under Waterfall* (Source: Thinkstock.) Bottom: *Ocean and Sky* (Source: Thinkstock.)

page 138 • Banner: *Street sign* (Source: Thinkstock.)

page 139 • Banner: *Checkmarks* (Source: Thinkstock.)

page 140 • Banner: *Jesus Statue in Rio de Janeiro* (Source: Thinkstock.) Bottom: *Road to Emmaus*, Sweet Publishing released these images, which are taken from now-out-of-print *Read'n Grow Picture Bible Illustrations* (Biblical illustrations by Jim Padgett, courtesy of Sweet Publishing, Ft. Worth, TX, and Gospel Light, Ventura, CA. Copyright 1984), under new license, CC-BY-SA 3.0. (Source: Wikimedia Commons.)

page 142 • Banner: *Thunderstorm* (Source: Thinkstock.)

page 143 • Banner: *Tower of Babel*, Wilhelm von Kaulbach (1805–1874). (Source: Wikimedia Commons.)

page 144 • Banner: *Dream of Three Wise Men*, Capital from Autun Cathedral. Sculptor: Gislebertus (Year unknown). (Source: Wikimedia Commons.) Bottom: *Joseph (son of Jacob)* Illustration from The *Holy Bible* published by Holman in 1890. (Source: Wikimedia Commons.) Bottom: *Joseph's Dream*, Jacques Stella (1596–1657). (Source: Wikimedia Commons.) Bottom: *Jacob's Ladder*, Gerard Hoet (1648–1733). (Source: Wikimedia Commons.)

page 145 • Banner: *Nail in the Cross* (Source: Thinkstock.) Bottom: *Stations of the Cross*, original artist and date unknown. This image is licensed under the Creative Commons Attribution-ShareAlike 3.0 Unported license. (Source: Wikimedia Commons.)

page 146 • Banner: *Assyrian Army* (Source: Thinkstock.) Bottom: *Moses During the Battle*, James Tissot (1836–1902). (Source: Wikimedia Commons.) Bottom: *Fall of Jericho*, Published as a Bible card by the Providence Lithograph Company in 1901. (Source: Wikimedia Commons.) Bottom: *David and Goliath*, Michelangelo Buonarroti (1475–1564). (Source: Wikimedia Commons.)

page 147 • Bottom: *Jericho* (Source: Thinkstock.) Bottom: *Rescue of Lot*, Image taken from the *Morgan Bible*, published ca. 1250. (Source: Wikimedia Commons.)

page 148 • Banner: *Doctor with Felt Heart* (Source: Thinkstock.)

page 149 • Banner: *Statue of Moses* (Source: Thinkstock.) Bottom: *African Giant Bullfrog* (Source: Thinkstock.) Bottom: *Hail* (Source: Thinkstock.) Bottom: *Flies* (Source: Thinkstock.)

page 150 • Banner: *Parched land* (Source: Thinkstock.) Bottom: *The Prophet Elijah*, Daniele da Volterra (1509–1566). (Source: Wikimedia Commons.) Bottom: *Bread* (Source: Thinkstock.) Bottom: *Elisha Refusing Gifts from*

Naaman, Pieter de Grebber (ca. 1600–1652). (Source: Wikimedia Commons.)

page 151 • BANNER: *Saints Peter and John Healing the Lame Man*, Nicolas Poussin (1594–1665). (Source: Wikimedia Commons.) BOTTOM: *St. Peter and St. John Heal a Man* (Same as banner image) BOTTOM: *Peter's Shadow*, original artist unknown, ca. 1425. (Source: Wikimedia Commons.) BOTTOM: *St. Paul before the Proconsul*, Raphael (1483–1520). (Source: Wikimedia Commons.)

page 152 • BANNER: *Loaves and Fishes* (Source: Thinkstock.) BOTTOM: *Manna*, original artist unknown, ca. 1460–1470. (Source: Wikimedia Commons.) BOTTOM: *Moses and the Water from the Rock of Horeb*, Bartolomé Esteban Murillo (1617–1682). (Source: Wikimedia Commons.) BOTTOM: *A Widow's Son*, unknown artist, ca. 1625. (Source: Wikimedia Commons.)

page 153 • BANNER: *Baby pictures* (Source: Thinkstock.) BOTTOM: *Manoah and His Wife*, Image from the *Morgan Bible*, published ca. 1250. Original artist unknown. (Source: Wikimedia Commons.) BOTTOM: *Mary and Joseph* (Source: Thinkstock.) BOTTOM: *Jacob Encountering Rachel with Her Father's Herds*, Joseph von Führich (1800–1876). (Source: Wikimedia Commons.) BOTTOM: *Mary Visits Elizabeth* (Source: Thinkstock.)

page 154 • BANNER: *Egyptian Hieroglyphics*, photo by Guillaume Blanchard. This image is licensed under the Creative Commons Attribution-ShareAlike 3.0 Unported license. (Source: Wikimedia Commons.) BOTTOM: *The Ten Plagues, Quickview Bible* © 2012 Zondervan Publishers (www.zondervan.com). Used by permission.

page 155 • BANNER: *The Vision of the Valley of Dry Bones*, Gustave Doré (1832–1883). (Source: Wikimedia Commons.)

page 157 • BANNER: *Heart in the Sky* (Source: Thinkstock.)

page 158 • BANNER: *Cross in the Sky* (Source: Thinkstock.)

page 159 • BANNER: *Fire* (Source: Thinkstock.) BOTTOM: *Hades*, From the library of TheBiblePeople.com. Used by permission.

page 160 • BANNER: *Masks* (Source: Thinkstock.) BOTTOM: *Isaac Blessing Jacob*, Govert Flinck (1615–1660). (Source: Wikimedia Commons.) BOTTOM: *Judah and Tamar*, Aert de Gelder (1645–1727). (Source: Wikimedia Commons.)

page 161 • BANNER: *Escape Sign* (Source: Thinkstock.)

page 162 • BANNER: *Tombstones* (Source: Thinkstock.) BOTTOM: *Death of Uzzah*, James Tissot (1836–1902). (Source: Wikimedia Commons.) BOTTOM: *The Assyrian Army*, unknown artist, ca. 1372. (Source: Wikimedia Commons.) BOTTOM: *Lion* (Source: Thinkstock.) BOTTOM: *Nadab and Abihu Are Killed*, James Tissot (1836–1902). (Source: Wikimedia Commons.)

page 163 • BANNER: *Burning Bush* (Source: Thinkstock.) BOTTOM: *The Outpouring of the Holy Ghost*, Luis Tristán de Escamilla (ca. 1586–1624). (Source: Wikimedia Commons.) BOTTOM: *Fiery Furnace*, Toros Roslin (1210–1270). (Source: Wikimedia Commons.) BOTTOM: *Balaam and the Angel*, Gustav Jaeger (1808–1871). (Source: Wikimedia Commons.)

page 164 • BANNER: *Jonah* (Source: Thinkstock.) BOTTOM: *Israeli Spies* (Source: Wikimedia Commons.) BOTTOM: *The Escape of David through the Window*, Gustave Doré (1832–1883). (Source: Wikimedia Commons.) BOTTOM: *Journey of the Magi*, James Tissot (1836–1902). (Source: Wikimedia Commons.)

page 165 • BANNER: *Top Secret Envelope* (Source: Thinkstock.) BOTTOM: *Photo*

Paper Borders (Source: Thinkstock.) BOTTOM: *Woodcuts of Samson* (Source: Thinkstock.)

page 166 • BANNER: *Angel Wings* (Source: Thinkstock.)

page 169 • BANNER: *Line of Babies* (Source: Thinkstock.) BOTTOM: *Crayons* (Source: Thinkstock.) BOTTOM: *Pregnant Woman with Name Tag* (Source: Thinkstock.)

page 170 • BANNER: *The Feast of Herod* (Source: Thinkstock.) BOTTOM: *Salome*, Movie still. Salomé was a silent film produced by William Fox in 1918 and starring actors Theda Bara as Salome and G. Raymond Nye as King Herod. (Source: Wikimedia Commons.) BOTTOM: *Herod Archelaus*, Guillaume Rouillé (ca. 1518–1589). (Source: Wikimedia Commons.) Bottom, *Massacre of the Innocents*, unknown artist, ca. 1308–1311. (Source: Wikimedia Commons.)

page 171 • BANNER: *Spies Returning with Grapes*, photo by Rudolphous. This image is licensed under the Creative Commons Attribution-ShareAlike 3.0 Unported license. (Source: Wikimedia Commons.) Date and artist of original sculptor unknown. (Source: Wikimedia Commons.) BOTTOM: *Spies with Grapes* (Source: Thinkstock.) BOTTOM: *Ox Pulling the Ark* (Source: Thinkstock.)

page 172 • BANNER: *Men's and Women's Restroom Signs* (Source: Thinkstock.)

page 173 • BANNER: *Legal Documents* (Source: Thinkstock.) BOTTOM: *Heart* (Source: Thinkstock.)

page 174 • BANNER: *Man with Name Tag* (Source: Thinkstock.)

page 176 • BANNER: *Cross* (Source: Thinkstock.) Bottom, *Girl with Father* (Source: Thinkstock.) Bottom, *Lightbulb* (Source: Thinkstock.) Bottom, *Sheep* (Source: Thinkstock.) Bottom, *Church*, photo by David Castor. (Source: Wikimedia Commons.)

page 177 • BANNER: *Mary* (Source: Thinkstock.) Bottom, *Postage Stamps* (Source: Thinkstock.)

page 179 • BANNER: *Numbers* (Source: Thinkstock.)

page 183 • BANNER: *Hand Holding the Number Five* (Source: Thinkstock.)

page 184 • BANNER: *Digits* (Source: Thinkstock.)

page 186 • BANNER: *Calendar* (Source: Thinkstock.)

page 189 • BANNER: *The Number Ten* (Source: Thinkstock.) BOTTOM: *Foolish Virgins,* James Tissot (1836–1902). (Source: Wikimedia Commons.) BOTTOM: *Moses and the Ten Commandments,* James Tissot (1836–1902). (Source: Wikimedia Commons.) BOTTOM: *The Ten Lepers,* original artist unknown, ca. 1035–1040. (Source: Wikimedia Commons.)

page 190 • BANNER: *Clock* (Source: Thinkstock.)

page 191 • BANNER: *The Last Supper,* Giampietrino (probably also known as Giovanni Pietro Rizzoli, 1495–1521). (Source: Wikimedia Commons.)

page 192 • BANNER: *The Forty-Yard Line* (Source: Thinkstock.) BOTTOM: *Moses* (Source: Thinkstock.) BOTTOM: *Great Flood,* Gerard Hoet (1648–1733). (Source: Wikimedia Commons.) BOTTOM: *Isaac Meets Rebekah, Bible Pictures with Brief Descriptions* by Charles Foster, published in 1897. (Source: Wikimedia Commons.)

page 193 • BOTTOM: *Jonah,* original artist unknown, ca. 14th century. (Source: Wikimedia Commons.) BOTTOM: *Saul and David,* Nikolai Petrovich Zagorsky (1849–1893). (Source: Wikimedia Commons.) BOTTOM: *David* (Source: Thinkstock.) BOTTOM: *Jesus* (Source: Thinkstock.)

page 195 • BANNER: *Donkey* (Source: Thinkstock.) BOTTOM: *Zedekiah,* unknown artist, ca. 1670. (Source: Wikimedia Commons.) BOTTOM: *Balaam and His Ass,* Rembrandt

Harmenszoon van Rijn (1606–1669). (Source: Wikimedia Commons.) BOTTOM: *Elymas Struck Blind by St. Paul before the Proconsul Sergius Paulus,* Giulio Clovio (1498–1578). (Source: Wikimedia Commons.)

page 196 • BANNER: *Samson* (Source: Thinkstock.) BOTTOM: *Jephthah's Daughter,* Bon Boullogne (1649–1717). (Source: Wikimedia Commons.) BOTTOM: *Deborah beneath the Palm Tree,* James Tissot (1836–1902). (Source: Wikimedia Commons.) BOTTOM: *Samson,* Joseph Ignaz Mildorfer (1719–1775). Photo by Wolfgang Sauber. This image is licensed under the Creative Commons Attribution-ShareAlike 3.0 Unported license. (Source: Wikimedia Commons.)

page 197 • BANNER: *Wood Chain* (Source: Thinkstock.)

page 198 • BOTTOM: *The Arrogance of Rehoboam,* Hans Holbein the Younger (1497–1543). (Source: Wikimedia Commons.)

page 199 • BANNER: *People Network* (Source: Thinkstock.)

page 200 • BANNER: *Crystal Ball* (Source: Thinkstock.) BOTTOM: *Saul and the Witch of Endor,* Washington Allston (1779–1843). (Source: Wikimedia Commons.) BOTTOM: *Stars* (Source: Thinkstock.) BOTTOM: *Divination Text,* This image is licensed under the Creative Commons Attribution-ShareAlike 3.0 Unported license. (Source: Wikimedia Commons.)

page 201 • BANNER: *The Apostles* (Source: Thinkstock.)

page 202 • BANNER: *Wheat Field* (Source: Thinkstock.)

page 203 • BANNER: *Melchizedek and Abraham Meet,* original artist unknown, ca. 1560–1600. (Source: Wikimedia Commons.)

page 204 • BANNER: *Daniel, Hezekiel, Jeremiah, and Isaiah,* Statues. Photo by Jose Goncalves. This image is licensed under the Creative Commons Attribution-ShareAlike 1.0 Generic license. (Source: Wikimedia Commons.)

page 205 • BOTTOM: *Nahum Title Page* (Source: Thinkstock.) BOTTOM: *Ezekiel* (Source: Thinkstock.) BOTTOM: Jeremiah (Source: Thinkstock.) BOTTOM: *Nathan* (Source: Thinkstock.) BOTTOM: *Zechariah Title Page* (Source: Thinkstock.)

page 206 • BANNER: *Lamp* (Source: Thinkstock.) BOTTOM: *Altar of Incense; Table of Showbread; Altar for Offerings,* photos by Ori229. These images are licensed under the Creative Commons Attribution-ShareAlike 3.0 Unported license. (Source: Wikimedia Commons.)

page 207 • BANNER: *Chalkboard* (Source: Thinkstock.) Bottom, *Teachers and Mentors,* From the library of TheBiblePeople.com. Used by permission.

page 209 • BANNER: *Jesus Sign* (Source: Thinkstock.) Bottom, *Rainbow* (Source: Thinkstock.)

page 210 • BANNER: *Baptism of Christ,* original artist and date unknown. (Source: Wikimedia Commons.) BOTTOM: *Baptism of Christ (far left)* Brazilian artist in the 18th century (name and date unknown). (Source: Wikimedia Commons.) BOTTOM: *Baptism of Christ (left of center)* Russian artist in the early 18th century (name and date unknown). (Source: Wikimedia Commons.) BOTTOM: *Baptism of Christ (center)* Original artist and date unknown (19th century). (Source: Wikimedia Commons.) BOTTOM: *Baptism of Christ (right of center)* José Ferraz de Almeida Júnior (1850–1899). (Source: Wikimedia Commons.) BOTTOM: *Baptism of Christ (right)* Bartolomé Esteban Murillo (1618–1682). (Source: Wikimedia Commons.)

page 211 • BANNER: *Life Button* (Source: Thinkstock.) BOTTOM: *Broken Chain* (Source: Thinkstock.)

page 212 • BANNER: *Flooded Village* (Source: Thinkstock.) BANNER: *Poor Village* (Source:

285